# LEDYARD

# LEDYARD

## In Search of
## the First American Explorer

## BILL GIFFORD

HARCOURT, INC.
Orlando  Austin  New York  San Diego  Toronto  London

www.HarcourtBooks.com

Library of Congress Cataloging-in-Publication Data
Gifford, Bill.
Ledyard: in search of the first American explorer/Bill Gifford.—1st ed.
p.  cm.
Includes bibliographical references and index.
I. Ledyard, John, 1751–1789.  2. Explorers—United States—Biography.
I. Title.
G226.L5G55  2007
910.92—dc22    2006017064
[B]
ISBN-13: 978-0-15-101218-3   ISBN-10: 0-15-101218-0

Text set in Centaur MT
Designed by Linda Lockowitz

Printed in the United States of America
First edition

A C E G I K J H F D B

*For Leonard Welles*

# CONTENTS

*Only death remains*
*To tell us*
*How great we were*

*Speaks the voice of the voyager*
*From fading bronze letters,*
*Great with desire.*

—from "John Ledyard,"
by RICHARD EBERHART

# INTRODUCTION

# Damned to Fame

O N THE MORNING OF MAY 21, 1789, THOMAS JEFFERSON
sat down at his desk in Paris, greatly troubled. Revolution was in the air; the French monarchy's days were
clearly numbered. Just two weeks earlier, the Estates-General—
the first representative body in French history—had met for the
first time; the storming of the Bastille was less than two months
away. As American minister to the court of Versailles, Jefferson
was torn between his passion for liberty and his fear of violence.
At the same time, he was busy with political and personal matters.
As he prepared to return home to Virginia for the first time in five
years, his new nation was dangerously in debt, and so was he. He
was so preoccupied that he had been neglecting his special friend,
the beautiful and married Maria Cosway, to whom he dashed off
an apologetic note that day.

But Jefferson's mind was not really focused on any of these
situations. Rather, what alarmed him was a rumor. People were
saying that his friend John Ledyard was dead. Reaching into a
stack of papers, he found a letter he'd drafted two days earlier to
Thomas Paine in London. He dipped his pen into a well of black
ink and added an urgent paragraph. The stories of Ledyard's death
could not possibly be true, he insisted. "I this moment receive a
letter from Ledyard dated Cairo, Nov. 15," he wrote. "He therein
sais 'I am doing up my baggage & most curious baggage it is, & I

leave Cairo in two or three days. I travel from hence SW about 300 Leagues to a Black king. There my present conductors leave me to my fate. Beyond I suppose I go alone.'"

"This seems to contradict the story of his having died at Cairo in January," Jefferson concluded hopefully, "as he was then probably in the interior parts of Africa." But if Paine learned otherwise, he was to notify Jefferson immediately.

Jefferson had met Ledyard four years earlier, when the young man from Connecticut had washed up in Paris, broke but full of wild dreams. He was an extraordinary character, broad chested and garrulous, his arms and hands marked with tattoos that he had acquired in Tahiti, on Captain James Cook's third and fatal voyage. On that trip, Ledyard had become the first American to set foot on the western coast of North America. Jefferson was fascinated by him. In his autobiography, written four decades later, Jefferson remembered Ledyard as "a man of genius, some science, and fearless courage and enterprise."

Their conversations helped convince the future president of the need to explore the interior of the continent, the vast unknown territory between the Appalachian Mountains and the Pacific Ocean. Such an expedition, Jefferson believed, was of vital importance to America's future—far more important, in the long run, than any of the other problems afflicting him that spring day in 1789. And Ledyard was just the man to do it. He was as strong as a plowman, and he shared Jefferson's insatiable love of walking. Ledyard sometimes hiked all the way from Saint-Germain-en-Laye, a small town outside Paris where he lived, to the Hotel de Langéac, Jefferson's home, a trek of twelve miles in each direction.

At Jefferson's urging, Ledyard had attempted the transcontinental journey himself, more than fifteen years before Meriwether Lewis joined William Clark on their famous voyage of discovery. Unfortunately, the stubborn Ledyard had insisted on going the

wrong way around the world, traveling east from Paris toward
Russia and Bering Strait rather than taking the more obvious
route—west from, say, Virginia. In the late fall of 1786, he had
set off across Europe to St. Petersburg, and from there made his
way across Siberia toward the Pacific, where he hoped to catch a
Russian trading vessel to what is now Alaska. He got as far as
Yakutsk, deep in the Siberian permafrost, when Empress Catherine the Great had had him arrested as a spy, which he probably
was: Jefferson found his missives highly informative, to say the
least.

Jefferson still hoped that Ledyard would be able to complete
the journey—perhaps, as he suggested, by starting in Kentucky
and heading west this time. In the meantime, however, the impulsive Ledyard had taken an assignment from a group of British
gentlemen led by none other than Sir Joseph Banks, the forward-
thinking aristocrat and naturalist who had sailed with—and
funded—Cook's first voyage in 1768. Now retired from traveling, Banks had become the leading patron of exploration of his
day, and he had just founded a group called the Association for
Promoting the Discovery of the Interior Parts of Africa. As Jefferson understood it, Ledyard was to ascend the Nile into present-
day Sudan, and then make his way overland to the mythical Niger
River, whose exact location was still unknown to Europeans in the
late eighteenth century.

Ledyard's errand for the British had annoyed Jefferson to no
end; the Crown was still behaving haughtily toward the young
United States of America, as well as toward Jefferson personally.
Jefferson had been somewhat mollified by Ledyard's apology in an
earlier letter, accompanied by Ledyard's characteristically keen observations of Egypt, which he'd passed along in violation of his
confidentiality agreement with Banks et al. He had done this sort
of thing quite often for Jefferson, who regarded Ledyard as having

"a talent for useful & interesting observation." In the context of the eighteenth century, when information was scarce and traveled slowly, he really was a kind of spy.

In one of his last letters to Jefferson, Ledyard had vowed to complete his North American journey just as soon as he returned from Africa. But even he knew that he might never come back. "I shall not forget you," the younger man had written, in that final missive from Cairo. "Indeed it would be a consolation to think of you in my last moments. Be happy."

Four weeks after Jefferson had written him, Paine replied, confirming the worst. Ledyard was dead. The sad fact had been reported by Banks himself, who wrote that Ledyard had been about to leave Cairo for the interior in early January 1789 when he was taken ill with dysentery. He had swallowed a dose of tartar emetic—potassium antimony tartrate—but as often happened in eighteenth-century medicine, the cure proved worse than the ailment. Ledyard had burst a blood vessel and died, in the bleak Franciscan convent where he had been staying. He was thirty-seven years old.

"That man," Sir Joseph had said to Paine, "was all Mind."

Nobody who met John Ledyard ever forgot him. That much became instantly clear to his first biographer, an upright Unitarian minister named Jared Sparks, as he scoured New England and Europe in the 1820s, looking for people who had known the great American traveler. Even the Marquis de Lafayette, after all the bloody tumult of the French Revolution and the Napoleonic reaction, still warmly recalled the "good & extraordinary man" whom he had befriended in Paris before the upheaval. "Mr. Jefferson & myself, I am proud to say, had indeed a great share in his affections," he wrote to Sparks, in the twilight of his life. "I am proud to say"—it sounded almost like a boast.

Blond-haired, well-built, and a fabulous raconteur, Ledyard was the kind of man who drew stares when he entered a room, from men and women alike. "He appeared to be formed by Nature for achievements of hardihood and peril," marveled an English admirer, recalling their first meeting. "The Virginian gentlemen here call me Oliver Cromwell," Ledyard had written home from Paris, proudly, "and say that like him I shall be damned to fame." The Virginian gentlemen—Jefferson and his Paris circle—were right, and even before he died Ledyard was renowned as a traveler and explorer. He knew all the right people, and he owed most of them money: Jefferson, John Adams, Banks, Cook. After his death, Ledyard's fame exceeded even his own lofty expectations. Within months, newspapers and magazines in Britain and the United States were already publishing articles about "the Celebrated Traveller." Jared Sparks's 1828 biography firmly installed Ledyard in the pantheon of American heroes, for Sparks put him alongside (literally, on a bookshelf) George Washington and Benjamin Franklin, biographies of whom Sparks had also authored. In turn, Sparks's volume provided grist for generations of Sunday newspaper hacks. It was impossible to live in nineteenth-century America and not know all about John Ledyard.

He even appears in perhaps the greatest classic of American literature, *Moby-Dick*. At breakfast at the Spouter-Inn, while waiting to board the whaling ship *Pequod*, the narrator Ishmael compares himself and his fellow sailors to "Ledyard, the great New England Traveller." One literary scholar thinks Ledyard might even have been the model, or at least a model, for Ishmael, whom he resembles in some particulars: Both men were the black sheep of respectable New England families, who had severed their ties to roam the earth. Travel was their tonic. "Whenever I find myself growing grim about the mouth," Ishmael tells us, "then I account it high time to get to sea as soon as I can." Ledyard was the same way: Time after time, he fled precarious situations and emotional dead-ends by embarking on some new voyage.

In his brief life, Ledyard participated in three of the greatest expeditions of his day, journeys that helped shape our under-standing of the world: Captain Cook's voyage to the Pacific, the expedition across North America ultimately completed by Meri-wether Lewis and William Clark, and the exploration of inner Africa that brought the Scottish explorer Mungo Park such renown. In modern terms, it was as if he had crossed both the North and South Poles and walked on the moon.

Yet, famous as he was, one wonders if anyone ever really knew John Ledyard. He traveled light, and it shows. He put down no roots, kept few possessions, and tended to neglect his own friends and family members, even his widowed mother. He never spent more than a few months in any one place. As a result, his paper trail is maddeningly sparse. "I ought to apprize you," one of Led-yard's Dartmouth classmates warned Jared Sparks, "that as Mr. Ledyard was a locomotive machine, no one person, and the people of no single Town, will be able to give much information respect-ing the Events of his life." Even Ledyard's own family was re-luctant to help Sparks, fearing that his randy exploits might scandalize their good name. He left only a handful of letters and a few scattered journals, most of which were bowdlerized by his relatives; others have been "lost" altogether. Thus the details of his life flutter down to us in tantalizing bits: a letter here and a ledger entry there, an excerpt from a journal over here. Each morsel leaves us hungry for more.

We don't even really know what he looked like, apart from his friends' somewhat vague descriptions of him: He was "scarcely above the middle stature," one recalls, contradicting others who remember him as tall. The Royal Marines measured him at five feet seven inches tall and recorded his gray eyes and "fresh" complexion. The British recruiter also remarked that he was "small," although none of his friends remembered him that way. It is generally agreed that his nose was aquiline, his chest was broad, and his hair was so blond (in his youth) that it was nearly white. But the black-and-white portrait of Ledyard that hangs in Dartmouth's Baker Library is a fake, commissioned at the turn of the last century by a Dartmouth alumnus. The oil portrait in the Ledyard National Bank in Hanover, N.H., is also imagined, as is the illustration on the cover of the book you are holding in your hands right now. The one known original portrait of Ledyard, painted in London by a Swedish pupil of Sir Joshua Reynolds, the society painter, has been lost.

Who was Ledyard really? The *Boys' Life* Ledyard of the nineteenth century—the gallant adventurer who never swore and led a life of noble ambition—was largely a creation of Sparks, who feared offending the Ledyard clan. But this Ledyard seems as irrelevant to our own time (and unrepresentative of his own) as a marble statue in a park. There was much more to Ledyard than the romantic figure of "the Traveller," as he was known throughout the nineteenth century. He was a complicated man—idealistic and mercenary, restless and lazy, chivalrous and decidedly uncelibate. His flaws were legion: He had a lifelong history of tantrums and fistfights. He proudly wore the British uniform during the American Revolution, when British forces killed and wounded literally dozens of his own relatives. He wrote a book that tarnished the reputation of a man he had considered a friend. While visiting a hospital for fallen women in Paris, he tried to seduce a young nun. His only loyalty, it seems clear, was to himself.

Yet his extant writings hint—tantalizingly—of an extraordinary and perceptive mind, one perhaps more suited to our age than to his own. His account of Cook's voyage was the first to attempt to see events from native peoples' point of view, and the first to suggest that the celebrated captain's behavior may have contributed to his death at the hands of angry Hawaiians. He was a rarity among Western writers of his own or any other age, in that he refused to presume the inferiority of non-Christian civilizations. Indeed, he anticipated by nearly a century Mark Twain's own revelation—that a God who intended Christians to rule over all so-called savages was not one he wanted to have anything to do with.

In some ways, John Ledyard was the first modern American. His life was a series of self-reinventions: from divinity student to sailor to entrepreneur to explorer. While his new nation emerged from its colonial torpor, Ledyard was already looking out at the world beyond, and preparing to take it on. He took the principles of the American Revolution literally, and he sought to spread those ideals around the globe, as one of America's earliest missionaries of democracy. "Little attentive to differences of rank, he seemed to consider all men his equals," one of Cook's English officers later marveled. Ledyard himself never quite understood how anyone could see things otherwise.

Yet at times it was less the Rights of Man than the pursuit of happiness that seemed to have motivated him. A lifelong ladies' man, Ledyard consorted with native maidens, Parisian demimondaines, and society women alike; jealous men tended to hide their wives from him, while his Victorian biographers politely ignored his bawdy comments and bouts with venereal disease. In a passage from his journals that became the most famous thing he ever wrote, he celebrated the kindness of the fairer sex: "In wandering over the barren plains of inhospitable Denmark, through honest Sweden, and frozen Lapland, rude and churlish Finland, unprincipled Russia, and the wide spread regions of the wandering Tartar, if hungry, dry, cold, wet, or sick, the women have ever been friendly to me."

Even after his death, women swooned for him. Helen Augur's 1946 biography, *Passage to Glory*, reads like a breathless valentine to Ledyard: "He stood, his close-knit body braced against the shock of the primeval land, his blond head lifted to the surge of mountains rolling their white crests like mighty waves against the sky. Like the land, there was pride in him and a radiant strength." ("The man had a way with these women," one more recent Ledyard scholar noted.)

Yet today John Ledyard is all but unknown. Until very recently, *Passage to Glory* was the most current biography of the Traveller. He is not a hero for fearful times, but for optimistic ones, when America is engaging the world without reservation. He appeals to the romantic in us, not the pragmatist. Ledyard's impact, though, can still be seen all over American life. He almost single-handedly established the archetype of the restless American wanderer, a figure that abounds in our literature, from Ishmael on the *Pequod*, to Huck and Jim on the Mississippi River, right down through Dean Moriarty, the rootless, wild, life-embracing hero of Jack Kerouac's *On the Road*. Like them, Ledyard is a catalyst for the imagination. He embodies that uniquely American urge to pull up stakes and go, taking to the river or the sea or the road, reinventing ourselves in some new place. No matter how settled we may be, a part of us longs to follow his path. And so I did: Over a period of four years, I pursued John Ledyard's ghost from the Connecticut River to the North Atlantic Ocean, from the libraries of New England to the archives of Britain, and from the streets of Paris to the farthest reaches of "unprincipled" Siberia. This book is the result.

# PART ONE
# Landlocked

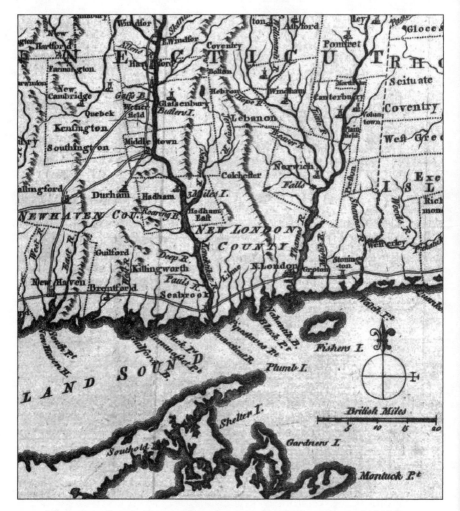

The craggy Connecticut coastline, shown in this 1758 map, proved ideal for smuggling, a Ledyard family trade. John's mother, Abigail Hempstead, came from Southold, Long Island. *Courtesy of the Library of Congress*

# The Squire's Revenge

ONE MORNING IN THE SPRING OF 1773, A SHOUT WENT UP in the center of Hartford, Connecticut. A canoe of some sort was making its way up the Little River, a sluggish stream that flowed through the middle of town, about where Arch Street is today. The craft was apparently being paddled by . . . a bear. The creature aimed its craft toward the riverfront house of Thomas Seymour, a prominent middle-aged lawyer and future mayor of Hartford. As the Seymour family gathered on the bank with a crowd of onlookers, the vessel drifted slowly to shore. It was a large Native American–style dugout, hewn from the trunk of a single tree. Finally the bear stood up, cast aside its skin, and leaped onto a rock—revealing itself to be none other than Seymour's own nephew, John Ledyard. He had paddled all the way down the Connecticut River from Dartmouth College in New Hampshire, negotiating several tricky rapids and two major waterfalls during the 140-mile journey; his was the first recorded descent of the river by a white man.

In the years to come, the story of the great canoe trip would become the cornerstone of Ledyard's legend; when Jefferson heard the tale, years later in Paris, he laughed uproariously. At the time, though, it did not seem so amusing. Instead of greeting him with pride and joy, Ledyard's family rolled their eyes in dismay. Young men from good families simply did not travel by canoe. And why was he coming home from college before the end of the term? What had gone wrong now?

A week or two later, the answer arrived, in the form of a blistering letter from the Reverend Eleazar Wheelock, the former Connecticut preacher who had founded Dartmouth College in the wilderness of New Hampshire in 1770, just three years earlier. Wheelock had agreed to accept twenty-one-year-old John as a student, since he was the grandson of an old friend. But the Reverend had recently learned that the young man couldn't pay his tuition, and he was now very angry. He had taken Ledyard in out of the goodness of his heart, he wrote to Tom Seymour, so furious that his pen practically tore through the paper in places; he had only hoped to save Ledyard from, as he put it, "total ruin." But his charity had limits, and Wheelock lamented that he had failed to achieve "the humbling of that youth, & fitting him for usefulness in the world—but as he secretly got his legacy into his own hands to waste as his Pride & Extravagant Humour dictated, & all out of my sight and without my knowledge, it was not possible for me to restrain him."

Inevitably, John saw the letters between his Uncle Tom and Reverend Wheelock. He had little idea of what was being said about him behind his back—by both Wheelock and Seymour, who, evidently, had admitted some unflattering things about his nephew's character. Ledyard was shocked. "Total ruin"? He needed to be "saved"? One of Wheelock's spies passed by the Seymour place in mid-May and saw Ledyard sulking. "He seems to avoid all Company and Conversation," he reported back.

In truth, both Ledyard and Wheelock were victims of the man who had brought them together: John Ledyard Sr., John's grandfather, who by then had been dead for two years. The elder

Ledyard had done some free legal work for Wheelock, years ago, so Wheelock gladly accepted the grandson at Dartmouth. Since Ledyard Sr. had been quite wealthy, Wheelock naturally assumed that the young man could afford to pay for his education. Before old man Ledyard died in 1771, however, at the advanced age of seventy, he had practically disinherited his namesake, the eldest son of his eldest son.

Nobody knows the cause of the grandfather's spite, but the roots seemed to reach deeply into his own past, well before the future explorer was born. In later life, John Ledyard Sr. styled himself a Squire, but in fact he'd had a humble beginning in America, in part because he had practically been disinherited by his own family in England. He was born in about 1700 in the port city of Bristol, where his own father was a relatively well-off merchant, but his father had died when he was about sixteen, and his mother, a stern unbending lady, had insisted that he be "placed" to work in a store. The young man balked at this, since he had planned on attending university. But having no means of his own, he was forced to roam the world to seek his fortune, just as his grandson later would. He appears to have arrived in the town of Southold, on the eastern tip of Long Island, in 1717.

Though little more than a teenage runaway, the future Squire Ledyard was an adept social climber, and not long after he landed on Long Island he fell in with the oldest and most powerful clan on the North Fork, the family of Judge Benjamin Youngs, whose father had been among the first settlers (and whose wife, like Ledyard, hailed from Bristol). Ledyard started out as a Latin teacher, but soon abandoned that to work for the Southold merchant Benjamin L'Hommedieu, a Huguenot emigré in his sixties. He also apprenticed in the law under Judge Youngs. His true occupation, however, was wooing the judge's daughter, Deborah, whom he eventually married in 1727. With his new wife's substantial dowry, he moved across Long Island Sound to Groton, Connecticut, on the tidal Thames River, where he purchased an estate next to the ferry landing, directly across from the bustling port of New London. Within two years Deborah bore him a son, whom they named John Jr.

The elder Ledyard quickly established himself in his new community. In 1732, his name appears on the charter of a local merchants' group dedicated to expanding trade with Great Britain; he had a warehouse and a pier on his property in Groton, full of Gloucester cheese and raw sugar. By 1733, he evidently had two brothers living in New London as well—Benjamin and Isaac, who at age thirty-two married a wealthy forty-seven-year-old widow, daughter of the old colonial governor, Gurdon Saltonstall (Ledyards married well, or not at all). Benjamin and Isaac owned ships together—one of their vessels burnt to the waterline one terrible night in 1735. John Ledyard Sr. dabbled in New London's lucrative shipping industry, as well. The New London diarist Joshua Hempstead has him leaving for London in October 1738, aboard Captain John Jeffrey's brand new snow (a type of schooner). He became justice of the peace in 1739, and represented Groton at the General Assembly of Connecticut for most of the 1740s, while steadily accumulating property that eventually totaled several hundred acres.

This was the time of the Great Awakening, the religious revival movement that swept New England in the wake of a charismatic young English preacher named George Whitefield, who toured the Connecticut coast in 1740 and 1741. Whitefield believed that total salvation, marked by a powerful personal experience of conversion, was the only path to grace. At his sermons, often delivered from a hastily erected scaffold in some farmer's field, to crowds numbering in the hundreds and thousands, women fainted and men spoke in tongues. After Whitefield left, the spiritual flames he had ignited were stoked by a band of evangelical itinerant preachers. One of the most sought after of these "New Lights" was a young minister from Lebanon, Connecticut, named Eleazar Wheelock, who, along with Jonathan Edwards, became the leading voices of the movement. Edwards's classic sermon, Sinners in the Hands of an Angry God, with its harrowing images of divine wrath and damnation, was the movement's intellectual apotheosis. "The God that holds you over the pit of hell, much as one holds a spider, or some loathsome insect over the fire, abhors you, and is dreadfully provoked," he told his terrified audience: "He looks upon you as worthy of nothing else, but to be cast into the fire."

By far the most impassioned, and most controversial, of these new preachers was James Davenport, formerly of Southold, who took up residence in New London in 1741. A fiery, intemperate speaker, Davenport often castigated the establishment clergy for their own allegedly incomplete salvation. After one New London meeting, his followers built a great bonfire in the street, onto which they tossed books written by rival divines. According to one contemporary account, things became so frenzied that people began removing articles of clothing and tossing them on the flames as well; Davenport even removed his own breeches, which a horrified young woman promptly tossed back at him. This sort of thing ultimately got him banished from Connecticut for a year. Not even Squire Ledyard was immune to the religious fervor: Joshua Hempstead reports that during one particularly lively service in April 1742, "mr. ledyard caryed it on. He Prayed & Exhorted, it was the 3d time of his performing in [that] form."

Hempstead was a carpenter, merchant, farmer, arbiter of disputes, scribe of legal contracts and wills, and engraver of headstones, as well as a compulsive diarist (not to mention John Ledyard's maternal great-grandfather). He recorded births and deaths, comings and goings, transactions and conflicts, and the weather—for every single day of his life between 1711 and his death in 1758, at the extreme old age of eighty. His terse entries rarely ran longer than a sentence or two, but they give an evocative picture of daily life in eighteenth-century coastal Connecticut. It was a rural world of hay-mowing, sheep-shearing, and barn-raisings, as well as births and marriages, disease, and especially death: of infants, children, young men in their twenties and mothers in childbirth. Hardly a week went by when Hempstead didn't record a passing or two, from smallpox or tragic accident or—very rarely—old age. In March of 1747, Hempstead reports, the Squire's wife, Deborah Youngs Ledyard, succumbed to the measles, not long after giving birth to her tenth child, a girl named Experience. With ten children on his hands, the Squire needed a new wife, and after an interval of only a few months, he married Mary Ellery, a wealthy young widow from Hartford (who would bear the prolific Squire another five offspring, bringing his total to fifteen). Before long, he moved to Hartford with her and turned his Groton interests over to his eldest son, John Jr., who was well on his way to becoming a sea captain.

The occupation of ship captain was lucrative but hazardous, occupying a foggy region between piracy and commerce. The New London vessels were single-decked sailing ships, small and fast, which carried lumber, livestock, and provisions south to the Caribbean (or east to England), and returned home with sugar, rum, molasses, and coffee. It was a simple enough trade, but the fleet also had to pick its way between French privateers and British revenue cutters. Typically, ships would unload their illicit cargo at one port under cover of night, before sailing on to the nearest customs house, where the legitimate cargo would be declared the next morning. From 1733 to 1765, according to British colonial tax records, not a single barrel of molasses officially entered the Rhode Island and Connecticut colonies. The British crackdown on unpaid taxes would lead directly to the American Revolution.

Captain John often took briefer voyages across Long Island Sound, to see one Abigail Hempstead, a pretty and passionately religious girl who happened to be the daughter of his mother's sister, and thus his first cousin. Her parents refused to give him permission to marry her, and his own parents were not pleased with the idea either, but in early May of 1750 the dashing John—just home from a voyage—snatched Abigail off to Setauket, some sixty miles west of Southold on Long Island, and persuaded a physician there named Dr. Muirson to marry them civilly on a Sunday night. (He had blank marriage license forms lying around, according to Hempstead.) As the happy couple returned to New London the following Wednesday on the ferry, they chanced to meet Abigail's father, Robert Hempstead, who'd spent the past five days fruitlessly searching up and down the Connecticut coast for his twenty-year-old daughter. Joshua Hempstead doesn't elaborate on the scene that transpired, but this uneasy union of cousins, with censure on both sides, likely sowed the seed of the trouble to come.

We don't know exactly when John Ledyard the Traveller was born, but church records indicate that he was baptized "in infancy" on November 10, 1751, a rainy day eighteen months after his parents were married. On that same day, his parents, John and Abigail Ledyard, joined the First Congregational Church of Groton, making it undoubtedly a very costly day for the young family. John was probably born a few months before his baptism, since Joshua Hempstead reports that his father, now Captain John Ledyard, returned from a sea voyage in April 1751. A typical Caribbean voyage could last anywhere between two and six months, and Captain John may very well have departed around December 7, 1750, when Hempstead observed "above 20 sail of vessels in the harbour Mostly bound to the West Indias & several of them Sayled this day." So John was likely born in September 1751 or earlier.

Groton was rapidly growing into a wealthy town, fueled by the lucrative Caribbean trade, and it became (and remains) a center of American shipbuilding; in the twentieth century, it was the longtime home of General Dynamics' nuclear submarine factory. As John roamed the rivers and hills, he could not have missed the reservation, just up the river in North Groton, where the last remaining Pequots lived. Once a proud, warlike tribe, they had had little fear of the English; the Pequot War of the 1630s had been almost a fair fight, with significant casualties on both sides, before the English and their Mohegan allies finally prevailed. By 1750 the Pequots had been reduced to a miserable band of 150-odd souls, trying to scrape a living from their swampy, rocky land. Ledyard would have seen them in their poverty, paddling their long dugout canoes on the Thames. (The Mohegans, who had long ago agreed to accommodate the invading settlers, fared only slightly better, and had their own reservation a few miles away.) Aside from these remaining Native Americans, however, there was little that was exotic to the boy about sleepy and provincial Groton.

On the other hand, New London, located directly across the river, was a tempting, worldly place. By 1750 it was the busiest port on Long Island Sound, its streets crowded with ship captains and crews recently back from far-flung voyages. The first lighthouse on the Connecticut coast was built there in 1760. And the population was growing, from 3,171 in 1756 to almost 6,000 by 1774. Where landlocked Hartford looked inward, at its own incestuous society, New Londoners ventured out all over the world. It was actually easier to reach (old) London or the Caribbean island of St. Kitts by sea than it was to travel overland from New London to, say, Boston or Philadelphia. "It was remarked by the inhabitants of other towns," writes an early historian, "that something bold, uncommon and startling was always going on at New London."

When John was growing up, New Londoners were still telling the tale of the 200-ton Spanish ship that had foundered on the rocks just beyond the harbor mouth in 1752. Both the crew and her cargo had been saved, even the gold and silver (thirty-seven chests of silver, by one account, and three of gold doubloons), and the Spanish sailors had spent several months in New London, drinking and fighting and hanging about while waiting for a ship home. Before they could leave, however, a gang of locals conspired to steal the Spaniards' heavily-guarded treasure, which nearly led to a diplomatic incident between Britain and Spain. The culprits were soon caught, but not all of the loot was recovered, and for decades afterward, doubloons were turning up in farmhouse cupboards and in the surrounding swamps and fields. John and his cousins Benjamin and Isaac probably spent many afternoons searching for the Spanish treasure, while wondering when their fathers would come back from the Caribbean.

The Ledyard boys had been born into a dense web of cousins— Averys and Hempsteads and Youngses, with intertwining families and business interests, all focused on shipping. Understandably, given the sub-rosa nature of the Connecticut trade, vessel records are somewhat sparse, but Joshua Hempstead and other sources place Captain John in the Caribbean periodically: He appears in

Barbados in 1753; in St. Christopher, with his brother Youngs Ledyard, also a captain, in 1757. He certainly spent time in St. Eustatius, the Dutch colony that was the epicenter of the quasi-legitimate Caribbean trade, thanks to its local officials' carefree attitude toward paperwork. Squire Ledyard and his sons often partnered together. In 1761, for instance, the Squire's brig, *Neptune*, left for Barbados with a cargo to deliver to William Ledyard, the Squire's third son, who was stationed there at the time.

The New London fleet was sailing into the thick of the Seven Years' War, between England and France, and the ships faced danger from both sides. On one voyage in November 1757, Captain John's ship, *Greyhound*, was seized by a French privateer, then retaken by a British naval vessel, whose captain generously gave some (but not all) of his cargo back. Others were not so lucky. "Many vessels and their cargoes were condemned and confiscated," writes Frances Manwaring Caulkins in her definitive history of New London, first published in 1852. "Bankruptcies were the consequence." Hurricanes and nor'easters were another hazard. As Joshua Hempstead recorded in October 1753: "Jno Ledyard was just now come from Sea having met with a violent Storm which Carryed away their Boom & Mainsail & gaff & 2 cables & 17 Horses & 40 Sheep & many other things." Luckily, he added, there was "no life Lost of any humane Creature."

During his father's long absences, young John became quite close to his mother. Like her father (and father-in-law, the Squire), Abigail Hempstead Ledyard had been swept up in the Great Awakening as a teenager, and she remained prone to swooning and speaking in tongues. A fervent, pious woman, she shared her faith with her young son, but he later tired of what he saw as her religious excesses: "Remember Madam," he admonished her in a letter from Paris, written when he was in his midthirties, "that I am ready to go out of life with this assertion, that you carry your notions of religion, to the most ridiculous & absurd lengths." Nevertheless, family members noted the strong similarity between mother and son. "[She] possessed unusual vigour of intellect—brilliant talents and Christian urbanity which greatly adorned a beautiful person (and if allow'd the expression, in a generous Mind)," one of her nieces wrote to Jared Sparks. "Whoever knew them most, have ever observed a remarkable parity of disposition between mother & son."

When his father returned from his voyages, John sometimes gained a new sibling: His sister Frances (Fanny) was born in 1754, followed by a brother named Thomas two years later. A boy named Charles, born in 1759, died before he was four months old and there seems to have been something wrong with his youngest brother George, born in 1761. Later in life, John would describe him, without explanation, as having been "so negatively blessed by Nature that he should not ever want for any thing." John spent most of his time with his cousins Benny and Isaac, both born within three years of him; while their fathers went to sea together, they wandered in the woods and sailed on the Thames. "Shall I ever spend such hours again?" he wrote longingly, years later, after everything had changed. "Will fortune renew the pleasurable scenes? My fears dictate an unfortunate reply."

In the winter of 1762, the Ledyard captains departed on yet another voyage, and this time they didn't come back. Captain John died at sea of a tropical fever, probably malaria, on March 17. Three weeks later, on another ship, Youngs Ledyard succumbed to smallpox in St. Eustatius. Family tradition holds Benedict Arnold responsible for both men's deaths: Many years later, Youngs's granddaughter claimed that Arnold had been the ship's apothecary and had prescribed her grandfather some lethal remedy, after which he stole the ship's cargo and sailed back to Connecticut. In time, Arnold would perpetrate more than his share of villainy on the Ledyard clan—more than twenty of John's cousins would die in his traitorous 1781 raid on New London—but this charge lacks evidence. In the spring of 1762, Arnold was in London, purchasing supplies for his New Haven apothecary shop.

John's world was shattered. At least Captain Youngs Ledyard had died solvent: He had owned a house, a wharf, some cargo, and a couple of slaves, including a man named Cuff and a woman named Jenny. But a long list of creditors waited to peck at what remained of Captain John's estate. He seems to have borrowed money from nearly everyone he knew, a skill his son would later perfect. The roll call of creditors includes friends, acquaintances, and his brothers William and Ebenezer, who proved to be the family's true businessmen. The Squire himself had also helped out in a small way, taking promissory notes from John's creditors totaling about forty pounds, worth a little more than $8,000 today. Times were tough, in the Connecticut of 1762, and an economic depression was around the corner. Looking around at this time, Squire Ledyard saw "a Strange scene of Bankruptcy and ruins," that didn't spare his own family. Captain John had died almost penniless. As administrator of her dead husband's estate, Abigail painstakingly listed the household's assets, down to the last brass button. There were five beds, a coffee pot, Captain John's sword and arms. He didn't have much more than personal property, the total value of which amounted to just 133 pounds, barely one-third the sum of his debts. Abigail was forced to beg the executors for an allowance on which to raise her four small children, the oldest of whom (John) was barely ten. And she cosigned a bond with her uncle John Hempstead, guaranteeing 500 pounds to cover the debts of the estate. Among the other items of property Abigail listed were an old sorrel mare, a cow and calf, the family Bible, and a handful of other books, only one of which she listed, pointedly, by name: *The Reall Christian.*

Even worse, the widow Ledyard soon found herself evicted from her home. She had placed the deed with her cousin Ebenezer Avery, but it had somehow been lost (the story goes), so she had no choice but to move back to her native Southold, with four children in tow and a fifth on the way, while the property wound up in the hands of the Squire—"by an unheard of Fraudulency," as one of John's cousins later put it to Jared Sparks. In fact, the Squire may have felt entitled to the land since, as he subsequently declared in his will, "I consider my son John to have already had a large portion out of my estate." He later gave the Groton place outright to his surviving sons, Ebenezer and William, "in consideration of the love and good will that I have and do bear toward [them]."

The Ledyard captains were laid to rest within thirty feet of each other, in Groton cemetery, at the top of the hill, not far from the tiny marker for Charles, John's dead infant brother. Though he died bankrupt, Captain John's headstone is the larger of the two, inscribed with a sunburst and a suitably romantic epitaph:

> *Once did I stand amid Life's busy throng,*
> *Healthy and Active, Vigorous and Strong.*
> *Oft did I traverse Ocean's briny waves,*
> *And safe Escaped a thousand gaping graves.*
> *Yet dire Disease has stopped my final Breath,*
> *And here I lie the Prisoner of Death.*
> *Reader, expect not length of days to See,*
> *Or if thou dost, think, think, ah think of me.*

About eight months after the captains died, Squire Ledyard apparently had a change of heart, and he sent for their eldest boys: Isaac, Benjamin, and young John. He wanted them at Hartford, he reportedly said, to replace the sons he mourned. John's mother let him go, for she could hardly afford to keep her remaining children. The three cousins went to live with their grandfather, in the attic of his big-timbered house on Arch Street. They were very much outsiders there, and this bonded them together for life, but John missed his mother and sisters. Abigail Ledyard eventually remarried to a widowed Long Island doctor, Micah Moore, with whom she had three more girls. After Moore died in 1776, she would open a boarding house and tavern catering to British soldiers. Though it was clear she could take care of herself, John would forever think of himself as "the leading descendant of a broken and distressed family."

By all indications, John hated his life in exile. Compared to cosmopolitan New London, Hartford was a stifling place, where appearances and manners were prized above all. This was the Connecticut of "steady habits," and it lived up to the colony's staid reputation. Once again, the Squire had established himself in a new town, leveraging his wife's family connections to make himself one of Hartford's leading citizens. By the time John and his cousins arrived, he had accumulated a robust portfolio of properties, including the big house in town as well as farms, livestock, and mills (not to mention children: five more with the second Mrs. Ledyard). And, of course, he was prominent in the First Church of Hartford, presided over by old Reverend Elnathan Whitman—a contemporary and kindred spirit of Jonathan Edwards. When the Squire died, Whitman praised him (in a nineteen-page eulogy, published in pamphlet form) for the "inflexible integrity" that made him "very much a terror to evildoers."

This was certainly no news to John, who had always had an

impulsive, pranksterish side to him that the Squire must have found maddening. One day, when the teenaged John was out walking on a road outside Hartford, he saw a team of fine horses thunder past. On an impulse, he stopped the driver and bought the horses on the spot, for a note drawn on his grandfather, who was not amused. The Squire made him return the horses, casting some unkind words in John's direction. And then there was that unexplained and tragic disaster that took place in Hartford, on the day after the hated Stamp Act was repealed in 1766. There was to be a celebration with fireworks at the brick schoolhouse at the center of town—which held a large shipment of gunpowder for the colonial militia that had been delivered the same day. The delivery had been sloppy, and that night, somebody managed to ignite some stray powder on the grass, which ultimately detonated the entire supply. The explosion shook the whole town, killing six young men—including John's twenty-six-year-old uncle Nathaniel, who was studying to become a doctor. Also seriously injured was Austin Ledyard, twenty-five, the Squire's favorite and most favored son. His death a decade later was thought to have been the result of his injuries that night. Nobody knows who or what caused the fire, but suspicions settled on a group of unnamed boys who had been seen playing near the schoolhouse. Was John among them?

As Ledyard matured, his uncle Tom Seymour began to take an interest in him. Seymour was a flinty character who reportedly swam in the Little River every single day of his life, even breaking the ice to swim in winter. He was also a shrewd lawyer who served as king's attorney for the Connecticut colony, and would later become mayor of Hartford, a post he held for decades. His wife, John's aunt Mary, was more forbidding. She wore her hair pulled back tightly, and her mouth was twisted into a permanent frown. John later mocked them as "Lord and Lady Mayoress," but when John was fifteen, Uncle Tom gave him a chance, inviting the boy to study law in his offices. He was a bright lad, Seymour saw, with a dramatic flair that might prove useful in court. "Uncle Seymour promises me as fair and kindly as an Uncle can," he wrote excitedly to his mother in 1767: "He sayeth that if I will (which I hope I shall) be steady and mind my business that he will do well by me & if my life should be spared he will let me & Cozen Thos. [Tom Seymour Jr.] Up to his law business (as he does not intend to follow the business long)." But John preferred to be outdoors in the sunshine rather than grinding down his soul on the millstone of the law. To his credit, Tom Seymour understood this, but not the Squire, who derided the boy (behind his back, of course) as "no great lawyer."

Nor did Ledyard wish to become one. His options were limited, however, particularly after his grandfather's death in September of 1771. Ordinarily, such a man would have left most of his property to his eldest son, but Captain John was gone. John would have been next in line, as the eldest of the eldest. Instead, the Squire left the vast bulk of his property—farms, mills, houses—to Austin Ledyard, his first son by his new wife, and evidently the favorite of his children. The Squire by then had amassed an enormous family, with fifteen children and (ultimately) eighty grandchildren, but the message to Captain John's family couldn't have been clearer: The Squire clearly bore a grudge, probably for some business debacle (the seizure of the *Greyhound*, perhaps) for which he held Captain John responsible. He generously forgave the debts of his other dead son, Youngs Ledyard, while also granting Youngs's children the "double portion" traditionally reserved for children of the eldest son. Meanwhile, Captain John's children were to split the interest on 150 pounds—out of a 5,000-pound estate.

It's not clear just when John realized that he had been stiffed by his grandfather, but when he finally did he must have marveled at the inscription on the old man's tombstone, a sandstone slab in the shady churchyard at the center of Hartford. "The memory of the just is blessed," it reads.

Dartmouth
College

This 1784 New Hampshire map, printed a dozen years after Ledyard arrived, shows no roads leading to Dartmouth College. *Courtesy of the Library of Congress*

# Shut Out and Set Free

FIVE DECADES AFTER THE FACT, JAMES WHEELOCK STILL VIVIDLY recalled John Ledyard's arrival at Dartmouth College in the spring of 1772. Wheelock, the son of Dartmouth's founder, was just fifteen years old when Ledyard rode out of the woods in, of all things, a horse-drawn sulky, a two-wheeled buggy like those now used in harness racing. Most students arrived alone, on horseback, after a lengthy trek over mud-choked, bridgeless roads. As Wheelock noted, Ledyard's was "the first carriage of this kind ever on Dartmouth plain," which had only recently been cleared out of the northern wilderness. It was like showing up in the Yukon behind the wheel of a Porsche.

Ledyard knew how to make an entrance. As if the sulky weren't sufficiently attention grabbing, he was dressed like some sort of self-styled sultan, wearing enormous, baggy Turkish breeches (loose in the legs, "but snug withal," as he had instructed Ebenezer Avery, his Groton cousin and the family's tailor). He left his shirts open at the collar, without a cravat, baring his chest even in the chill of a New England spring, when ice still covered the ground. Unlatching a trunk, the twenty-one-year-old freshman revealed bolts of colorful fabric that he said he planned to use for theatrical productions—an utterly bizarre notion, at this rugged school intended to train missionaries. Where did Ledyard think he was, Yale?

Though Dartmouth is today a member of the Ivy League, in 1772 it was a very different place from the four established American colleges—Harvard, Princeton, the College of William and Mary in Virginia, and Yale, which was where anyone who was anybody in Connecticut went to school (including Eleazar Wheelock himself). Tom Seymour had graduated from Yale, and so would his two sons, Henry and Tom Jr. Ledyard, however, was dispatched to the log-cabin school in the north woods. Dartmouth was then quite literally a rough-hewn place, where young men were expected to work in the cornfields and woodlots as well as in the groves of knowledge. Such labor, Wheelock believed, would prepare them for their careers as missionaries to the Native Americans, and it might also help keep them out of trouble.

Dartmouth had actually grown out of the remains of another institution, Moor's Charity School, which Wheelock had established in Lebanon, Connecticut, in 1756. Named for its chief benefactor, Moor's had been intended exclusively for Native Americans, mainly members of the nearby Pequot and Mohegan tribes. (Squire Ledyard had been an early supporter.) Wheelock hoped to train Native American boys to become missionaries to their own people, but he had grown disillusioned by "the bad conduct and behaviour of such as have been educated here, after they have left the school."

One pupil who didn't disappoint him was a bright Mohegan named Samson Occom, who had come to Wheelock in 1743 as an eager twenty-year-old, and soon became one of the most famed preachers in Connecticut, Indian or white. An impassioned, well-read, and articulate speaker, Occom represented the model for what Wheelock had hoped to achieve, and drew huge crowds wherever he preached. (Ledyard had certainly seen him, long before he went to Dartmouth.) In 1765 Wheelock dispatched Occom on a two-year fundraising tour of England, where he proved quite an exotic sensation. His trip yielded some 12,000 pounds and the support of influential English clergymen and lords, including the Earl of Dartmouth. With their backing, Wheelock decided to pull up stakes and move north, closer to the Native Americans he hoped to convert. There Moor's would be reborn and repurposed as Dartmouth College, a unique hybrid institution for English and Native American boys alike. He would charge tuition from those white boys whose families could afford to pay, but native students would be educated for free. Occom, meanwhile, had grown disillusioned with Wheelock; having raised so much money for educating (and Christianizing) his own people, he soon realized that Wheelock planned to turn Moor's into a school for whites. He was also annoyed that Wheelock had allowed Occom's family to live in poverty while he was away, and the two men never repaired their relationship. (Occom died, drunk and embittered, in 1792.)

In the summer of 1770, Wheelock and his little band of students and servants trudged nearly two hundred miles north to Hanover Township in New Hampshire, where Governor John Wentworth had granted Wheelock about 1800 acres situated on a plateau above the Connecticut River. Wheelock rode in a grand English coach, with various household articles and a barrel of rum, since enshrined in a college song. About thirty students followed on foot, as well as sundry servants and at least one slave, a black man named Exeter.

At the time, the northern New England woods were still very much a frontier. The early settlers had mostly abandoned the upper Connecticut Valley in the wake of the Deerfield Massacre of 1704, in which a small Massachusetts farming village had been brutally attacked by Mohawks and French soldiers, who killed fifty settlers, including women and children, and took 112 captives. The prisoners were marched three hundred miles north to

Canada through deep snow; twenty of them died or were killed en route. The Connecticut Valley remained a kind of no-man's-land, with few farms and almost no roads linking the tiny, hardy settlements that persisted in the wilderness, despite the danger of Native American attacks; Deerfield continued to be harassed as late as 1746.

The site Wheelock chose for his college lay some thirty-five miles upriver from the northernmost British military outpost on the Connecticut, the Fort at No. 4, near Charlestown, N.H. Built in the 1740s to protect against Native American attacks, the fort had seen action during the French and Indian War of 1754–1763, still a fresh memory. With the defeat of the French and the retreat of the Native Americans, new settlements had sprung up along the Connecticut River, many of them founded by emigrants from Connecticut, such as Wheelock. The first settler had arrived in Hanover in 1765, only a few years before Wheelock.

The land was still largely wooded, so Wheelock set about clearing fields and building a gristmill, a sawmill, and a log house that measured eighty by thirty-two feet, with sixteen rooms on two stories. Students and servants and laborers were set to work building stone walls and stump fences, and sending newly-cut logs down the Connecticut River, marked DC to identify them as having come from Dartmouth College. One of the trees felled to clear what is now the Dartmouth Green measured over 270 feet tall. (The tallest of the trees, the straight white pines, were marked and reserved by the Crown as masts for the king's navy.)

It was difficult work, and Eleazar Wheelock showed the strain of every one of his sixty years. He was tormented by eczema, asthma, and painful flatulence. His arthritis was so bad he employed students to write his letters for him. As a younger man, at the height of the Great Awakening, Wheelock had been unstoppable, sometimes preaching more than 400 sermons in a year.

He was such a powerful speaker that his audiences often burst into spontaneous tears and cries, or simply stood trembling. After one such meeting, he wrote in his diary in 1741, "I was forced to break off my sermon before done, the outcry was so great." Now he was in charge of a brand-new college—as well as a frontier farm and a busy logging operation. Despite his ailments, he maintained a huge correspondence: with his English sponsors, his impatient creditors (the logs brought in a little money, but Wheelock still watched with anxiety as his original endowment dwindled), the townsfolk, and with the occasional deadbeat student. "Henceforth he was a harassed administrator, a harassed farmer, and a harassed provider," notes the Dartmouth historian James McCallum. "All things converged on Wheelock."

By the time Ledyard arrived in the spring of 1772, the college was in a full-fledged crisis. It was the end of a hard winter, and provisions were running low. Most food had to be imported from great distances, over extremely bad roads. There was only one formal road, in fact, a newly cut track from the coast, which ran via Plymouth. Fodder for livestock also had to be brought from afar during winter months. In April 1772, the month Ledyard arrived, Wheelock had sent some men to Walpole, thirty miles downriver, to get provisions. Their mission was so urgent that he had given them special permission to travel on the Sabbath.

Dartmouth was a lonely, purgatorial outpost; it was probably the only American college where students had to be careful of wolves. The campus was prowled by "wild beasts double the number of both the inhabitants and the domestic animals together, which were a great annoyance," recalled one of Ledyard's classmates, Nathaniel Kendrick. It was cold, too: "The fireplaces were generally from six to eight feet wide, and as the dwellings were cold and clothing scarce, the wood, which was plenty, was used unsparingly. In the winter the last thing before retiring to rest was to fill the chimney and make a lordly fire." Until John Payne opened his notorious tavern on the north side of the Green, there was little for the students to do besides study and work in the fields. This was just fine with Reverend Wheelock. Such labor, he hoped, would provide "the principal or only diversion" for his students.

Although he almost certainly joined his classmates in raising a large barn, during the summer of 1772, Ledyard had other ideas about recreation and diversions. He and two classmates signed a cheeky petition to the old reverend in the fall, asking that, like their colleagues at Harvard and Princeton, the young gentlemen be allowed time "for stepping the Minuet and learning to use the Sword." Wheelock's response is not recorded.

Ledyard always found a way to make himself the center of attention. His whole tenure at Dartmouth constituted a sort of theatrical performance, much to the annoyance of the sober Reverend Wheelock. "[He] had an independence & singularity in his manner, his dress, & appearance," James Wheelock recalled, "that commanded the particular attention & notice of fellow students." His classmate Nathaniel Adams also found his manners "singular." Time and again, throughout Ledyard's life, his friends and acquaintances would alight on that particular word: He was not merely unique, or odd, or even strange, but . . . singular. It started with his dress, those poufy Turkish breeches and the open shirts, which all but begged young James Wheelock to slip a "cold frosty iron wedge" down Ledyard's shirt one day during class, causing him to swear an "oath": "Come, come, Wheelock! Is the Devil in you?"

Wheelock ran a tight ship, and one of the many things he could not tolerate was swearing. "I have not heard a profane word spoken by one of my Number, nor have I Reason to think there has been one for three years past," Wheelock declared to his English trustees in his annual report for 1773, in all apparent sincerity. Students who broke the rules—by getting drunk, by cursing, by going to nearby Lebanon on the Sabbath (to drink, naturally)—were expected to make a public apology. Even one of Wheelock's sons, Eleazar Jr., had to confess his own "bad and disrespectful conduct," at least once. Wheelock wielded a sharp pen, and those who crossed him could count on receiving a slashing broadside, usually citing the specific commandments they had violated. And he launched a crusade against two local tavern keepers, John Sergeant and John Payne, who had established a thriving student trade. (Dartmouth's reputation as a hard-drinking party school, it seems, was earned long ago.) Wheelock was not above trying to sabotage a former student's career with a damaging recommendation, as he did to one Francis Quarles, who was attempting to transfer to Yale. Quarles replied to Wheelock with a vow to tell a court of law "[how] you treat your men that are sent to your college. Sometimes to blow stinky horns eat stinking provisions kill dogs &c &c. And many other things scandelous to relate." Ledyard's classmates in the class of 1776 included Ebenezer Mattoon, later a lieutenant colonel in the Continental Army and a member of the Massachusetts legislature; and John Sherburne, a future congressman and federal judge. A good number of the other boys went on to become ministers.

It was unclear where young Ledyard was headed in life. He was an undistinguished student, less interested in his studies than in various extracurricular activities. "He was much addicted to reading plays," a fellow student recalled. After a few months, he even managed to stage a production of Joseph Addison's five-act tragedy, *Cato.* The play had been hugely popular since its first performance in 1713, and it was a particular favorite of George Washington's, perhaps because it involves a colonial rebellion against the power of Rome. True to form, Ledyard played the tragedy as a farce. His own role as the gray-bearded Numidian general Syphax "afforded much hilarity," James Wheelock recalled. The elder Wheelock tolerated Ledyard and his plays, so the young man found other ways to challenge authority. When it came his turn to blow the hated conch horn, which was used (instead of a bell) to summon students to classes and prayers, the best he could manage was an exaggerated sort of bleating, which amused his classmates but annoyed Wheelock no end.

Although Wheelock was too harried to keep formal student records, he did maintain strict accounts, and Ledyard's name first appears in the college ledgers on April 23, 1772, recording his purchase of "6 sheats paper." While his personality was extravagant, his spending habits, for the most part, were modest and sparing; he was far more frugal than some of his classmates. Perhaps even then he was perfecting the art of living off others. He bought paper, quills, and ink, perhaps to write letters home; a load of wood for heating his room; thread and fabric to repair his clothes. He earned a few shillings, now and again, for "services in writing" (likely helping Wheelock with his letters) and he spent a few more shillings at John Payne's tavern. He also bought a pair of Indian moccasins from the well-traveled missionary David Mc-Clure, who had just returned from the Ohio River Valley.

At the time, Wheelock was trying hard to recruit Native American students, with mixed results. Out of thirty students when Ledyard arrived in April 1772, only five were Native American; by the following spring, there were seventeen Native Americans among a student population of eighty. The tribes closest to Dartmouth, the Six Nations or Iroquois (living in present-day Vermont, New York, and Quebec), also proved the most resistant to conversion, forcing Wheelock to send his missionaries farther afield, to western Pennsylvania and beyond. One of his emissaries, Sylvanus Ripley, brought back ten Native American boys during the 1772 school year, eight from the Caghnawaga tribe (near Montreal) and two from the Hurons. The Hurons adapted well and learned to read and write, but the Caghnawagas had more difficulty: "They soon discovered the Indian Temper, grew impatient of Order and government in the School, [and] shew'd a great Inclination to be hunting and rambling in the Woods," Wheelock wrote disgustedly. Within months, four of them were gone.

Some Native Americans who stayed became good students; the Dartmouth archives contain several examples of their handwriting, proudly preserved. Others, though, caused Wheelock nothing but headaches. He complained often about drinking, and still more often about ingratitude, the worst of all possible sins in his view. There were conflicts between the white students and the Native Americans as well, which is not surprising since they came from vastly different cultures. Four students (three white, one Native American) wrote to Wheelock in January of 1773, complaining about their Native American neighbors, who liked to stay up all night "hollowing and making all manner of nise."

In later life, Ledyard impressed both Thomas Jefferson and Captain Cook with his knowledge of Native American customs and languages. Intentionally or not, Ledyard fostered the strong impression that he had actually lived with the Native Americans for several months during his time at Dartmouth. "He had not been quite four months in college, when he suddenly disappeared without notice to his comrades, and apparently without permission from the president," wrote Jared Sparks, apparently based on his interviews with Tom Seymour and his son Henry. "He is understood to have wandered to the borders of Canada, and among the Six Nations. It is certain, that he acquired in this excursion a knowledge of Indian manners and Indian language, which was afterwards of essential service to him in his intercourse with savages in various parts of the world."

If he did go, it was likely without Wheelock's knowledge, as there is no mention of such a mission in any of Wheelock's copious letters. And if he went without permission, surely the reverend would have remembered that when he later catalogued Ledyard's sins. There is no evidence that Ledyard performed any such mission; moreover, the Six Nations had already made it clear to Wheelock that they wanted no more missionaries or teachers. Ledyard does appear to have left Dartmouth at the end of August 1772, when he settled his college accounts. August marked the end of the term, so he may simply have gone home after commencement. Governor Wentworth even attended, making the trip from his country estate at Wolfeboro, near Lake Winnipesauke, via the newly constructed royal road. Shortly afterward, some of Ledyard's classmates, including his friend Sam Stebbins, traveled south to Hartford. Ledyard might have gone with them and spent time in Connecticut. On November 2, 1772, at any rate, we know he left Hartford on a horse, headed back to Hanover carrying a letter to Wheelock from Wheelock's son-in-law William Patten. The infamous "stepping the Minuet" petition was submitted to Wheelock that same month, bearing Ledyard's unmistakable signature (with a flamboyant, swooping *L*). A few weeks later, on December 1, his account was credited with seventeen shillings for "6 yds greenbays," or fabric—perhaps he sold the cloth used in his theatrical productions.

Although he had ostensibly gone to Dartmouth to learn to teach Native Americans, Ledyard seems to have learned more from them. Over the winter and spring of 1773, he showed himself quite well acquainted with native peoples' ways. A few weeks into the New Year, for example, he rounded up a group of students and, with Wheelock's blessing, marched them to the top of a nearby peak (probably Velvet Rocks, a 1,250-foot knob a few miles east of Hanover), through swamps and deep snow. Wheelock agreed to the idea because he felt it would help prepare the young men for the rigors of missionary life. They left at noon, breaking trail through heavy drifts, and reached the mountaintop shortly before dark, just in time to build a fire and to dig snow caves, which they lined with pine boughs. Then they climbed into the burrows, covered themselves with blankets, and snuggled together for warmth through what one recalled as a "sleepless night." The next morning, they struck camp and hiked home in time for classes—"all of us, except it might be Ledyard, well satisfied not to take such another jaunt," according to James Wheelock.

That he could persuade a dozen of his classmates to take a camping trip in midwinter testifies to Ledyard's charisma and his emerging role as a student leader. His name appears on several petitions to Wheelock, as well as on a bond to secure the release of a black servant named Caesar, who had been jailed on charges of defamation against another servant named Mary Sleeper, for claiming that two other servants "have had carnal knowledge of her the said Mary," according to the complaint, "and that she was fond of it." Furthermore, according to the charges, "the said Caesar said that he knew something which if known to the world would ruin the character of the said Mary to her dying day." Ledyard and the other petitioners were able to raise ten shillings, enough to spare Caesar the prescribed penalty of seven lashes across his bare back.

Years later, James Wheelock told Jared Sparks that he couldn't remember why Ledyard left Dartmouth. "I think probably, however, it was, that he was too restless to be long in any one place, and that his mind was not adapted to close application, & that he could not patiently submit to the restraints, nor comply with the strict & uniform regulations of a College government," Wheelock theorized. The truth was that things were not going well for Ledyard at Dartmouth. Since January, Wheelock had been writing to

Tom Seymour, who was now Ledyard's guardian, wondering (politely at first) when and how he might be reimbursed for young John's education. Although he told Seymour that Ledyard "[has] been pretty steady, & bids fair to make a good scholar," it was probably quite clear to him by then that young Ledyard was a poor candidate for the clergy. Later in life, Ledyard admitted that he'd had little interest in "preaching the everlasting Gospel to the cursed Indians." Even before he left for Dartmouth, he had penned an Easter-season letter to his spinster aunt Elizabeth in New York, mocking the religious zeal of provincial Connecticut: "*Christ crucified* is no news surely in N York," wrote the jaded young man.

> What a melancholly worn out tale is this same—indeed stand I not unreprov'd, quite, to call it ungenteel Entertainment—nay as who should say is it not much to be thought of that one could not after having been quite satisfied with the disappointments of Pleasure enter the Kingdom Above without—the tasteless repasts of—the New Testament. Faith, regeneration, repentance, & whats worse than all—Humility.

Meanwhile, Wheelock's three-year-old college was on the brink of financial ruin. The original endowment from Lord Dartmouth and others was steadily dwindling, with no hope of replenishment. Of his eighty-odd pupils, half paid no tuition. He was besieged by applications from prospective students, all of whom seemed to want a free education. In response, he resolved to stop taking any more white charity students. Meanwhile, the tone of his letters to Tom Seymour in Hartford grew more urgent, and in March he dispatched an agent to collect several debts in Connecticut, including Ledyard's.

April was, and still is, a good time to escape Hanover. During the long weeks of New England's mud season, the trees remain stubbornly bare, the sky bleak, the land cold and soggy. A measles epidemic raged through the college during the spring of 1773, there was trouble in the kitchens, and fresh food again grew scarce. And, of course, Ledyard had no money. Letters had been flying back and forth between Wheelock and Ledyard's uncle Tom Seymour, who ultimately informed the old man that young Ledyard had, in fact, no inheritance left.

This news apparently shocked Wheelock. Squire Ledyard had been a wealthy man, and Wheelock felt that John should have been able to pay tuition, which amounted to a fairly modest twenty pounds per year. But his share of his grandfather's estate, which he received sometime around his twenty-first birthday, in the summer or fall of 1772, had apparently disappeared, and Ledyard had no good explanation. After a year at Dartmouth, all he had to his name was a few personal possessions, including his blanket, which he returned to the college on April 15 for a credit of one pound, and a bundle of candles, for which he was credited four and a half pence. The only other asset he possessed was a horse, which unfortunately was in Connecticut at the time. Ledyard gave Wheelock a bill of sale for the horse, and then went down to the river, axe in hand.

Ledyard began to build his canoe, on the bank of the Connecticut River, sometime in early April 1773. His fellow students naturally drifted down to watch. According to legend, he felled the biggest old-growth tree he could find, but more likely, college loggers had already done the job for him. With the help of some of the onlookers, he set about hollowing the trunk into a dugout, like the impressive double-prowed craft that his Connecticut neighbors, the Pequots and Mohegans, paddled on the Thames River and Long Island Sound. In the telling and retelling, Ledyard's canoe would grow to thirty, forty, even fifty feet, but such a long, unstable craft surely would have killed him; more likely it was about fifteen or twenty feet long. At one point his axe slipped and he cut himself badly on the thigh, but after a few days' rest he went back to work. None of the other students, some of whom were mere boys of fourteen or fifteen, suspected the real reason for his urgency; to them it was all a great "frolick," as one later wrote. When, finally, the canoe was ready, he stocked it with cheese, bread, and dried venison, and a bearskin for warmth, as well as two great books to peruse during his voyage: Ovid, in Latin, and the New Testament, in Greek. While his young admirers looked on, Ledyard leaped into the canoe and pushed off from shore. But he didn't row or paddle at all; he simply lay in the stern of the vessel, ostentatiously reading Ovid while the current carried him around the bend and out of his amazed classmates' sight.

That could have easily been the last anyone ever saw of John Ledyard. A day's float downstream from Hanover, the river poured over Bellows Falls, a turbulent series of cascades and rapids that dropped more than forty feet in Ledyard's day (now buried under a hydroelectric dam). Even if he survived the falls, he surely would have drowned in the turbulent, rocky gorge below. Ledyard was so engrossed by his reading, he later claimed, that he didn't hear the roar of the falls until it was almost too late. In his panic, he managed to tip over the canoe, and just barely avoided being swept over the falls to his death. Apart from the bearskin, of course, he lost nearly everything—his food and most of his possessions—when the canoe capsized.

The canoe trip was much more than an escape from Eleazar Wheelock's Dartmouth; it marked the beginning of a new stage in Ledyard's life. Of course, he didn't realize this at the time. He was broke and desperate to leave, and his horse was in Hartford. The canoe simply offered the cheapest way out. Yet it was also his maiden voyage as an adventurer, his first sally into the unknown.

When Thomas Jefferson heard the story of the canoe trip, years later, Ledyard reported that "our minister laughed most heartily, observing that it was no unworthy prelude to my subsequent voyages."

He was not home long before reality caught up with him. Eleazar Wheelock's final letter to Tom Seymour, written on April 26, likely arrived in early May. The old man was apoplectic, and not only because Ledyard had fled on a day when Wheelock happened to be out of town. While the reverend normally employed an amanuensis, he was so furious that he wrote this letter himself, in his crabbed, arthritic hand. "I had no [motive] to induce me to attempt to give him a college education with such a pittance," Wheelock raged,

> but Compassion to your Nephew (whom I hoped to be instrumental to save from utter ruin, to whom I owed nothing more than to any of my fellow creatures) and respect to the Family of my deceased friend his grandfather, nor could you suppose I had any other, or that I could expect one farthing reward for all I proposed to do for him, more than the pleasure of being instrumental of saving him from total Ruin.

Nevertheless, he did expect to be paid—not much to ask in return for rescuing the young wastrel from "total Ruin." And, Wheelock intoned darkly to Seymour, "I am far, very far, from thinking you clear from blame." As king's attorney, Seymour was surely not used to being addressed this way. Soon it seemed like everyone had turned against Ledyard. He spent a week brooding over his own response to the reverend, which he revised and extended a few times before he posted it on May 23, 1773. "When I sit down to write," Ledyard began, "I must confess I know not where to begin or where to end, or what to say." He had quite a lot to say, however, and his letter matches Wheelock blow for blow: "Who's this that assumes the Pose of compassion, kindness, benevolence & charity," the young man demanded of his elder, "& writes as he writes?

> Is he honored with preferments, is he cloathed with Authority from God, & Man, is he a Scribe well instructed in the Law, giving to every one a portion in season, is he one that brings the glad tidings of peace, is he a Steward of the mysteries of Heaven, is he dealt with by the laying on of Hands?—yes.—is he a *Man*?

And so on, for seven tightly scribbled and often rambling pages. Despite Ledyard's disjointed syntax, the long dashes like jouster's lances—revealing the influence of his favorite novel, Laurence Sterne's *Tristram Shandy*—the letter's significance is clear. Ledyard is standing up to the old man at last, addressing him as an equal, "with the freedom of a younger brother," which must have driven Wheelock to new heights of fury. The old divine was used to handing down judgments, not receiving them from lessers. "For not to you, but to my Master do I stand or fall," Ledyard declared, "—your eyes discerning no further than the coat & breeches."

Then he gets to the point: "You begin Sir with a surprise that my Legacy was so exhausted—justly might you Sir, but not more so than my unfortunate self." He added solemnly, "I now, under the most sacred obligations, bona fide, declare I was *not aware* of it." He goes on: "When I saw the Letters & Accts, I was ever after so asham'd of my inadvertancy & so justly culpable before you Sir that I could not compose myself to come before you & answer for my misconduct." Therein lay the reason for hasty departure in the canoe—or so it seems.

In closing, Ledyard at least absolves his alma mater, if not its founder: "Farewell dear Dartmouth—delightfull repose for Innocence & true felicity . . . that you may flourish in immortal green." He closed with a cheeky postscript: "Was sorry the Doctr [Wheelock] happened to be out of town when I came away." On the envelope next to Ledyard's name, the Doctor assessed the young man's character concisely: "Saucy Enough," he wrote.

The next day, May 24, probate records show that John received twenty-three pounds four shillings from his grandfather's estate. So the joke might have been on Wheelock, too.

Sometime after he returned from Dartmouth, Ledyard got his hands on a coat that had been made for his grandfather. The Squire's coat was too large, so Ledyard had it shortened by Ebenezer Avery, the family tailor in Groton. But he refused to have it hemmed, the old tailor recalled to Jared Sparks, and so it slowly began to unravel. It was made of a rough woolen fabric called duroy, and John wore it constantly, strutting down the Hartford streets and Groton lanes as it quite literally fell apart on him. Ledyard's life also seemed to be unraveling. Having failed at the law, he had now failed at Dartmouth, and there seemed to be little chance of his joining the family merchant business, most of which was by then under the control of his half-brother Austin Ledyard. The rest of the Ledyard clan was eager to get John settled into a position, and it really didn't matter what that might be.

Once again, powerful family friends were enlisted in the cause. Within a week of mailing his letter to Wheelock, Ledyard was on his way to see the Reverend William Hart, of Preston, Connecticut, followed by the famed Reverend Joseph Bellamy of Old Saybrook. Both of these prominent preachers encouraged him to pursue a career in the ministry, a suggestion he adopted with his usual enthusiasm. That had been his mother's fondest ambition for her eldest son, whom she adored but had hardly seen in the last decade; he would do anything to please her. Back in Hartford, his Seymour relatives were surprised to discover John preaching aloud in the woods, practicing his diction to the foxes and rabbits. A few weeks later he was off to Long Island, where he was to begin his studies while looking for a prelate who would be willing to tutor and eventually certify him.

His first stop was his mother's house in Southold, where he stayed just one night, being in a great adolescent hurry to get on with his life. Then he ferried over to East Hampton and the ample library of Reverend Samuel Buell, where he spent a month studying with another hopeful young preacher. The other candidate's fate is not known, but at the end of his stay, Ledyard was gently encouraged to look elsewhere, and perhaps consider teaching school. He mounted his mare and rode east. "I bestride my Rosinante with a mountain of grief upon my shoulders but a good letter in my pocket," he confided to his cousin Isaac, "and jogged on groaning, but never desponding."

He worked his way down Long Island, from Southampton to Smithtown to Oyster Bay to Huntington, where he stopped in to see the old minister there, Ebenezer Prime. There he spent "twelve days feasting upon his great library"; Ledyard continued to be a voracious reader. But in the end, he found himself unable to find a school or a church that would take him. By the time he reached Elizabeth, New Jersey, he was seriously dejected. Two local ministers, Reverend James Caldwell (later known by the British as the "High Priest of the Rebellion") and a Reverend Rogers, attempted to cheer him up, no doubt over a few glasses of wine. "They told me that the sufferings I met with, and the contemptuous ideas the people where I was born and educated had of me, were nothing strange, but projected honor on me," he reported; "that a prophet is not accepted in his own country, and the like."

So the prophet made his way back to Connecticut, with "warm letters" of recommendation but no job. He crossed over from Long Island on the ferry, but was too ashamed to visit his uncles William and Ebenezer, who still lived in Groton. "[I] thought it most prudent not to stop there, no, not where I was born," he wrote melodramatically. "I dropped a tear upon the occasion, and rode on toward Preston till eleven at night, when, feeling quite exhausted, for I had been severely sea-sick, I dismounted, left my horse to graze, looked up to heaven, and under its canopy fell asleep."

He returned to Reverend Hart, who explained the situation to Ledyard as diplomatically as he could. While he didn't doubt the young man's "probity," he said he had to consider his own public position before he approved the young man for the clergy, and his mind would be greatly eased if John could obtain two things. The first was a letter from the Reverend Elnathan Whitman in Hartford. This should pose no problem, since Whitman had been his grandfather's great friend and beneficiary, as well as his prolix eulogist. The second requirement was a "regular dismission" from the president of Dartmouth, confirming Ledyard's good standing with the Congregational Church. "There are four ministers standing ready to advance me once this is done," Ledyard boasted to his cousin Isaac, "among whom the Rev. Bellamy is one."

But Ledyard knew it would not be so easy, especially after his "coat & breeches" screed. Wheelock was well aware that his students' futures depended on their admission to the church, which he had the power to grant or withhold. He was so vague about the criteria for admission that in October 1772 a group of students had submitted a petition of protest, asking him to clarify the rules. Ledyard had apparently approached him in person, not long before he left, and the meeting had not gone well. When he asked

Wheelock for admission to the church, Ledyard writes in his letter, "You Sr then said I should you feared dishonour my profession &c—a great a peice of charity this!" He goes on, wondering why "tho the rich were not denied & others that were possessed of those same things for which I was condemned were admitted yet because their settlement to human estimation was more sure—I was shut out."

As to why he was "condemned" and "shut out," and why Wheelock had told him that he would "dishonour" the clergy, the record is silent. Whatever Ledyard's sin might have been, it was either too trivial—or too scandalous—to merit one of those public confessions that Wheelock's charges were forever being forced to make, for such offenses as "bringing the College into disrepute" and getting drunk on the Sabbath. "Doctr," he pleaded, "my heart is chaste as the new-fallen snow." But on the basis of his behavior during the rest of his life, it's likely that other parts of his body may have been somewhat less chaste.

Or perhaps there was no sin at all, and that Wheelock simply knew Ledyard better than he knew himself. A black churchman's suit would have fit Ledyard as poorly as his grandfather's oversized coat, and would in time have unraveled just as thoroughly. As Wheelock had seen, Ledyard marched to his own "singular" rhythm, and could not be expected to conform to a congregation's taste. So while the reverend may have believed that he was punishing young Ledyard once and for all, he had in fact given him a tremendous gift: his freedom. Ledyard was now completely liberated—from the expectations of his family, the constraints of his social rank, and his very homeland itself. There was nothing tying him to Connecticut anymore, and like many another rootless New Englander before and since, he took to the sea.

# PART TWO
# Voyages

This map of Captain Cook's third voyage, from Ledyard's unauthorized journal, was lifted from an earlier anonymous voyage account (as was a substantial amount of the text). *Courtesy of the John Carter Brown Library*

# Seven Years' Ramble

THE NEW MAN HAD DISAPPEARED NOT LONG AFTER THEY made landfall. Captain John Deshon was eager to weigh anchor and leave Gibraltar, the British garrison at the gate of the Mediterranean, but he couldn't; the missing crewman was the son of his dead friend back in Groton, the late Captain John Ledyard. Deshon was starting to regret his kindness toward the lad, whom he'd taken on in the fall of 1773 for a voyage across the Atlantic and back. The ship carried lumber and other New England goods to trade in Gibraltar for North African mules, which they would then sell in the West Indies, returning to Connecticut with unspecified Caribbean cargo—probably molasses or rum (duty-free, of course). Until now, the young man had promised to make a fair seaman, perhaps even a captain someday, like his father. Seawater practically ran in his veins. But the father, wild as he was, would have never pulled a stunt like this.

Captain Deshon sent a man to the British barracks—and lo, there was John Ledyard, already dressed in royal red, stepping as fancy as a palace guard. As Deshon's nephew told Jared Sparks, Ledyard was found "armed and equipped from head to foot, and carrying himself with a martial air, which proved that, to whatever vocation he might be called, he was not to be outdone by his comrades." Deshon and his crew must have been horrified. Bunker Hill was still more than a year away, but for New London sailors, the British were already the enemy. British press-gangs roamed all the ports and the high seas, forcing Americans into the Royal Navy (or worse, the Army) against their will. Ledyard sheepishly explained that he was "partial to the service" and wished to enlist. If the captain insisted, however, he would return to the ship. Deshon insisted, the British commander relented, and Ledyard doffed the uniform. His little caper was not without consequence, however. He had delayed the ship's departure, and by the time the ship reached the West Indies, well behind schedule, Deshon could find no cash buyers for the mules. He was forced to unload them on twelve months' credit, to the great disappointment of his employer, the powerful New London shipowner Nathaniel Shaw.

Ledyard was apparently oblivious to the trouble he had caused. His newfound freedom intoxicated him: After "a rough passage of forty days," the mere sight of Gibraltar looming up over the turbulent strait had inspired him beyond words. His crewmates hadn't seen the last of his strange behavior, either. One night, on this same voyage, the crew was awakened by a commotion on deck. They rushed up the companionway, thinking someone had attacked the ship, only to discover Ledyard, sword in hand, fighting a mock duel with the mainmast while declaiming verses from Shakespeare. Later, a shipmate told Jared Sparks, Ledyard was among a party of sailors who discovered a slave's corpse on the shore of Île-à-Vache, near Haiti. Feeling playful, Ledyard removed the head from the body and brought it back to the boat wrapped in a handkerchief, this crewman recalled. A day or so later, while the rest of the crew went ashore for a few hours, Ledyard stayed on the ship. His colleagues returned to find him busy cleaning the cooking kettle, having just boiled the man's head right down to the skull.

He seems to have returned to Connecticut by April 15, 1774, when probate records show him receiving the remaining thirty-six pounds of his inheritance. He spent his newfound wealth that summer and fall in New London and Groton, where his chief occupation (as he told Ebenezer Avery) was "going over to Stonington to visit the Ladies." There was one in particular who caught his fancy, a twenty-year-old he later identified only by her initials, R.E., but who Ledyard biographer James Zug identifies as Rebecca Eells, daughter of the Stonington minister Nathaniel Eells. Dressed up in his custom-made linen breeches, he paid her many visits that fall, so smitten that, a decade later and a continent away, he still pined for R.E. We can only guess what the Reverend and Mrs. Eells thought of this young man, with his fancy breeches and utter lack of prospects—not even of becoming a sea captain. Ebenezer Avery found Ledyard "odd, loquacious, good-natured and civil," but that did not necessarily make him husband material. The relationship with Rebecca went nowhere, and in March of 1775, Ledyard shipped out again, this time aboard a different vessel, from New York.

He had nothing left but his freedom, and he intended to use it. "I allot myself a seven years' ramble more," he had declared in a letter to his cousin Isaac, written from and inspired by the dramatic outcrop of Gibraltar. Moreover, he would do it on the cheap, for "the past has long since wasted the means I had, and now the body becomes a substitute for Cash, and pays my traveling expenses."

Nearly eight years later, in early December of 1782, a British naval officer walked into a small boarding house in Southold, near the far end of Long Island. Cornwallis had surrendered more than a year before, at Yorktown, but Long Island was still under a desultory British occupation (as was New York City). The lady of the house, twice a widow, earned her living by lodging and feeding British officers in her modest saltbox home. Every now and then, it was rumored, fifty-five-year-old Abigail Ledyard Moore would help to spirit a deserter to safety; smuggling evidently ran in the family blood. She showed the new arrival where he could stow his bags, and then he came down and took a seat by the fire, keeping his hat tipped low over his brow.

There was something familiar about the young man, the landlady thought, stealing glimpses at him whenever she passed through the room. When he called for a glass of punch, she mustered her courage and put on her glasses. Approaching the familiar-looking stranger, she apologized for her rudeness and told him that he looked just like one of her sons who had been gone to sea seven years and hadn't been seen since. Ledyard's poker face broke down instantly, as a younger cousin recalled, and he "fell weeping upon his mother's neck."

Ledyard had a good enough excuse for not writing: For most of the past seven years he had been beyond the reach of any kind of mail service. In July of 1776, he sailed from Plymouth with the celebrated Captain James Cook, on his third and last voyage to the Pacific. Even in the former colonies, Cook was renowned, and his death in Hawaii was the subject of great curiosity, ever since it had been reported in the London papers in January 1780. Cook's expedition was considered so important that the warring powers of the time—including the rebellious American states—had granted him safe passage over the seas.

The only sign that Ledyard was still alive, during his long silence, was a tortured letter to Isaac written in January 1782 and smuggled from Ledyard's British warship, a frigate then anchored in still-occupied New York Harbor. "Believe me I know not what to write or what I ought to write," he'd lamented in that letter. "Thou companion from my youth, shall I lose thee?" It was another ten months before Ledyard finally managed to extricate himself from the Royal Navy, escaping the ship at Huntington Bay, Long Island, with a week's shore pass. He had no intention of returning. He left nearly all of his possessions on board, and sacrificed most of his accumulated pay, but he did manage to salvage a few treasured books, including his ten-volume set of the works of Laurence Sterne. Within a few days of his reunion with his mother, he had ditched the British uniform for good and slipped across Long Island Sound.

He was thrilled to be home again, but Connecticut was much changed. While Ledyard was serving the Crown, his hometown of Groton and neighboring New London had suffered one of the worst British raids of the war. Both towns still bore the smoky scars of September 6, 1781, when a British fleet led by Benedict Arnold sailed past the New London lighthouse and attacked the town, burning New London to the ground. That was just a diversion, for a second force soon materialized and laid siege to Fort Griswold, which guarded the river from atop a high hill in Groton, just yards from John's childhood home. Arnold knew his way, having grown up in Norwich, a few miles up the Thames. The Redcoats soon overran the small rebel garrison, which was commanded by Colonel William Ledyard, John's uncle. As his men lay wounded and dying around him, Colonel Ledyard gallantly handed his sword to the British commander, who accepted the surrender and then allegedly skewered the American with his own weapon. More than two dozen of John's relatives were killed or wounded that day, including his guardian and uncle, Tom Seymour, who took a bullet to the knee. His sister Fanny had made a heroine of herself, tending the wounded and dying men, including their cousin Ebenezer Avery, who had been bayoneted fourteen times and left for dead, with his skull bashed in. He somehow survived, and lived into his eighties, but the Ledyard family never really recovered from that terrible day.

Ledyard had spent at least a year sailing in American waters under the British flag. It's not clear whether or not he saw any actual combat, and he doesn't say, but as a marine, he was essentially a ship's soldier, and he would have had to fire on and board American ships if need be. Clearly, he had some explaining to do. True to form, he did so in extremely public fashion, presenting a "Memorial" to the Connecticut Assembly dated January 6, 1783, in which he explained his whereabouts during the Revolutionary War. In March 1774, he said, he had signed on as a crewman aboard a merchant ship out of New York, but it apparently hadn't been as grand an adventure as his cruise with Captain Deshon. By the time the ship reached Falmouth, Ledyard had had enough. "Finding his situation unprofitable & unpleasant in the ship to which he then belonged," he wrote to the Assembly (referring to himself in the third person), he ran off once again, this time for good. Hitchhiking with an equally destitute Irishman, he made his way to Bristol, the city from which the Squire had run away as a teenager almost six decades before. His luck did not improve there. "He was however so unfortunate then as to be apprehended by a kind of Police in that city," he informed the Assembly, "who obliged him either to ship himself for the coast of Guinea or to enter the British Army: Your Memorialist, young, inexperienced & destitute of friends, chose the latter as the least of two evils."

He remained in the army until early 1775, Ledyard said, when he was ordered to Boston. "To this your memorialist objected being himself a native of that Country & desired he might be appointed to some other duty, which ultimately was granted: Matters continued thus until July 1776 when the equipment for discovery came round from London to Plymouth & your memorialist esteeming this a favorable conjuncture to free himself forever from coming to America as her enemy & prompted also by curiosity & disinterested enterprise embarked on that expedition."

As usual with Ledyard, there are some holes in the story: In March of 1774, Ledyard was still on Captain Deshon's ship, en route from Gibraltar to the Caribbean and thence to New London; he probably meant 1775. There is no record of his ever having served in the British Army. Royal Marine files, however, show that John Ledyard of New London was "recruited" into the 21st Company of the Plymouth division of the marines in April 1775. He gave his profession as "labourer," and the recruiter noted that he had a "wen" over his left eye, either a cyst or a swelling, perhaps the result of a fight. Three months later, private Ledyard was promoted to corporal and transferred to the 24th Company, from which the marines for Cook's voyage were drawn.

John Ledyard's name first appears in the ledger of the *Resolution*, as corporal of marines, on July 9, 1776. How he was chosen for this assignment is not quite clear. But his mere presence aboard the *Resolution*, with her celebrated commander, indicates that by then, he was far from eager to escape British military service. With two successful Pacific voyages to his credit, Captain Cook was already an icon of exploration, the eighteenth-century equivalent of an astronaut. (It was no accident that the captain of *Star Trek*'s starship *Enterprise* was named James Kirk, echoing Cook.) He had ventured twice into the still almost-unknown Pacific Ocean, where he discovered new lands and strange peoples, from vicious cannibals to nubile island women, who were the subject of much London gossip after the first voyage accounts appeared. Yet for all his accomplishments, the captain was humble and reserved, a quintessential Yorkshireman: The writer and Samuel Johnson biographer James Boswell, who met Cook in April 1776, described him as "a grave steady man," and found it "strange" to think that this fellow was about to leave his plump English wife to sail around the world. Boswell had hoped to come along on that third voyage, but Johnson talked him out of it, a huge loss to the literature of exploration.

The son of a day laborer in gritty northern Yorkshire, Cook had risen from the merchant marine to the officers' ranks—normally reserved for young gentlemen—based solely on his skills as a sailor. Largely self-educated, he was a keen judge of character and one of the best navigators and marine surveyors of his day. Some of his Pacific charts were still in use just a few decades ago. He was also expert at keeping his crewmen alive. Before Cook, sailors enlisting for Pacific voyages would have had better odds at Russian roulette. Some ships lost half their crews, or more. But Cook had carefully studied the arts of maintaining his sailors' health and morale. His men ate fruits and vegetables whenever possible, and even local grasses and homebrewed spruce beer, to ward off scurvy, the great killer of eighteenth-century seamen. As a result, nearly all of the *Endeavour's* crew had survived his first voyage—until the return trip, that is, when ships pulled into the mosquito-infested Dutch port of Batavia (now Jakarta, Indonesia) and nearly a third of the men succumbed to malaria and other plagues. He did better on his second voyage, losing only three sailors from the *Resolution*. (Her sister ship, the *Adventure*, had fared less well, losing an entire landing party—eleven men—to cannibals in New Zealand, much to the regret of her captain, Tobias Furneaux.)

Equally important, Cook staved off madness and mutiny by keeping his men busy and directed. "Able in the technical sciences, Cook was also no mean practical psychologist," writes J. C. Beaglehole, author of a doorstop-sized Cook biography and editor of four equally imposing volumes of Cook's journals. "He knew how to command: he knew, almost always, how to humour. On his own leisure he set little store, and no officers and men laboured harder than his; but there was a purpose in the labor, and the measure of the affection he drew is the willingness of many to sail with him again." More recent scholars have noted that Cook's voyages were far from pleasure cruises: The Captain had a reputation for stretching his provisions to the point of inciting mutiny, and his officers and midshipmen privately complained of his despotic, irrational behavior. Still, it was a mark of honor to have served with Cook, and as a result he had a fairly decent pool of potential crewmen from which to choose—several cuts above the scoundrels and drunkards who typically manned long voyages. Nonetheless, more than three dozen men had already fled the *Resolution* before Ledyard went on board in July 1776.

While there is no record of his meeting Cook before the voyage, it seems improbable that John Ledyard, an ordinary marine, would have simply been assigned to the *Resolution* at random. Young gentlemen were prepared to sacrifice a great deal to win a coveted midshipman's spot. Throughout his life, Ledyard had a knack for meeting the right people. He was also the sort of man who would have marched straight up to Cook's quarters, refusing to be turned away. He apparently made enough of an impression to get the job. Cook could not have failed to note the young man's skill with Native American languages, which would prove useful when the expedition reached its top-secret destination. Three days after Ledyard came on board, on July 12, 1776, the

*Resolution* weighed anchor and sailed, bound for the edge of the known world.

Now back in Connecticut, Ledyard was proud of what he had done. Cook's final voyage to the Pacific was the subject of intense curiosity even in the former colonies. The true purpose of his petition to the Connecticut Assembly was not merely exculpatory, but something rather novel: He planned to write an account of the voyage, and so he requested "that the memorialist may have the exclusive right of publishing this said Journal or history in this State for such a term as shall be thot fit." Copyright law as we know it did not yet exist in the United States (nor in the former colonies). Colonial publishing had been a thoroughly piratical business, with printers lifting material from one another and distributing it as their own. Writers often pillaged other writers' words, as well. Ledyard knew that he had a valuable piece of intellectual property on his hands, and he felt that his rights as author should be protected. The assembly agreed, and soon passed an "Act for the encouragement of Literature and Genius" that was a precursor of other states' and federal copyright laws.

Ledyard then repaired to his uncle's study in Hartford, and began to write. The resulting work, *A Journal of Captain Cook's Last Voyage to the Pacific Ocean, and in Quest of a North-West Passage, between Asia & America; Performed in the Years 1776, 1777, 1778, and 1779*, was published in two installments, in June and July of 1783, totaling 208 pages. (A final version included both parts bound together.) He earned some twenty guineas for the book, from the Scots-born publisher Nathaniel Patten, whose printing house lay "a few rods north of the State-house" where the assembly met. Although it was cheaply printed, with broken type, Ledyard's book nevertheless sold quite well and was advertised everywhere from Boston to Philadelphia, more than earning back its advance; a relative told Jared Sparks that Patten had made "no inconsiderable sum" on its publication.

As the only work he published during his lifetime, Ledyard's *Journal of Captain Cook's Last Voyage* was literally an advertisement for himself. It proved that he had finally accomplished something. Not only had he taken part in Cook's famed last voyage, but he had apparently witnessed firsthand the navigator's brutal death at the hands of Hawaiian natives, in February 1779. His account of Cook's murder is so deftly written that it was considered authoritative for nearly 150 years. Mark Twain relied on Ledyard's journal to inform his own writings from Hawaii, and even Jefferson wrote that Ledyard's account, with its unflattering portrayal of the captain, had the effect of "lessening our regrets at [Cook's] fate"—a view that annoyed J. C. Beaglehole to no end. As "a patriotic as well as free-born American," he wrote scornfully, Ledyard's loyalties were suspect. "He did not omit to slip in a few episodes discreditable to the British in the persons of Cook and [Second Lieutenant James] King," complains Beaglehole, a Canadian, "and he did not hesitate to enlarge on his own part in the voyage." And he dismisses Ledyard's journal itself as "a worthless production, badly printed, with some importance in American bibliographical history, and in helping to give Cook the bad press he traditionally had for many decades in Hawaii."

Contemporary critics and historians have begun to appreciate Ledyard's journal anew, for some of the same qualities that so irritated Beaglehole. Ledyard's was the only account of the voyage to offer the perspective of the ships' "people," the ordinary seamen and noncommissioned officers (as well as marines) who were generally assumed to be illiterate. Where the ships' officers and naturalists filled pages and pages of their journals with descriptions of islands and oceans, plants and animals, Ledyard focused his almost exclusively on human beings. His great subject was the clash of cultures between the "civilized" seamen and the "savage" natives; Ledyard was one of the only white writers of his time who even attempted to understand native peoples' perspective. So when academic historians in the 1990s began to reexamine Cook's voyages, revisionist scholars such as Gananath Obeyeskere, a professor of anthropology at Princeton, relied on Ledyard as an invaluable source for their critique of the captain's behavior.

Ledyard's *Journal* occupies an important place in American literary history, as well, and not only because of its distinction as the first copyrighted work of nonfiction to be published in the United States. Larzer Ziff, a scholar of nineteenth-century American literature, places Ledyard's work at the very headwaters of American travel writing, as a kind of precursor—and foil— to the likes of Mark Twain and Henry James. He was the first American to go abroad, to seek new lands and people, even as the American nation was itself coming into existence. And he took a particularly American view of what he witnessed. Ledyard had no fealty to the Crown, nor was he a career navy officer. He was unconcerned with the imperial aims of Cook's voyage, or the physical, "scientific" description of mountains and coastlines and islands, or plants and animals that so fascinated the voyage naturalists; he focused only on people, English and native. Unlike most travel writers, Ziff observes, "[who] presented the 'face of the country' as an essentially unoccupied landscape, Ledyard regarded the occupants as the very essence of the lands he visited."

Beaglehole did have a point. Ledyard's *Journal* is far from an eyewitness account. He certainly kept some kind of regular journal during the voyage, but it was almost certainly seized when the ships returned, along with all other journals kept by the ships' officers and seamen. The Admiralty had been badly embarrassed by unauthorized accounts of the first and second voyages and wanted to avoid a repeat. So while Ledyard's title page promised that the work had been "faithfully narrated from the original MS.," in all likelihood there was no such thing: All the crew's journals had been confiscated before the ships reached England. (Many of those journals ended up in Admiralty archives, but apparently not Ledyard's; he may have smuggled some private notes off the ship, however, but it seems unlikely.) To refresh his memory for names and dates, and sometimes more, he consulted his copy of John Hawkesworth's accounts of Cook's two prior voyages. He relied even more heavily on an anonymous account of the third voyage that had already been published in London in 1781, and republished in Philadelphia in 1782. Ledyard stole that book's title, and more. The last third of Ledyard's journal, in fact, was "faithfully narrated" from his source, verbatim. The books are so similar that Ledyard was long thought to have been the author of the anonymous *Journal* as well, but in fact it was written by John Rickman, a midshipman on the *Resolution*'s sister ship, *Discovery*. (The Cook scholar F. W. Howay made that discovery in the 1920s, granting Rickman his belated due.)

Aside from his own journal, John Ledyard appears only a few times in the official records of Cook's last voyage. The captain mentions him by name just once—when he dispatched Ledyard on an arduous mission in Alaska. While Cook does credit Ledyard as "an inteligent man," the other officers seem to have overlooked the presence of the man who would later become known as the Traveller. This may have more to do with the officers' snobbery than any lack of distinction on Ledyard's part. The "people," such as Ledyard, were largely regarded by their superiors as illiterate, uneducated drunks, but Ledyard did attract the notice of Burney. "With what education I know not, but with an ardent disposition, Ledyard had a passion for lofty sentiment and description," Burney wrote, years later, in a passage that echoes Ledyard's Dartmouth classmates' recollections of him. He seems to have contributed to the informal ships' newspapers that were exchanged between *Resolution* and *Discovery* (sadly, also lost), but even there, his highfalutin talk was lost on his fellow sailors, as Burney hints: "His ideas were thought too sentimental, and his language too florid. No one, however, doubted that his feelings were in accord with his expressions."

This fellow sounds a lot like the Ledyard who went to Dartmouth: flamboyant, talkative, iconoclastic. He may have tamped down his mischievous side because of his role on the ship; it wouldn't do for a marine to pick a swordfight with the mast. But when he sat down to write, he often found himself coming down on the side of natives. On the voyage itself, his job involved protecting the ships from unruly islanders, and he seems to have performed well enough, though he does not often go into detail. As a result, Ledyard is a shadowy presence even in his own *Journal*, appearing only at isolated moments: shooting fowl in Alaska with some of the gentlemen, or climbing a volcano in Hawaii. Cook's last voyage was the defining episode of Ledyard's adult life: It exposed him to the world (the whole world), and it set the course for the rest of his days. So we cannot understand him without at least attempting to see Cook's voyage—not merely as Ledyard wrote it, many years and thousands of miles removed, but as the twenty-five-year-old marine corporal would have lived it.

# Resolution and Discovery

ON A PERFECT ENGLISH SUMMER EVENING NEARLY 230 YEARS to the day after John Ledyard sailed out of Plymouth Harbor aboard the *Resolution,* I stood on the deck of a nearly identical sailing vessel and watched the green Yorkshire coastline dissolve in the dusk. This was a replica of the *Endeavour,* the ship that Cook had commanded on his first Pacific voyage in 1768. Like the *Resolution,* she was a Whitby collier, the type of vessel on which Cook had learned his trade. Broad-beamed and blunt-bowed, she was the sailing equivalent of today's bulk carriers, built for hauling huge cargoes of coal across the temperamental North Sea. Sturdy and unglamorous—like her captain—she suited Cook's purposes beautifully. With her enormous hold and shallow draft, she could carry vast quantities of supplies without fear of running aground. That she proved "but a heavy sailor," in the words of Sir Joseph Banks, was a small price to pay. Cook was in no hurry.

This modern *Endeavour,* launched in Australia in 1993, was a faithful re-creation of the original, almost down to the last wooden peg. Her lines were made of hemp, her cleats and pulleys of wood, her sails of canvas. She was similar to the *Resolution,* only smaller, weighing in at 392 tons compared to *Resolution's* 462. Measuring just under one hundred feet at the waterline (versus 110 for her successor), and 143 feet from the tip of her bowsprit to her rudder, *Endeavour* carried three stout wooden masts, each as big around as Pavarotti, and her bluff bow pushed a great pile of seawater before her, like an oceangoing snowplow. "She's a box," acknowledged Captain Chris Blake, a lean Australian in his fifties who seemed to have sea salt encrusted into his eyelids. He commanded a permanent crew of about a dozen sailors, mostly sunbleached Aussies in their twenties; far below them in status were the voyage crew, a motley assortment of some thirty-odd Captain Cook enthusiasts and tall-ship buffs who'd paid about $200 a day for the chance to play sailor for the week. I was one of these: I was hoping to get at least a taste of Ledyard's life aboard *Resolution*, his home for four crucial years.

Belowdecks, everything was almost (but not quite) exactly as it had been in the eighteenth century. We were each issued a canvas hammock and assigned a place to sling it from the crossbeams in the main open area. As prescribed by Admiralty regulations, our berths were fourteen inches apart. My heart sank when I realized that most of my fellow sailors were quite a bit wider than that. Luckily, our replica ship carried barely half the original *Endeavour*'s complement of ninety-four sailors, officers, and marines. (The slightly larger *Resolution* carried a total crew of 112.) Even better, we had access to hot showers on the deck below. Known as the "twentieth century," this deck—the former cargo hold—also held a modern galley and dining booths, as well as men's and women's locker rooms and balky pump toilets that tended to overflow when they weren't watched. Better those than the eighteenth-century heads—two thick wooden planks projecting from the forward rail, one on either side of the bowsprit, each with a twelve-inch-diameter hole cut into it for the obvious purpose, and no handholds of any kind. To relieve oneself in heavy weather on these so-called "seats of ease" would have been like using an outhouse in a hurricane.

The *Resolution* had no space for fancy plumbing, had it even existed in 1776. When she left England, her cargo hold was crammed with three years' worth of supplies for more than a hundred men, including 580 pounds of beef, forty bushels of salt, 3,400 pounds of dark muscovado sugar, as well as 1,800 gallons of spirits and another 600 of port. Under navy rules, each sailor was allotted an astonishing pint of rum per day, which they usually diluted with water to make a longer-lasting, more palatable drink called grog. Whether this helped to maintain ship's discipline or erode it is subject to debate: Drunkenness on duty was a floggable offense, while sobriety off watch was rare indeed.

She carried, as well, all the sundries that 112 men could conceivably need, including extra winter clothing and 800 pairs of shoes. And of course there was the livestock. King George III was eager to introduce proper British husbandry to the Pacific Islanders, so *Resolution* carried several horses, a bull, and two cows with calves, which the ships were to leave wherever Cook thought they were most needed. If he'd had his choice, Cook would have left them all on the dock at Plymouth, since they proved a constant nuisance on the voyage, requiring frequent stops to gather fresh fodder. There were also uncounted sheep, rabbits, pigs, fowl, dogs, and cats. Goats roamed the decks at will, including the captain's cabin, which was off-limits to most of the ship's human occupants. "Thus did we resemble the ark," Ledyard wrote, "and appear as though we were going as well to stock, as to discover, a new world."

Ledyard was one of six American-born crewmembers aboard *Resolution*, including gunner's mate Simeon Woodruff, also from Connecticut, and the first lieutenant, Virginia-born John Gore, who would become Ledyard's fast friend. Like Cook's crew, we on *Endeavour* were a motley assortment, mostly English but with a smattering of Irish and Americans. We'd come to the voyage from all walks of life, and together our varied accents comprised a virtual Babel of the British Empire. But there our similarities with Cook's men ended. As fine a captain as Cook may have been, his men were more than a little rough around the edges. Only a certain type of person—whatever their social status—tended to sign up for a multiyear sea voyage in the first place: one who was either running from something, or terminally and dangerously bored with civilized life. "Too often the expedition of discovery was manned from the dregs of piracy, prison, and dockyard inn," writes J. C. Beaglehole. Cook merely drew a better sort of misfit.

Compared to this bunch, we were a pathetic lot, less like Blackbeard and more like Sir Joseph Banks, the twenty-six-year-old aristocratic dandy and amateur naturalist who decided to go along with Cook's first voyage, perhaps since he was paying for it, anyway. Sir Joseph spent the first several days of the voyage huddled in his cramped, windowless cabin, vomiting, and probably regretting his decision to come along. There were few if any aristocrats among us, but we were just as pale-skinned and soft-palmed as Banks, with wives, and children or dogs or both, from whom we'd be absent just a week. (Banks brought his hounds with him.) There were even four or five women, who got as much attention as Tahitian princesses. Some of us were Captain Cook geeks, others had tried a bit of blue-water sailing, but we were all basically dilettantes, and almost entirely clueless about what lay ahead. Unlike Cook's men, who were sailing to the far side of the world, we were only going to Norway.

And then there was the fellow I'll call Peter, since that was his name. He was one of the last to board, driving right up onto the pier in a funky Citroën, into which his lanky frame barely fit. He strode down the gangway, resplendent in an oiled canvas overcoat and straw hat; he wore his hair in a sailor's ponytail and his face was craggy and severe. Most of us figured he was part of the show—

some sort of Captain Cook reenactor—especially after a quartet of crewmembers unloaded two heavy brass cannons from his car and carried them aboard. Was he supposed to be Cook? Or was he portraying Banks? And what was the deal with the cannons? We didn't know we were supposed to bring our own artillery.

There was no time to worry about that: As we cruised out of Whitby, Cook's home port on England's northeast coast, we gathered around the permanent crew to literally learn the ropes. There were dozens of them, if not hundreds, running this way and that way, up and down the masts, so dense they nearly blotted out the sun. Not a single one was labeled, so it was impossible to tell a clew from a bunt, a sheet from a halyard. The only thing that was clear was that we were going to have to climb the rigging, via a series of tar-covered rope ladders, ascending all three masts to perilous heights. It didn't look too bad, while we were still in port; now, as the ship began to roll, the masts swayed back and forth. The eighteenth century was starting to seem like a lot of bloody dangerous work, and I already felt a little queasy.

The voyage crew, like Cook's seamen, had been divided into three watches, each group working four hours on and eight hours off. I was on foremast watch, and that first evening it was our turn to scramble up the rigging to put out more sail. We had each already taken a practice climb, clawing our way up the shrouds to a wooden platform on the mainmast, about thirty feet above the deck. Called the fighting top, this was the marines' favored perch during close-quarters combat; Ledyard would have spent time up there on guard duty. But that was while we were still tied at the dock. Now the ship was heeled over on her right—starboard— side, rolling gently over the waves. A couple of the permanent crew clambered skyward, and a handful of us greenhorns followed, too excited to think about what we were doing until it was too late. With every foot we climbed, the motion of the ship became more exaggerated. It was a relief to clamber onto the nice, flat platform, but the excitement was only beginning. From there, we would have to maneuver our way onto the main yardarm, standing on a one-inch-thick footrope that ran along its underside. As each new person stepped on—shouting "stepping on!"—the line tensed and heaved. I threw my weight over the top of the spar, and clipped my safety harness—a belt of nylon webbing wrapped around my waist and attached to a carabiner—onto another rope running along the top of the yard. Rather than reassure, the harness only added to the feeling of danger, as I imagined it popping my ribs one by one before I fell screaming to the deck.

I'd hoped to avoid going out all the way to the end of the yardarm, and through a bit of foresight and manipulation, I made sure that the honor went to my friend Stuart, a thirtyish sewage-treatment engineer from Kent. As we inched out along the yardarm, staring between our feet at the blue water rushing below us, I could feel him trembling through the footrope, while the crew shouted incomprehensible commands. The basic gist was that we had to untie the sail and prepare to drop it, a task that required both hands (leaving exactly zero hands with which to hold onto the yardarm). "I'm fucked," Stuart gasped, as we swayed wildly over the foaming waves, while his father snapped photos from the deck below. Amazingly, it seemed to me afterward, not one of Cook's "tars," or sailors, died from a fall off the rigging (though a few were injured). Ledyard himself took a tumble from the yardarm, though not by accident: When the *Resolution* crossed the equator, he and all the other first-time equator-crossers were subjected to three ritual dunkings, a typically drunken affair presided over by a tar dressed as the god Neptune.

Already some of us were perfecting our Joseph Banks impersonations. The first night, I'd been washing dishes with a bespectacled Chicagoan in his midtwenties named Jack, when he suddenly stopped working and gazed mournfully into the bouillon-colored water sloshing around in the greasy sink. "I can't do this," he said, and bolted for the deck. Jack was hardly the first. The ship already seemed a lot less crowded, as crewmembers succumbed to the ship's ceaseless rolling the way Cook's men fell to venereal diseases after nearly every island stop.* Above and below decks, the victims hunched over their blue and red buckets, trying to keep out the icy wind. As if by some unwritten rule, the rest of us ignored them, stepping over their prostrate bodies on our way to perform important tasks that would, we hoped, forestall our own inevitable trips to the lee rail. I still felt fine because I'd pasted scopolamine patches behind both ears, which gave me blurry vision and a strange disembodied feeling but kept my stomach calm. (I was also gobbling capsules of ginger, the ancient sailors' remedy.) "Some of you will get seasick," warned George Lemann, the sandy-haired Australian first officer, on the first afternoon. "But as you're hanging over the rail, remember that you're providing entertainment for the rest of us."

Captain Blake was a taciturn character who'd been with the ship since she was launched. During that time he had sailed almost as far as the real Captain Cook, making two round-trip voyages between Britain and Australia—even rounding Cape Horn, a nightmarish passage that Cook braved on his first two voyages. (Footage from the *Endeavour*'s Cape Horn crossing appeared in the film version of Patrick O'Brian's *Master and Commander*.) Like Cook, Captain Blake was reserved and somewhat stern. You didn't speak

---

*Sexually transmitted diseases had most likely been introduced to the South Pacific by Cook's men and other Europeans, including the English under Captain Samuel Wallis in 1767, and the French under de Bougainville, who visited Tahiti in 1769.

to him unless addressed, and that usually only happened when you were doing something wrong, like steering the ship off course, toward Iceland. It took two men to control her six-foot-diameter helm, as the wind and waves pushed the ship around. Yet despite the chilly North Sea wind, the Captain often emerged from his cabin wearing nothing but a thin cotton sarong. While the rest of us stumbled around the deck like intoxicated Philadelphia Eagles fans, clutching the rail or rigging for dear life, he swayed and rolled with the ship, as if he were riding his very own hundred-foot surfboard.

Two weeks after the *Resolution* sailed, John Ledyard's class graduated from Dartmouth College. But Cook's voyage, not Dartmouth, gave Ledyard his true education. With Cook he saw far more of the world and its peoples than any Dartmouth missionary ever dreamed. And in the person of Cook, Ledyard had found a role model quite unlike the Squire, or Reverend Wheelock, or anybody else he'd known in Connecticut, including Captain Deshon and his own father. Captain Cook was a driven, purposeful man, with loftier goals than the mere accumulation of money and property. In the spirit of the Enlightenment, Cook quite literally embraced the entire world, and sought to share his knowledge for the benefit of mankind. No longer was Ledyard's life a string of disappointments and failures; he was now part of an important project, one with consequences for all humanity.

But Ledyard's great adventure had gotten off to an ill-omened start. Within a few days of setting sail, the *Resolution* had begun to come apart at the seams. She leaked constantly, even through her decking, and in wet weather the men were actually rained on in their hammocks. In strong winds, her masts and yardarms snapped like rotten tree limbs. The *Resolution* had already sailed around the world once, on Cook's second voyage, and she had been sent to the naval shipyard at Deptford for refurbishment, but the corrupt and lazy navy carpenters there had done an extremely poor job, using rotten wood and inferior caulk. (They were also quite busy preparing the royal fleet for war with America.) Cook ordinarily would have supervised the work himself, but he had gone off into retirement after his second voyage and hadn't expected to sail in her again. The poor condition of the ship would be a constant annoyance, requiring Cook to put in for repairs frequently, further delaying the voyage and ultimately contributing to his death. "If I return in the *Resolution*," John Gore wrote to Sir Joseph Banks from the Cape of Good Hope, "the next Trip I may Safely Venture in a Ship Built of Ginger Bread."

Our ten-year-old replica *Endeavour* was in near-perfect repair, despite her two voyages around Cape Horn. She kept to a strict timetable, which required her to keep an average speed of 4.5 knots. If the wind died down, or blew unfavorably, she was equipped with mighty diesel engines; a battery of modern navigational equipment was concealed in one of the officers' cabins. But as the sun went down, it became easy to imagine sailing in Cook's day, steering by the compass and the stars, taking bottom soundings with lead weights attached to very long ropes. Late-eighteenth-century navigation was still a highly complicated and inexact art. Finding one's latitude was easy, but longitude was still nearly impossible to determine, requiring a complex series of observations and calculations. One of the cutting-edge pieces of technology carried on Cook's third voyage was a new ship's chronometer designed by the late Greenwich clockmaker John Harrison. An extremely complicated machine, the longitude clock—"our Watch," the appreciative Cook called it—kept constant Greenwich time (losing a second or two each day). By calculating the precise local time (via observation of the moon and sun), and subtracting the difference, navigators could determine the ship's position. Without this knowledge, they were practically sailing blind. (Harrison had died in March 1776, only three years after finally collecting the 20,000-pound prize offered by Parliament.)

Even in relatively familiar waters, potential disaster was never far away. Nautical charts of the time were notoriously inaccurate, and often the ship's survival was a matter of dumb luck. Leaving England in July, the *Resolution* stopped in Madeira and the Canary Islands, nearly reaching the coast of Brazil before turning southeast towards the Cape of Good Hope, at the southern tip of Africa. On the night of August tenth, barely a month into the voyage, as the *Resolution* was cruising through the Cape Verde Islands off the coast of West Africa, the helmsman heard the unmistakable and deadly sound of breaking waves. It was a well-known reef off the island of Boa Vista, one of the southern Cape Verdes. Someone had miscalculated the ship's course—perhaps William Bligh, the sailing master, later of *Bounty* fame. The helmsman spun the wheel to starboard, and the crew sprang aloft to rearrange the sails. The *Resolution* struggled against the wind for a very tense night before she finally cleared the sunken rocks. "To bring a ship into so alarming a situation . . . certainly deserves the severest reprehension," fumed ship surgeon William Anderson in his private journal. Though Ledyard's published *Journal* established him as a severe critic of Cook, he doesn't even mention this incident, perhaps because he was writing six years after the fact, and so much more was yet to come.

Cook knew that his crumbling, leaky "ark" was headed for the Arctic. According to his sealed sailing instructions, the real purpose of the voyage was to seek the fabled Northwest Passage, a body of water thought to link the Atlantic and Pacific Oceans, which would allow British merchants to reach China without risking the deadly passage around Cape Horn, at the southern tip of

South America. The only alternative was the extremely long route via the Cape of Good Hope and the Indian Ocean. After delivering Omai, a Pacific Islander who had accompanied Cook's second voyage home to England, to his home in the Society Islands, Cook was to head for the coast of "New Albion," as Sir Francis Drake had dubbed the western coast of North America in 1579. Beginning at about the forty-fifth parallel, the ships were to head north along the coast, searching for inlets and sounds that might lead, somehow, to the Atlantic Ocean. Already, the expedition had fallen dangerously behind schedule, thanks to the hungry livestock and to the *Discovery*, whose commander, Captain James Clerke, had been detained nearly a month in a London prison because of his brother's debts, which he had guaranteed. On her voyage to the Cape of Good Hope, the *Discovery*'s corporal of marines, Ledyard's counterpart, had fallen overboard and drowned, which surely gave Ledyard pause. The expedition had left too late to reach America by the following summer, as Cook's instructions specified, and so the Northwest Passage would have to wait.

The modern *Endeavour* was well ahead of schedule, thanks to near-perfect winds. We had no livestock to slow us down, other than the hunks of meat in the galley freezers, which the ship's cook would soon turn into a pretty decent beef stew—vastly preferable to the *Resolution*'s staple diet of rat-nibbled biscuit, sauerkraut, and constipating salt pork. On the downside, we also carried no grog, and were forbidden to drink alcohol of any sort, despite two very large wooden casks marked "Madeira Wine" lashed underneath the main stairway. This was generally felt to be quite inauthentic, but actually it was not: The *Resolution*'s initial supply of rum was barely enough for six months at sea. When Cook tried to substitute homemade concoctions made from spruce or sugarcane, the men grumbled mutinously. (Ledyard, a

lifelong wine drinker, would have done well to befriend the officers, whose rations included ample amounts of port and Madeira
rather than rum.)

Most of us could not have handled alcohol, anyway. We were
too busy working on the ship and trying to avoid seasickness. The
worst job was the morning cleaning, after breakfast, when all
hands were ordered below deck (the most dangerous place for the
almost-seasick). An officer opened a coffinlike chest, and buckets,
mops, and brushes were handed out. It seemed a terrible idea to
stay belowdecks in rough weather, but we had no choice. In contrast to the wide-open main deck, with its limitless views to the
horizon, the ship's quarters were positively claustrophobic; in
some areas, notably the officers' cabins, the overheads were barely
four feet six inches high (the ship fitters had installed an extra
deck to accommodate the officers' cabins). Only Cook's cabin
qualified as truly spacious, with a dining table and a grand chan-
delier swinging from the ceiling.

I'd already bumped my head several times and was verging on
seasickness, so I grabbed a mop and slunk off to the area that
would have been occupied by the marines in Ledyard's day: a little
cavelike space with dwarf-height ceilings, between the officers'
quarters in the stern and the ordinary sailors in the main cabin.
As I pretended to scrub the floor, I imagined Ledyard spending
months and months in that cramped little space, with a dozen
other smelly, drunk, hairy English marines. Ledyard would not
have minded too much, I suspect. This was much better than the
hard duty he'd known on New England merchant ships, and now
he knew he was off to a great adventure; he even, later in the
voyage, applied for the job of expedition historian, supplying a
sample passage describing the manners of the Society Islanders,
but Captain Charles Clerke turned him down. "He was not aware
how many candidates he would have had to contend with, if the

office to which he aspired had been vacant," wrote James Burney. Ledyard won out in the end; his became the most famous account of the voyage.

Ledyard would have had plenty of free time on his hands while the ship was at sea. The *Resolution's* marines were not required to help in the sailing of the ship, except for all-hands-on-deck jobs such as raising the ship's anchors, an arduous chore requiring more than a dozen men to turn the heavy capstan, a giant winch that dominated the midships. By and large, they left the sailing to the ordinary seamen. The marines were sea soldiers, responsible for protecting the ship from outside threats—and from her own crew. They enforced ship discipline, a job for which Eleazar Wheelock surely would not have recommended his former student. When a crewman broke the rules, the marines doled out the lashes, even when the offender was a fellow marine. The marines, in effect, were the captain's only bulwark against mutiny. And when Cook and the officers went ashore, a detachment of marines always went along. So Ledyard had a perfect seat from which to watch the drama of the voyage unfold.

The job of marine corporal, on this important voyage, was also Ledyard's first meaningful position. By donning a uniform and shouldering arms, he became a man, discovering a sense of purpose and clarity that he'd previously lacked. Forever after, it was his claim to fame: He had been with Cook, and he would spend the rest of his life pursuing dreams that he had shaped right here, swaying in his hammock, perfectly situated between the common crew and the officers, the English and native people, observing them all—especially the steely and enigmatic captain—and thinking and scribbling in his notebooks.

Ledyard feuded with Omai, a Polynesian who had been brought to London and "civilized"—shown here riding ashore with his armor and pistol—perhaps because they were alike in some ways.

# Noble Savage

THE MEMBER OF THE VOYAGE WHOM LEDYARD LIKED THE least was also the man he most resembled in certain ways: Omai, a native of the Society Islands who had come to England in 1775 with Cook's returning second voyage. Omai, or Mai,* had been a hit with London drawing-room society, as an authentic exemplar of the then-fashionable "noble savage," though in truth he was neither truly noble nor particularly savage. Mai and his British shipmates had seen real savagery in New Zealand, where the *Adventure*'s watering party had been cannibalized. In truth, Omai was a commoner, from a family of middle rank. Originally from the island of Raiatea, near Tahiti, his family had been driven to exile in Huahine, a couple of dozen miles to the northeast. Mai's own father had been killed by Bora Borans in some kind of interisland skirmish. Mai himself had been greatly impressed by his first encounter with the English: As a teenager, he had been wounded by musket fire from the *Dolphin*'s crew. He may have seen the British as potential allies in his quest to reclaim Raiatea. None of his fellow islanders were sorry to see him go.

The English were intensely curious about this South Seas

---

*Though he was universally called "Omai" by the English (just as Tahiti was "Otaheite"), his name was really Mai.

native. Ever since Captain Samuel Wallis of the *Dolphin* had sailed into Tahiti in 1767, the exotic islands and their tawny, good-looking inhabitants had captured the public imagination. Sir Joseph Banks's account of Cook's first voyage, published in 1773, caused a flurry of gossip, with its titillating hints of the beauty and generosity of Tahitian women. (Banks's male companions also caused a stir.) Other voyage journals fairly sizzled compared to Banks's, but Sir Joseph was an aristocrat and had been engaged when he left; shortly after he returned, the engagement was broken off.

Mai was hardly the first "savage" London had seen. Two centuries earlier, two explorers working for Sir Walter Raleigh had brought home two Native Americans from North Carolina, named Wanchese and Manteo, who both died in England. More recently, Samson Occom had preached the Gospel and raised money for Eleazar Wheelock. Another Tahitian, Tupaia, had agreed to come back to England with Cook's first voyage, but he died en route. Unlike other native people brought to Europe, Mai thrived in cosmopolitan London. "[Mai's] advantage was not that he was a wild man of the woods," writes his biographer Michael Alexander, "but that he was to act from the start like a civilized Englishman."

Mahogany-skinned and slender, with small, fine hands, Mai was both exotic and ingratiating. During the yearlong voyage to England, he had learned to speak English well enough to get along, and his idiosyncratic expressions were highly prized. In Mai's English, a wasp was a "soldier-bird," while a cow was "the hog that gives milk." His chief patron, Sir Joseph Banks, showed him off like a parrot. Shortly after he arrived, Mai was shuffled off to an audience at Kew with King George III, whom he greeted as "King Tosh." The king insisted that Mai be inoculated against smallpox, which no doubt helped him survive. He dined with

Samuel Johnson, attended the London opera and the horse races at Leicester, and learned to play a mean game of chess. He was a fixture of the gossip columns of the day, and he enchanted Fanny Burney, who found him "politely easy, and thoroughly well bred."

In Mai, these qualities were thought to be natural gifts rather than learned behaviors. The celebrated painter Sir Joshua Reynolds produced a lavish portrait of Mai, clad in a turban and flowing white robes against a backdrop of verdant palms, that exemplifies how the English saw the Tahitians: as natural men living in a state of luxuriant purity. To London society, Mai was Rousseau's "noble savage" personified, with more than a dollop of exotic sexuality. Flocks of women awaited his visits, and he reportedly even became engaged to a twenty-two-year-old English woman, but when Mai boarded the *Resolution* in July 1776 and took his place in the best cabin on the ship, right next to Cook's, no fiancée accompanied him. He did, however, have a raging case of the "French pox," or venereal disease.

Having seen the palaces and finery of the British upper classes, Mai now had similar aspirations for himself. Lord Sandwich, head of the Admiralty and patron of Cook's expeditions, had promised that Mai would have a fine house built for him when he returned to the islands. Savage or not, Mai was returning home very well equipped, with assorted tools, clothing, umbrellas, silver watches, and an "electrifying machine"—"amongst many other useless items," Cook noted tartly in his journal. He had also been given a stallion and two mares, which he did not yet know how to ride. While Mai seemed eager to return, he was quite concerned for his own safety, and had procured himself a brace of muskets and a full suit of armor, which he donned when he went ashore at the Cape of Good Hope, in a kind of strutting dress rehearsal for his eventual triumphant homecoming.

Unfortunately, Mai's social schedule in England had been so packed that he had failed to learn anything that would possibly be of practical use to himself or his countrymen. He could ice-skate, but knew nothing about modern British agriculture or the emerging science of medicine. He knew how to entertain, though, and David Samwell, the surgeon's mate, found him "a droll animal" who had become "very expert" at cards. "After a stay of two years," wrote the acerbic Georg Forster, naturalist on the second voyage, "he will be able to amuse his countrymen with the music of a hand-organ, and with the exhibition of a puppet-show."

Ledyard was unimpressed by Mai. He had seen the type before, most vividly in the person of Samson Occom. To Ledyard, the condescension of the "civilized" and the kowtowing of the "savage" were equally repulsive to behold. Mai's arrogant pretensions made him that much more difficult to take. Ledyard saw right through Mai's "proud empty ambitious heart," and had nothing good to say about him. Yet he might have disliked Mai precisely because they were so similar. Both men favored flamboyant dress and relished elaborate ceremonies. Far from home, they each had assumed a distinct persona. In a way, Mai was a kind of Polynesian Ledyard, an exotic traveler who had remade himself in a strange land. Later, when he traveled through Scandinavia and Siberia, Ledyard himself would assume the role of noble savage: an untutored wild man from an exotic land.

Yet despite his frivolity, Mai proved useful to the expedition on several occasions as an interpreter and as a diplomat, albeit a rather aggressive one. The Polynesian languages, from New Zealand to Hawaii, are all fairly similar, so he could make himself understood across most of the South Pacific. He was uniquely attuned to native peoples' moods and customs, but he also delighted in firing muskets to scare them—as he did when they reached Queen Charlotte Strait in New Zealand, where the *Adventure*'s men had been slaughtered just two years earlier. The Maori there believed that Cook had returned to take revenge on them; even the chief, Kahura, seemed to expect it. Mai urged Cook to kill the chief, but Cook stayed his hand, thinking he was doing the right thing. He would only allow his men to use deadly force if they were in immediate danger. This succeeded only in perplexing Kahura and his people, and the ships spent a very tense eleven days at anchor there. It wouldn't be the last time Cook failed to meet the locals' expectations as to how he should behave.

Although Cook had visited the South Pacific three times now, each new landfall was cause for great anxiety. They might be welcomed with gifts and food, or they might be robbed, killed, and eaten. At the island of Atiu, which the ships reached on April 1, the four-man landing party was thoroughly robbed and then treated to a magnificent feast. (Spotting suspicious-looking cooking fires, the quick-thinking Mai informed the king that the white men's guns could destroy the island with a single shot.) For a first time Pacific sailor like Ledyard, these encounters must have been stunning: to come ashore and immediately be surrounded by hundreds and sometimes thousands of half-naked men and women, sometimes carrying clubs and spears, chanting in their guttural language and pulling at the strangers' clothes, hair, and weapons. Cook had always enjoyed a friendly reception at the Tongan archipelago, which he had named the "Friendly Islands," so he next steered a course in that direction, east by northeast, across miles of warm blue ocean.

When the ships reached the Tongan islands, in late April of 1777, a flotilla of 200 canoes raced out to greet them from the island of Nomuka, laden with fresh fruit, live pigs, and beautiful half-naked women. Ledyard befriended a Tongan chief named Finau, who accompanied the ships as they sailed throughout the northern islands. On the island of Lifuka, he then met the king of all the islands, the Tui' Tonga, an enormously fat man named Paulaho, who invited Cook to make his anchorage at Tongatapu, the largest and most important of the Tongan islands, where the ships finally arrived on June 10. The two island chiefs vowed to protect Cook and his men as well as they could and urged their people to trade freely with the English. To celebrate the new friendship, the islanders staged boxing and wrestling matches, their favorite pastimes; Cook savored the sight of two "lusty wenches" tangling with each other in the dust. Those English sailors who joined in the wrestling were easily beaten and would have been humiliated, but Cook later ordered the marines to stage a parade at full arms, firing several volleys into the air. That night the ships launched an impressive display of fireworks, sending the terrified islanders fleeing for the hills—and reinforcing Cook's point.

After nearly a year at sea, the men surely felt like they had arrived in paradise. It had been a brutal crossing from New Zealand, and the *Resolution* had almost run out of fresh water (the ship did have a cutting-edge desalination machine, but the liquid it produced was brackish and unappetizing). The horses and cattle looked like walking skeletons, and the men were starved of fresh meat. Now they had all the hogs and yams they could eat, not to mention delicious bread fruit, a starchy tropical staple that smells like fresh bread. Beautiful brown-skinned women flocked to the ships, eager to trade favors. A night of pleasure could be had for the price of a steel hatchet, or a shirt, or in exchange for a few red feathers—oddly, the islands' most prized currency. As the ships settled in for a few weeks' refreshment, the officers and Mai took girlfriends, as did some of the men. Ledyard, too, participated in the sexual cornucopia; the ship's ledger shows that while at Hawaii, six months later, he was treated for venereal disease by Anderson, the ship's surgeon, paying fifteen shillings for the privilege. In all, more than half the *Resolution*'s 112 men were treated during the voyage for gonorrhea or syphilis. There were no antibiotics, so the stricken men were given either an ointment made of mercury and lard or crude mercury pills. This was called the "salivary cure," since it made the men's mouths water. The drooling was thought to help flush out the disease, but excess salivation is really an early symptom of mercury poisoning—followed by sickness, dementia, and eventual death.

Even in Tonga, Ledyard met the right people. He was stationed on shore with a detachment of marines, guarding the astronomers' tents that had been set up on the beach. One evening, early in their stay, the island king Paulaho invited the young corporal into his tent for a meal of baked yams and fresh fish cooked in plantain leaves, which Ledyard pronounced "most delightfully dressed." Then it was time for bed, and Ledyard sketched the idyllic scene for his readers:

> [I]n a few minutes there appeared a fine young girl about 17 years of age, who approaching Polahow [*sic*] stooped and kissed his great toe, and then retired and set down in an opposite part of the house. It was now about nine o'clock and a bright moon shine, the sky was serene and the winds hushed. Suddenly I heard a number of their flutes beginning at nearly the same time burst from every quarter of the surrounding grove: And whether this was meant as an exhilarating serenade or a soothing soporific to the great Polahow I cannot tell, though in fact from the appearance of the young girl and other circumstances I confess my heart suggested other matters; but my heart at that time was what Polahow's ought to have been and not what it was.

At the king's urging, Ledyard writes, he lay down on the mat beside him and watched the girl giving him a kind of massage, "pating him on the posteriors with the palms and back of her hands alternately in constant and quick succession of gentle strokes...until she found her lord fast asleep when she gently arose and went off." Reading Ledyard's account, one can't help but think of Melville's Ishmael, in the opening pages of *Moby-Dick*, famously bedding down with the South Seas harpooner Queequeg— "civilized" and "savage" joining in peaceful, equal slumber. ("[I] never slept better in my life," Ishmael remarks afterward.)

Ledyard was less sentimental about Polynesian chiefs' practice of keeping *Ikanes*, young men whose purpose, as David Samwell put it, was "to perform the sin of Onan upon the King." Ledyard's own tolerance was stretched: "Though we had no right to attack or ever to disapprove of customs in general that differed from our own," he wrote, "yet this one so apparently infringed and insulted the first and strongest dictate of nature, and we had...so strong a prejudice against it, that the first instance we saw of it we condemned a man fully reprobated."

Ultimately, however, he quite approved of the native peoples' pursuit of pleasure. "Of all the animals from the polypus to man," Ledyard goes on in his journal (borrowing a metaphor from Jonathan Edwards),

> the latter is the most happy and the most wretched, dancing through life between these two extremes, he sticks his head among the stars, or his nose in the earth, or suspended by a cobweb in some middle altitude he hangs like a being indigenous to no sphere or unfit for any, or like these Indians he is happy because he is insensible of it or takes no pains to be so.

The ships spent the whole month of June 1777 at Tonga-tapu, repairing and refurbishing—they had plenty of time, since they couldn't even start looking for the Northwest Passage until the following spring. The crew feasted on fresh pork and fish and plantains, then relaxed with a mildly narcotic native tea made from the kava root. The chief source of friction between the two cultures was the islanders' tendency to remove articles from the sailors and the ships without permission. The ships had dealt with thievery everywhere, but the Tongans proved to be expert pilferers, perhaps because of their imperfect understanding of European notions of property rights. The carpenters lost tools and the astronomers lost lenses (irreplaceable, in the South Pacific); in short, anything made of metal or glass was likely to disappear. James Burney even came to admire the islanders' "degree of genius" at stealing.

The culprits, when caught, were typically punished with a hearty whipping. As Cook lost patience, the punishments grew ever more "disgustful," according to Ledyard, who with his fellow marines had to carry out the sentences. Thieves were lashed to ribbons for stealing a single iron tool, and one unlucky fellow had a cross cut into his upper arm, all the way to the bone, which even shocked some of the Englishmen. Still the thieving continued. Two crewmen who went inland with their island girlfriends were beaten, robbed, and stripped naked. When someone snatched a pair of prized turkeys from the *Resolution*, Cook had had enough. He angrily ordered Ledyard and the marines to seize Paulaho as prisoner. It pained Ledyard to treat the friendly chief this way, and he chides Cook for his wrathful overreaction. But in Tonga and elsewhere, Cook found that hostage-taking was an effective way to get what he wanted, in the short run at least. On this occasion, Cook's measures very nearly resulted in disaster, for the island chiefs were massing on land, preparing a suicidal attack on the ships, before Finau intervened and returned the birds (which he had stolen in the first place). Cook graciously freed Paulaho, and the next day the captain went ashore with his officers "and made it a day of pleasure on his part" serenaded by two French horns, recalled Ledyard, who, with his fellow marines, stood guard over the scene.

Afterward, however, relations with the Tongans deteriorated rapidly once again. Soon it became dangerous to venture inland from the beach; reprisal was in the air, and sailors ashore were often pelted with coconuts and stones. With the wisdom of hindsight, Ledyard wrote that Cook "would perhaps have done better to have considered that the full exertion of extreme power is an argument of extreme weakness." The Tongans seemed to have caught on to that fact as well, Ledyard observed: "Before we quit Tongataboo we could not go any where into the country upon business or pleasure without danger."

It was time for the ships to leave, and the crews spent several busy days loading wood and water onto the ships, as well as several months' supply of yams and dozens of freshly killed and salted hogs, for the long voyage ahead. As for Mai, he had proved essential as a translator, but less effective at explaining island culture, particularly the key concept of tapu or taboo, and as a result, as Anne Salmond points out, Cook unwittingly committed numerous cultural faux pas. Among the worst was attending a sacred burial ceremony on Tonga, despite being told to leave. In matters involving theft, on the other hand, Mai favored strong retaliation, not merely because island justice was also often severe, but because he generally took a share of the prizes for himself.

The islanders treated Mai as Cook's equal, or nearly, but he had begun to lose favor with the men of the ship. At the outset of the voyage, Samwell had regarded him as a "droll animal," but now Mai was making a nuisance of himself. Not long after the ships arrived at Tongatapu, a drunk and frustrated Mai punched a marine corporal—probably Ledyard himself—who returned the blow. A shoving match ensued, and the two had to be separated. "At this Omai was highly offended & made his Complaint to

Capt$^n$ Cook," David Samwell reported in his journal, but Cook refused to punish the marine, as Mai had provoked the fight. He left the ships in a huff, with one of his servant boys, and it took a full day before he could be persuaded to return.

By the time the ships reached Tahiti, a month or so after leaving Tonga, Mai had worn out his welcome with almost everyone, including Cook, who fervently wished to rid himself of Mai and get on with his voyage. The ships' arrival was carefully staged to impress the Tahitians with Mai's importance: He rode onto the beach on horseback, clad in his shiny armor—"like St. George going to kill the dragon," as one chronicler remarked, only St. George didn't have an officer riding beside him to make sure he stayed upright. When the islanders became too rowdy for his taste, Mai fired his pistol over their heads, something that never failed to delight him. But he lost his balance and was promptly tossed off his horse.

Toote, as the Tahitians called Cook, was extremely well liked on the islands, which he had visited on both previous voyages. The Tahitians were so overjoyed at his return that they crowded aboard the ship. "Cook fairly gave it up as a day of festivity, not only to the Otaheiteeans but to his own people," Ledyard wrote, "[who were] as much and perhaps more pleased than if they had been moored in any part in Great-Britain."

They'd evidently landed in Spain, instead. The English were surprised to discover an enormous wooden cross planted on the island, with an inscription claiming it in the names of Jesus Christ and the king of Spain. The islanders said that after Cook's last visit in 1774, a pair of strange ships had come from a place called Rema, (probably Lima, Peru) and they had left behind a pair of priests, who had since returned to Peru. The Spaniards had also claimed to have sunk Cook's ship and killed the captain, which explains the islanders' surprise and joy at seeing him very much alive.

Cook had the carpenters reinscribe the cross with *Georgius tertius Rex, Annis 1767, 1769, 1773, 1774 & 1777,* leaving no doubt as to who'd been there first and most often.

Tahiti was the most beautiful place Ledyard had ever seen, with spectacular rocky peaks rising vertiginously from the hibiscus-scented, palm-fringed shore, like tropical Alps. The Tahitian girls were even more beautiful than the Tongans, and the ships were now well stocked with red feathers. The *Resolution* and *Discovery* anchored in Matavai Bay, near the present-day capital of Papeete, and the astronomers and workmen set up their tents and encampments on shore. The carpenters went to work repairing the leaky, battered vessels, and a lively commerce sprang up, as usual. The sailors knew they were bound for the icy Northwest Passage, and were determined to enjoy themselves while they could.

Meanwhile, Cook set in motion his plan to leave Mai behind on Tahiti, which seemed feasible because his sister already lived there. Accompanied by a guard of red-coated marines, Cook and Mai went to meet the king, Otoo (or Tu), bearing lavish gifts that included a linen suit, tools, a few yards of gold cloth, and other small luxuries. But right away, Mai irritated his host by giving a speech praising the wonders of another king, George tertius Rex. This wondrous ruler, Mai informed Tu, reigned over more people in one city than lived in all the islands put together. He had 300,000 warriors at his command, and ships of war equipped with enormous "poo-poos," or guns. Tu may have been impressed, but he was not amused, and he turned his back on Mai and went to talk to Cook.

Cook had hoped that Tu would take a liking to Mai, and perhaps let him marry one of his younger sisters. But Omai didn't like the sister, and Tu grew weary of Mai. Even Mai's own sister and her husband seemed mainly interested in his wealth. To make matters worse, he had apparently contracted a venereal disease from his island girlfriend. Cook pleaded with Mai to settle there anyway, he wrote, "[but] Omai rejected my advice, and conducted himself in such a manner as not only to lose the friendship of Otoo [the king] but that of every other person of note in the island. He associated with none but refugees and strangers whose sole Views were to plunder him and if I had not interfered they would not have left him any single thing worthe the carrying from the island." Ledyard agreed: "Omai had ever since our arrival among these isles been declining not only in our estimation but in the opinions of the natives, among whom he was envied for his underserved riches and dispised for his obscure birth and impudent pretentions to rule and command, in short his ignorance and vanity were insupportable."

In late September, after six weeks at Tahiti, the ships pulled anchor and sailed toward Huahine, one of the Leeward Islands, a few days' ride to the northwest. This was Mai's home island; he'd have no choice but to stay, Cook figured. The project of settling him there would consume a few more precious weeks, but the voyage was already so far behind schedule that it didn't matter anymore. After four months in the islands, the ships resembled oversized Polynesian war canoes more than British naval vessels. Many of the men brought their native girlfriends along; by this point, some of them spoke Tahitian well enough that they could actually converse. The Pacific sun had burned their skin to a nearly native shade of brown, and they dressed casually, unlike the starchy Spaniards. Like many of his shipmates, Ledyard had himself tattooed in the island way. Tahitian men often had their entire torsos covered in dense geometric designs that spread over their buttocks, lower legs, necks, and faces—and even, assistant surgeon David Samwell noted with horror, the penis. Ledyard made sure to get his tattoos on his hands and arms, where they would be noticed when he returned home. For the rest of his life, the strange marks on his wrists would attract interest and comment from strangers, not to mention the occasional free meal.

Even the ships had gone feral. Cook noted an "incredible" number of cockroaches aboard. Some of the men, though, were already plotting to leave the ships and their vermin and stay in the islands. They knew they were bound for the icy Arctic, which they might not survive. If they did, it was back to dreary England and its sad whores, probably forever. At another island, Ulietea, several of the men actually would desert, including Ledyard's fellow marine John Harrison (not the clockmaker), who stole off one night with his musket. He was soon captured, at the house of his girlfriend's parents, where she was "dressing his head with flowers," according to Ledyard, who was likely part of the search party. He was hardly the first to run off: Earlier, in New Zealand, a young sailor from the *Discovery* had disappeared with a local girl, and the searchers had discovered them in each others' arms, to the dismay of the romantic Ledyard (who lifted the tale from John Rickman's anonymous journal). "Love like this," he declared in his *Journal*, perhaps thinking of his failure with the Stonington ladies, "is not to be found in those countries where the boasted refinements of sentiment too often circumscribe the purity of affection and narrow it away to mere conjugal fidelity."

Fearing a mass desertion—or mutiny, as would later happen to the *Resolution*'s sailing master, William Bligh—Cook moved the ships to the middle of the bay, making it more difficult to escape. Two men managed to slip off anyway, including yet another of Ledyard's fellow marines, and Cook took several of the island chiefs hostage until the men were returned (which they were, four days later, bound hand and foot in the bottom of a canoe, as their women wailed and cried). "I would not have been the author of such grief for two deserters," Ledyard wrote. Cook's retaliations were growing ever more extreme. When they had stopped at

Moorea on the way to Huahine, Cook had punished the theft of two goats by ordering the marines to burn down every single hut in sight, and every canoe as well, in a two-day orgy of violence whose destruction "could scarcely be repaired in a century," according to one witness. One wonders what Ledyard thought of this duty, but his journal is silent on the subject.

The ships' arrival at Huahine, though, was a scene of rejoicing—outwardly, for the islanders and for Mai, and inwardly for Cook, who was glad to be getting rid of his distracting passenger. Mai arrived in grand style, riding alongside the ships in his own sailing canoe, with two other canoes in tow—prizes he had claimed in a raid, in retaliation for the theft of another goat. (He had capsized once, during the night, firing his musket as a distress signal, but by the time he reached the island his boat was upright and Mai was more or less dry.) The carpenters went to work building Mai's house, a one-story dwelling with a loft, built on a parcel of about an acre and a half that the islanders had granted to Cook. Mai overcame his initial disappointment (Lord Sandwich had promised him a two-story house), and soon set up housekeeping, with his English china, his organ and his "Lectrifying machine." He was a wealthy man now. In addition to his horses, cow, goats, and hogs, as well as a small cache of firearms and powder, he had brought along pots, kettles, and an assortment of toys, including a Jack-in-the-box that quickly held the entire island in thrall. He soon accumulated an entourage of eight to ten people, "without ever a woman among them," Cook noted dryly. "Nor did Omai seem disposed to take a wife."

Yet he had already managed to acquire an enemy on the island, a desperate character who Omai accused of having stolen the astronomer's sextant, a crucial piece of navigational equipment. Omai had helped to capture the man, and Cook punished him "with greater severity than I had ever done any one before," he admitted. The marines lashed him to shreds and sliced off both his ears. But the man insisted on his innocence, and vowed revenge on Mai as soon as the ships sailed. (He also turned out to be a Bora-Boran, and thus coincidentally an old enemy of Mai's people.) To prove his seriousness, he soon vandalized Mai's garden and stole from the ships again—two goats, this time. Cook clapped him in irons once more, intending to take him away to some other island, but he managed to escape, diving overboard, shackles and all. This time, the marine sentry who let him go was whipped.

On Huahine, Mai behaved a bit better than he had previously. He seemed to regret his dissolute life in England and his haughty conduct on the other islands. He wined and dined the ships' officers at his new house, further cementing his lofty status in the eyes of his countrymen. Several islanders volunteered to take Mai's place and return to England, but Cook turned them down. Mai, Cook wrote, "was so ambitious of being the only great traveler that he frequently put me in mind that Lord Sandwich told him no more were [to] come." After his exasperating time with Mai, Cook was not even tempted to create any future Mais.

When the ships finally sailed out of Huahine harbor, on November 2, 1777, Mai rode along until they were nearly out at sea. He said his good-byes to the officers, holding back his tears until he reached Cook, when he broke down totally and sobbed on the captain's shoulder. The ships sent him off with one last salute from the guns, as a warning to anyone who thought to harm Mai. Ledyard remembered feeling less sorry to see him go. "It is certainly to be lamented," he noted acidly, "that Omai will never be of any service to his country from his travels, but perhaps will render them and himself too the more unhappy."

And indeed he did not last very long. When William Bligh returned to Huahine in 1789, as temporary captain of the *Bounty*, he found that Mai had died a few years before. He had used his firearms only once, to fend off an attack by the ever-troublesome Bora-Borans. That had made him a bit of a local hero, but soon after, Mai had grown ill and died. His house had been destroyed (burnt, some said), and his English garden was now overgrown. There was almost no sign that he'd ever been there, or that he'd ever been to England, except that some of the islanders bore tattoos depicting a man on horseback. Mai, the great traveler, had learned to ride after all.

Cook relied heavily on this Russian-made map of a supposed Northwest Passage, and he was surprised to find that Alaska was not, as shown here (upper right), an island. *Courtesy of the Alaska State Library*

# Northwest Passage

NEARLY FIVE MONTHS AFTER THE SHIPS HAD LEFT MAI ON his home island, John Ledyard stepped out of the *Resolution's* launch onto the western shore of his own native continent. "Though more than two thousand miles distant from the nearest part of New-England I felt myself plainly affected," he wrote. "I was harmonized by it. It soothed a home-sick heart, and rendered me very tolerably happy."

After a long, lonely crossing, the *Resolution* and *Discovery* had first sighted the American continent at what Cook dubbed Cape Foul Weather, now in Oregon, and had worked their way up the coast for three weeks, somehow managing to miss both the Columbia River and the strait of Juan de Fuca, entrance to the Puget Sound, perhaps on account of "the ruggedest weather we had yet experienced," according to Ledyard. They'd barely seen a soul, not even the smoke of a cooking fire, until they moored in Nootka Sound, a smallish, three-pronged inlet on the western coast of Vancouver Island (Cook named it George's Sound, after the king). Now, at last, Ledyard spotted "that hardy, that intriped, that glorious creature man" paddling out to meet the ships, in more than thirty long dugout canoes. They were fierce-looking individuals, dressed in clothing made of tree bark and fur, their faces daubed in ocher and mud. They looked to Ledyard like the Pequots and Mohegans he remembered from Connecticut, only

unconquered and proud. He was captivated. "I had no sooner beheld these Americans," Ledyard wrote, "than I set them down for
the same kind of people that inhabit the opposite side of the
continent."

It was now early April of 1778. The ships had been out for
more than twenty months, and it had been almost two months
since they'd left their last haven, at the newly discovered islands of
Hawaii (which Cook had named the Sandwich Islands, in honor
of his benefactor, Lord Sandwich). The water casks were running
low again, and the howling offshore winds had made it impossible to reach any kind of harbor, which were few and far between
on the American coast, anyway. The crew was getting tired of
their diet of pickled pork; the Hawaiian yams that had once filled
the ships' holds were gone. By the time the ships sighted land,
the sailors had been reduced to eating "fricassee of rats, which
they accounted a venison feast," according to John Rickman's
journal. The rats were hungry, too, and had been gnawing holes
in the very hull of the *Resolution*, as the carpenters would shortly
discover.

So it was a relief when the Nootka natives came to trade with
the ships. They seemed to have seen white explorers before—
probably a Spanish ship that had passed along the coast in 1774—
and they already had some iron, which they especially prized; they
brought fishhooks and bone carvings, as well as some furs. The
pièce de résistance, though, was a curious-looking hunk of meat,
which the natives presented to their guests with great relish. It
turned out to be a fully roasted human arm. None of the other
journal keepers admitted to being the least bit tempted by the arm
(or hands, as recounted by Cook, who thought they seemed
freshly cut). They'd been offered roast arm before, in Hawaii, but
surgeon Anderson had been so appalled that the Hawaiians had
paddled off with their arm in embarrassment. Now, after starving

for weeks at sea, Ledyard dug right in. "I have often heard it remarked that human flesh is most delicious," he declared, gleefully shocking his Connecticut readers, "and there fore tasted a bit." He chewed it, savoring the flesh, and then he spit it out—he says—"without swallowing the meat or the juices, but either my conscience or my taste rendered it very odious to me." It probably tasted better than fricasseed rat.

Before long, the Nootka natives—the Mowachaht clan of the Nuu-chah-nulth tribe—brought forth real provisions, including venison and fish, much to the sailors' relief. Hungry as they were, however, the English turned down the natives' offer to sell them a young girl of three or four years, despite their promise that she would make very good eating indeed. More interesting to Ledyard and to some of the officers were the furs that their hosts brought to the ships, their canoes stacked high with a dozen different kinds of pelts, including bear, fox, and sea otter, which the English called sea beaver. The ships ended up buying more than 1,000 beaver skins, and hundreds of other kinds as well, intending to use them for extra winter clothing in the Arctic. When they arrived in China on the return voyage, a year later, the surviving crewmembers would be astonished when the furs sold for a thousand times what they'd cost, and they surely would have wished they'd bought more. Ledyard only belatedly realized the potential for profit, and when he returned to America, his countrymen would hardly believe his tales.

He was amazed to see that the Nootka natives not only had iron tools and weapons, but copper as well, which did not seem to have come from the local area. None of the native people knew the source of the metal, but Ledyard surmised that it must have come from Hudson Bay, like the copper used by the East Coast Native Americans that he had known. Something in the scene stirred his mercantile instincts. "Commerce is defusive and nothing will impede its progress among the uninformed part of mankind," he wrote, in a passage that later got the attention of Thomas Jefferson. "It seems intirely conclusive to suppose that no part of America is without some sort of commercial intercourse, immediate or remote."

This moment would come to define the rest of Ledyard's life. The ship-captain's son could not miss the opportunity that the Nootka Sound represented, not only in terms of trade with China. Ledyard looked in the other direction as well, to the east, and realized that if the tendrils of commerce spanned the continent, a traveler might possibly make the same journey, harnessing the engine of trade as his "locomotive machine." It was not difficult for him to imagine the day when America's Atlantic and Pacific coasts were as inextricably linked as New London and St. Kitts.

The rest of the ships' company, it seems safe to say, had their eyes on a more immediate prize: the £20,000 reward (about $2 million today) that Parliament had promised back in 1745, upon the discovery of a Northwest Passage between the Pacific and the Atlantic. Officially, the purpose of Cook's voyage was strictly scientific, but in truth it was primarily strategic. And now, two years after leaving England and almost a full year behind schedule, Cook had finally begun the most important part of his mission. According to his secret instructions from the Admiralty, he was to explore the coast of New Albion, beginning at about the Columbia River—safely north of any other settlements (the Spanish had already established a small mission at San Francisco Bay in 1775–76). When he reached sixty-five degrees north latitude, Cook was "carefully to search for, and to explore, such Rivers or Inlets as may appear to be of a considerable extent and pointing towards Hudsons or Baffins Bays."

He might have done better had he simply loaded up on furs, stopped off in China to sell them, and headed home with a shipload of money. Even before Cook had left England in search of the Northwest Passage, there was already more than 200 years' worth of evidence that no such thing existed. The English had been searching for the shortcut to China since 1497, when King Henry VII dispatched a Venetian navigator named John Cabot to Newfoundland, which he believed to be part of Asia. During the next century, Henry Hudson blundered into the huge bay that bears his name—aboard a ship called *Discovery*—but the voyage proved so unpleasant that his crew rebelled and cast him out on an island in the bay. (The *Discovery* returned a few years later, this time in company with a ship also called *Resolution*, but also to no avail.) In 1633 two English ships, the *Henrietta Maria* and the *Charles*, ventured further into the bay and explored several promising inlets, but the *Charles*'s captain returned home early while the *Henrietta* was shipwrecked with her crew on a deserted island. All of these expeditions were basically on the right track—there actually is a Northwest Passage, running along the north coast of Canada—but they all ran into the same problem: The passage has been ice choked until very recently, when it has cleared during the summer due to the effects of global warming.

A dozen years before Cook's third voyage, the Admiralty had renewed the quest for a Northwest Passage, this time from the west, dispatching John Byron to the Pacific in 1764. Byron, grandfather of the poet Lord Byron, was supposed to investigate the claims of the various Spaniards who claimed they had actually found the passage, including the sixteenth-century Greek-born navigator Juan de Fuca, for whom the strait leading to Puget Sound (and no further) is named. Byron did manage to claim the Falkland Islands for Britain, on the outward voyage. But after his ship *Dolphin* (the same *Dolphin* that Samuel Wallis later sailed to Tahiti) barely survived the rugged passage around Cape Horn, he abandoned the search for the Northwest Passage and made a beeline for the Marianas

Islands, and then the Dutch port of Batavia. He returned home in a scant two years, without ever glimpsing the North American coast.

Nevertheless, the idea of a water passage between Atlantic and Pacific had thoroughly seduced the English public, not to mention the Admiralty, primarily because it would allow ships to avoid the perilous, weeks-long rounding of Cape Horn, a nightmare which even the supremely able Cook chose to avoid on his third voyage, preferring the longer but calmer route via the Cape of Good Hope and the Indian Ocean. The nation that controlled the Northwest Passage would control the China trade—and the west coast of North America. The French and Spanish seemed well on their way, having already drawn up numerous maps showing plausible-looking Passages fissuring the American coast. Some depicted the great waterway beginning at San Francisco Bay, some at Juan de Fuca, others as far north as Anchorage. The hysteria had been fanned by the 1768 publication in London of a book titled *The great probability of a North West Passage,* a masterwork of disinformation based on the account of a Spanish admiral who, in 1640, had supposedly sailed into an inlet somewhere on the western coast of North America. He was vague on the inlet's exact location, but he followed it for hundreds of miles inland, where he claimed to have encountered a Boston trading ship, under a certain Captain Shapley. Oddly, this astonishing news had not reached Boston itself, and if Captain Shapley ever existed, he kept a very low profile.

Even more influential was the 1774 publication in English of a book by Jacob von Stählin of the St. Petersburg Academy of Science. Purportedly based on the latest Russian discoveries, Stählin's slim volume included a Map of The New Northern Archipelago, which depicted Alaska as an island separated from the American continent by a wide channel cutting northeast to the Arctic Ocean and then to the Atlantic. This passage supposedly

started at sixty-five degrees north latitude, near present-day Anchorage, but because the Arctic Ocean was believed to be free from
ice during the summer (ocean water was not thought to freeze),
Cook's ships were not even strengthened against icebergs.

Though Cook was not normally prone to speculation, the
notion of a Northwest Passage had appealed to him; it seems unlikely that he would have agreed to a voyage whose purpose was
merely to deliver Mai home and chart some of the already-known
Pacific islands. He was clearly a restless man, and while his sine-
cure job at Greenwich Hospital outside London had proved comfortable, Cook found retirement confining. He may also have felt
unfulfilled as an explorer. Strange as it may sound, his second
voyage had actually been somewhat unsatisfying: He'd gone in
search of the fabled southern continent, Terra Australis Incognita, which was said to be vast and fertile, a kind of southern
Eden. He sailed to the edge of the Antarctic ice zone, at seventy-
one degrees south latitude, before concluding that no such continent existed—"and not for want of looking," he noted bitterly.
Thus all he'd accomplished (besides charting the coast of Australia on his first voyage) was to prove that something wasn't
there. Now he had a chance to make a discovery of enormous
strategic and economic importance, something that would make
him famous for all time; it might even bear his name. He would
be wealthy, too, with his share of the Admiralty prize. By this
point in the voyage, the crew were also aware of the high stakes
involved—each crewman's share amounted to many years' worth
of naval wages—and all hands buckled to the job with newfound
determination.

The ships were in no shape for an Arctic voyage, especially the
*Resolution*. Her foremast was in terrible shape, and her mizzen, or
aft, mast was a mess of rotten, fractured wood that needed to be
completely replaced. One of the first orders of business at Nootka

Sound, therefore, was to fell a tree that could be used for the purpose. Much to Cook's astonishment, the natives insisted on being paid for the wood, as well as for grazing and other uses of their land—the first such insistence on property rights by any natives they had thus far encountered. This earned them the captain's grudging respect. "This is an American indeed!" the Captain exclaimed, according to Ledyard, as he grudgingly offered the chief his asking price.

There was no time to linger as they had in the South Pacific. Once the *Resolution*'s mast was repaired, she and the *Discovery* began to work their way north along what is now the British Columbia coast, leaving Nootka Sound on April 26th. Immediately they ran into a strong gale that pounded both ships and briefly separated them. The *Resolution* sprang yet another leak, "which was of an alarming nature," Ledyard noted. Yet Cook did not dare take the ships into port in such weather.

Even today, the coast north of Vancouver remains thinly settled, a few small hamlets and isolated port towns scattered along the rugged, rainy landscape. A few years ago, I took a sea kayak trip in the Queen Charlotte Islands of British Columbia, an archipelago north of Vancouver Island. As we paddled away from the last logging outpost on the main island and into a national park dedicated to the Haida natives, the coast began to resemble the place Ledyard had seen in 1778. Tall mountains plunged steeply into water that, in some places, was a thousand feet deep, just offshore. The forests had never felt the bite of a logger's axe. The bays and inlets teemed with energy and life. A fishing lure dropped into the water would never fail to hook a fish, often within a short minute. Whales breached in sheltered waters. The Nuu-chah-nulth had so impressed Ledyard with their ingenuity at fishing and whaling that he compared them to Newton and

Descartes, in a passage that the critic Larzer Ziff finds resonant with Melville:

> They have a harpoon made from a mushel shell only, and yet they have so disposed of it as to subdue the great leviathan and tow the unwieldy monster to their shores. Let not man think meanly of himself, but claim that glorious rank his amazing powers so justly entitle him to. If Descartes and Newton from the improvements of age could produce at last the magnificent system of Philosophy that hath immortalized them; why should not these glorious savages, who, without any of those great collateral assistances, without which THEY could have done nothing, have discovered such astonishing sagacity, and the name of Ben Uncus be as great as that of Isaac Newton.

Cook kept the ships safely offshore until they reached what is now southeastern Alaska—leaping over the fictitious rivers described by the Spanish. The first major inlet he explored, Prince William Sound, was also the site of a rare dispute between Cook and his first lieutenant, John Gore, the American who had accompanied him on all three voyages. Gore wanted to explore farther up the sound, but Cook turned the ships around—wisely, as it turned out, since it dead-ends against a wall of snowy mountains. They rounded the Kenai Peninsula on May 25 and found another inlet that seemed promising; within a few miles, though, it, too, began to close off, and the water turned browner, fresher, and shallower. Even so, Cook persisted, to Gore's bafflement. This was dubbed Seduction River—now known as Cook Inlet, leading to modern-day Anchorage.

Even the place names bestowed by Cook during this segment of the voyage reflected the growing sense of futility: Cape Flattery,

Cape Lost Hope. Yet another watery cul-de-sac was named Turn-again Arm. As if the rocky, irregular coastline and reef-studded bottom weren't bad enough, the unpredictable and gloomy weather made the crew's job vastly more difficult. One day, the *Resolution*'s lookouts spotted land, which promptly disappeared in a sudden, thick fog. The crew heard the sound of crashing surf, and fearing the worst, the *Resolution* dropped anchor and lit signal fires to try to warn the *Discovery*. When the fog cleared they found themselves sitting in a tiny bay, encircled by rocks, reefs, and islands. Once again, Cook had avoided disaster by a miracle. "We were . . . amazed," Ledyard notes, "to find ourselves in such a frightful situation."

Cook carried and often consulted von Stählin's map; his sailing instructions, in fact, were based on its promise of a passage at about sixty-five degrees north (never mind that fur-traders and surveyors such as Vitus Bering, a Dane working for the Russians, had already determined that Alaska was firmly affixed to North America). But as the English sailors followed the Alaskan coast, dutifully exploring nearly every sound, bay, and river mouth, they discovered to their dismay that it kept curving to the northwest rather than to the northeast, as the map promised it would. Cook spread out von Stählin's map on the table in his quarters: Nothing on it seemed to match up with what he observed. Von Stahlin's Alaska was an island, but this coastline seemed quite unbroken. There was no "new northern archipelago," except on paper.

The ships had sailed a very long way west before finally rounding the end of the Alaska Peninsula in late June and entering the Bering Sea, named for the Danish navigator (who himself had blundered around in the fog a good bit). Following the coast for six weeks, they passed through Bering Strait on August 10 and into the cold Chukchi Sea. Now things looked hopeful again: They had Asia to port and America on the starboard side as they sailed north at last. Within a few days, though, the ships came up against a low wall of ice, which seemed to present conclusive proof that seawater did indeed freeze. Even if a Northwest Passage did exist, therefore, it was probably not navigable. The ships sailed back and forth, picking their way among deadly icebergs, seeking a clear channel through the pack ice, but without success.

It was now late August, the end of Arctic summer. The officers' council met aboard the *Resolution*, and Cook reluctantly decided to abandon the search for that year. The ships were both badly damaged, and they were many hundreds of miles from the nearest safe haven. The crew, as well, was exhausted and half-starved— "pale languid and poor," in Ledyard's phrase, after months in the northern seas. On September 2, they sailed back through the Bering Strait, after reaching seventy degrees forty-four minutes north latitude without finding any sign of a Northwest Passage.

As they threaded their way through the Aleutian Islands, the ships stopped on October 2 and anchored in a vast sheltered bay of an island that Cook dubbed Providence, now known by its native name, Unalaska, one of the largest of the Aleutians. The *Resolution* had developed yet another leak that needed repairing. When they'd stopped there on the way north, a canoe had paddled out to greet them, with natives waving a piece of paper with strange lettering on it (probably a receipt showing that they'd already paid the Russians' harsh tribute). This time, a young chief was paddled out to the *Resolution* bearing a curious gift: a loaf of dark rye bread with a piece of salmon baked inside it, seasoned with salt and too much pepper.

The rye and the pepper could mean only one thing: Europeans. There was also a note, written in Russian, evidently addressed to the captain. On Gore's advice, Cook chose Ledyard to be his ambassador. The marine was to go with the chief, whose name was Derramoushk, in search of the Russians. Equipped only with some bread and several bottles of rum and wine, as well as a note from Cook, Ledyard set off with his guides. This way of traveling, alone and unarmed, relying on native conductors, suited Ledyard so well that henceforth it became his preferred mode of travel. "An armed body would move slowly," and attract potential enemies, he wrote in his journal. It was better to go alone, conducted by locals; by sacrificing himself, Ledyard heroically (in his own mind) lessened the danger to the expedition. "A single person would entirely risk his life," he wrote, "[but] if he should be killed the loss would be only one." Cook said he would wait a week. "If I did not return by that time he should wait another week for me, and no longer," Ledyard wrote.

On the first day, Ledyard and his guides hiked about fifteen miles into the treeless, windswept island's interior, until they reached a small village of some thirty huts, half-sunk into the ground for protection against the cold and lashing Aleutian wind. He was led into one of the largest huts, where he met more Aleutian people, men and women, who seemed quite familiar with blond Europeans. The women, in particular, he found "much more tolerable than I expected to have found them, and one in particular seemed very busy to please me, to her therefore I made several presents with which she was extremely well pleased." He was to spend the night there, so he broke out his bread and rum, to supplement his hosts' meal of dried fish, and although he was already quite tired, he evidently had quite an evening: "Ceremony was not invited to the feast," he informed his genteel readers, "and nature presided over the entertainment until morning."

Other scribes were more explicit, and less charitable, about the delights of Unalaskan women, who were free with their favors, although "very dirty & much infested with Vermin & smelled very strong of Brimstone," wrote David Samwell, the ship's surgeon— promoted to replace Anderson, who had finally succumbed to tuberculosis on August 3, in the Bering Sea. After a bit of scrubbing, the women were deemed acceptable, despite a lingering smell of sulfur. Samwell and two other men spent a day and night ashore, each taking a native "wife," while their husbands looked on: ". . . & so we pigged very lovingly together, the husband lying close to his Wife & her Paramour & exercising such patience as would have done Honour to a City Husband while we engrafted Antlers on his Head." As for Ledyard, he was treated for venereal disease (for the second time) not long after this encounter.

Awakened the next morning at daybreak, Ledyard found himself suddenly lame, his feet painfully swollen, perhaps on account of the previous night's entertainment. Nevertheless, he had to walk for several more hours over rough, hilly country until they reached a bay, where more natives met them in a large two-person kayak made of skin. By then it was nearly dark. There were two Aleuts with paddles and two seats in the kayak; their passenger was to ride inside the hull of the boat, "which I did not very readily agree to," Ledyard reports. There seemed to be no alternative, though, so Ledyard squirmed down into the coffinlike space, below the waterline with his head toward the bow, and was carried across the bay in this manner. When they landed, it was dark, and Ledyard felt the canoe being carried some ways up the beach. Strong hands reached in and pulled him out by the shoulders, wet and freezing. He heard a strange language, Russian, and he was led to a hut, which to his joy was lit by an actual lamp, by whose light he noticed that his new friends were light-skinned Europeans. They gave him fresh clothes, a blue silk shirt, boots, and a fur cap, and in return, he assembled his various bottles of liquor and tins of snuff, and presented them to his hosts. "Hospitality is a virtue peculiar to man, and the obligation is as great to receive as to confer," he wrote in his journal. He gladly kept up his end of that bargain.

Dinner was a sumptuous feast of smoked salmon, boiled whale, and fried fish. "They were very fond of the rum, which they drank without mixture or measure," Ledyard noted. Still feeling a bit piqued, he lay down in a comfortable bed of furs and skins. Before he fell asleep, he watched the Russians lead the locals in an Orthodox mass, the Aleut natives fondling their little crucifixes. He slept late the next morning, and before breakfast he was bundled into a separate little hut that housed a traditional Russian steam bath, or *banya*. Some of the Russians were already there, basking in the steam that billowed from a huge copper cauldron. Ledyard promptly fainted. The Russians revived him with cold water, and proceeded to whip his naked body with green branches. Afterward, still feeling faint, he needed a nip of brandy before he could face a morning meal that consisted "mostly of whale, sea-horse [walrus], and bear, which, though smoked, dryed and boiled, produced a composition of smells very offensive at nine or ten in the morning."

Given his shaky condition, Ledyard was relieved to see a snowstorm sweeping across the bay, which meant that he'd have at least one day to rest before he had to trudge back to the ships. The Russians wouldn't let him leave, anyway, he wrote, so he occupied himself by compiling a vocabulary of a few words in English, the Alaskan natives' language, and that of the "Asiatics" who'd come over with the Russians from Kamchatka. Ledyard was a talented linguist, and he would later teach himself French and Russian, and he also gave Thomas Jefferson a lesson in Native American languages. (In this case, however, he confused Russian and Aleut, as he later realized when he traveled in Siberia.) When he'd finished that, he went out and made a tour of the Russian outpost, which turned out to be a fur-trading station of impressive scale, employing some thirty Russians and another seventy-odd imported Kamchatka natives. There was a small ship in the harbor, and Ledyard was amazed that such a tiny vessel, less than one-tenth the size of the *Resolution*, could make the rough passage to Kamchatka.

The following day, Ledyard brought three Russians back to the ships, rowing in a large skin boat across the bay, and then retracing his hike across the island, arriving at the ships by sundown. "The satisfaction this discovery gave Cook, and the honor that redounded to me may be easily imagined," he bragged to his Connecticut readers. Cook's own journal, curiously, has Ledyard leaving on October eighth and returning to the ships on the tenth—only two days later, instead of four. Perhaps Ledyard's memory was faulty, or perhaps he was guilty, as Beaglehole charged, of enlarging his own part in the voyage. A little gentle exaggeration is understandable, though, since Ledyard wanted his readers to see every detail of the Russian fur-trading operation.

The Englishmen spoke no Russian, and the Russians no English, but a few rounds of drink rapidly lowered the language barrier. Eager to settle the question once and for all, Cook brought the visitors into his cabin, and spread out his precious map, on which he'd relied for the past three months—and, indeed, which had provided much of the basis for his entire voyage. The Russians looked at it, puzzled over it, but were unable to pinpoint Kamchatka, or Alaska, or any other known landmark. "Nor had they the least idea," Cook noted dryly, "what part of the world Mr. Staehlins map referred to."

In late October 1778, the ships weighed anchor and left Samnagoodha Harbor, and began sailing south toward the warm waters of Hawaii. The case for a Northwest Passage appeared to be closed.

The last moments of Captain Cook, as rendered by voyage artist John Webber. Ledyard's unsparing portrayal of the captain "lessened our regrets at his fate," Thomas Jefferson later wrote. *Courtesy of the Bishop Museum*

# Fatal Paradise

B Y THE SECOND MORNING ON THE *ENDEAVOUR*, THE WIND HAD cranked up to Force Seven, a sail-tautening thirty-eight miles per hour, and the ship was heeled over on her starboard side. The bigger swells would push her so far that her rail almost dipped into the water, sending plates flying and sailors reeling; at night, we swayed in our hammocks. During a particularly steep roll, I woke to find my shoulders pressed against the ceiling. Shaving was hazardous; showering was out of the question. I knew things were getting out of control one day at lunch, when all the soup sloshed out of my bowl and onto the table. "Ye might as well eat," the cook urged us. "Gives ye somethin' to heave!"

Cook's crews had been among the healthiest on the seas, but we had dwindled to a sorry, pale, hungry lot; every watch was at two-thirds strength, or less. More than two years out, the *Resolution* had lost only a couple of men, including Anderson, the surgeon, who succumbed to the tuberculosis that he had caught from his own patient, Captain Charles Clerke of the *Discovery*. But by late October 1778, when the ships finally headed south from Alaska, most of Cook's men were cold, tired, and mutinously sick of eating walrus meat. "We've been out three days, and already we're going mad," said Jack, my seasick dishwashing partner from the first night, finally emerging from below. Red-eyed and unshaven, he looked as if he'd been on a 72-hour bender. He shook his head. "Imagine three *years.*"

While her crew suffered, the replica *Endeavour* was sailing brilliantly. Captain Blake's sluggish, heavy "box" had transformed into a ballerina, floating gracefully over the ten-foot seas. We passed a small modern freighter whose steel hull was getting pounded by the same waves. According to the electronic instruments mounted discreetly by the wooden helm, *Endeavour* was making eight to nine knots as she surfed the swells. The only hitch was a small leak which she had developed below decks, which the crew set about patching, cursing and tumbling as they tried to work in the rough seas.

If there was one thing our *Endeavour*—like Cook's *Resolution*—could do well, it was to sail in a straight line. So long as the winds were perfect, blowing across the beam or slightly astern, she'd plow along gravely at four to six knots. We were lucky in that the wind was blowing directly across our intended course, so Captain Blake kept her on a straight track, to the north-by-northwest. At one point we threaded right between two North Sea oil rigs, ignoring the security boat sent out to intercept us. A bit later, we blundered into some sort of NATO submarine-hunting exercise. Captain Blake kept right on going, ignoring the dire warnings that crackled over the radio and the menacing destroyers on our flanks. It seemed possible that those twenty-first-century warships did not even register in his eighteenth-century eyes.

Late on the fourth day, the wind swung around and we learned the limitations of a Whitby collier: As sturdy as she was, capable of weathering steep seas and high winds, *Endeavour* was clumsy and difficult to maneuver. She could not tack or point into the breeze very well at all. The helmsman steered us at an angle to the wind, and crewmembers who had been lazing around the deck for days with little to do suddenly sprang into action, climbing aloft and hauling on ropes to adjust her sails. The Norwegian coast hove into sight, off to our right. But no matter how much we tacked, back and forth, we hardly made any progress at all; in fact, we seemed to be moving backward relative to the shore. Finally, the breeze died altogether. Captain Blake flipped a series of switches, and the ship hummed again with the vibration of the diesel engines. My watch-mates scampered aloft yet again, to douse the sails, and when we climbed back down we were back in the twenty-first century, motoring across a placid sea.

Like the replica *Endeavour*, the *Resolution* was almost completely at the mercy of the winds. Captain Cook did not have diesel engines, of course, which may have been one reason why the *Resolution* and *Discovery* spent more than six weeks cruising off the islands of Hawaii and Maui, which they'd spotted in late November 1778. The ships had first stumbled on the islands the previous winter, anchoring off Kauai for about two weeks. The English had enjoyed a warm reception there; shortly afterward, Ledyard paid for a second treatment for venereal disease. Now Cook had returned, having decided that the tropical islands would make a better wintering ground than the Siberian peninsula of Kamchatka.

After the four-week voyage from Alaska and a fruitless summer and fall searching for the Northwest Passage, the crew was exhausted but relieved to be back in the tropics. Now paradise was within sight but out of reach. The fierce Hawaiian winds kept the ships well offshore, cruising along the island chain in search of a decent anchorage. But the waters close to shore were fathomlessly deep, and huge winter swells made it dangerous to approach the land. The powerful winds—which Ledyard variously describes as a "gale," a "small hurricane," and a "tornado"—literally tore apart the *Resolution*'s well-worn sails, and in mid-December the ships were separated for almost three weeks. Native canoes paddled out to meet them, bearing hogs and fruit and even rope, which was much needed after the ravages of the North Pacific.

The Hawaiians displayed something else, too: As the first canoes approached, off Maui, the officers were horrified to see the men's enormously swollen penises, clearly the result of venereal disease that the sailors had introduced to Hawaii the previous winter. Cook was eager to prevent this sort of "commerce," another reason for keeping well offshore. Matters came to a head after Cook stopped the crew's grog ration. Instead he substituted a sugarcane brew seasoned with hops, which he pronounced quite good, and which the officers obediently tasted. The conservative crewmen would have none of it, however, and they wrote Cook a threatening letter, complaining about the beer and about their reduced food rations; he raged against "my mutinous turbulent crew," and had a man flogged for emptying a cask of sugar beer that had purportedly gone sour. In his journal, Ledyard accuses Cook of placing his own interests ahead of those of his men. "It appeared very manifest," Ledyard wrote, "that Cook's conduct was wholly influenced by motives of interest, to which he was evidently sacrificing not only the ships, but the healths and happiness of the brave men, who were weaving the laurel that was hereafter to adorn his brows."

But Cook had his reasons: He was trying to save his precious brandy and rum for colder climes; hence the beer. He also hoped, by preventing the sailors from trafficking in sex with local women, to keep the price of provisions down. And then there was the lack of suitable anchorages throughout the Hawaiian Islands (the ships evidently missed Pearl Harbor on Oahu). Finally, in mid-January of 1779, William Bligh reported that he had found a fine anchorage at Kealakekua Bay, on the southeastern side of the main island of Hawaii. The ships dropped anchor and delivered Captain James Cook to his fate.

———

Four years later, as he reflected back on the voyage and its disastrous climax, it seemed perfectly clear to Ledyard that Cook's demise had been almost preordained from the very moment of his arrival. Throughout Polynesia, the ships and their crews had been held in awe by islanders, but nowhere more so than in Hawaii, where no one had ever seen white-skinned Europeans and their enormous ships. The newcomers were exotic people to the Hawaiians: light-haired, wearing strange clothes with shiny metal buttons, and wielding dangerous weapons that exploded with deafening (and deadly) power. In other places, such as Tonga, Ledyard had seen how this initial reverence had inevitably turned toxic, as the sailors—and especially Cook—wore out their welcome. As a marine, positioned on the front line between the English and the Hawaiians, he was in an ideal position to sense the islanders' mood, particularly when they took to throwing stones. The more the English were worshipped at first, the worse the consequences would be for all concerned.

As for the English, they'd never seen anything like the scene that greeted them as the ships wore slowly into Kealakekua Bay. Literally thousands of canoes awaited the visitors, carrying 10,000 or more Hawaiians; thousands more swarmed the shoreline of the bay, climbing into trees or onto the tops of houses for a better view. They had seen the ships sailing counterclockwise around the islands for weeks, and their curiosity had become insatiable. As Cook came ashore with his officers and the marines, including Ledyard, it became clear that he was being welcomed as some sort of god. As Cook's boat approached, the dense thicket of canoes somehow parted to let him pass, as if by an invisible hand. Then the canoes closed ranks behind him (like in the scene from *Apocalypse Now* in which Captain Willard arrives at Colonel Kurtz's compound on the river). When Cook's boat touched the beach, the bargemen hoisted him onto their shoulders to carry him over the blazing sands. Ledyard picks up the scene from there, in an almost comical passage:

> As soon as he was set down, the multitude on the beach fell prostrate with their faces to the ground, and their arms extended forward. Those upon the adjacent hills, upon the houses, on the stone walls and in the tops of the trees also hid their faces while he passed along the opening, but he was no sooner past them than they rose and followed him, but if Cook happened to turn his head or look behind him they were down again in an instant, and up again as soon, whenever his face was reverted to some other quarter, this punctilious performance of respect in so fast a throng being regulated solely by the accidental turn of one mans head, and the transition being sudden and short rendered it very difficult even for an individual to be in proper attitude, if he lay prostrate but a second too long he was pretty sure not to rise again until he had been trampled upon by all behind him, and if he dared not prostrate himself he would stumble over those before him who did. This produced a great many laughable circumstances, and as Cook walked very fast to get off from the sand into the shades of the town, it rendered the matter still more difficult.

In the end, the crowd adopted a sort of compromise, which was to crouch on all fours and scuttle after Cook, alternately prostrating themselves and scooting along behind him. As Cook walked up the beach, anxious to get into the shade, the multitudes were calling Cook by a strange name: "Lono," (or "Orono" as Ledyard has it), the name of the Hawaiians' ancestor god. Cook had happened to arrive during the annual Makahiki festival, which welcomed Lono's return, and which was supposed to mark a time of peace and fertility. Normally, Lono was represented by a grass-stuffed effigy; now it seemed as if the god had returned in person.

Although today it is nearly deserted, and difficult to reach by road, Kealakekua Bay was then well-populated, with two villages, the priestly settlement of Kealakekua in the south and the warriors' town of Ka'awaloa to the north, each with about a hundred houses. Cook's first order of business was to ask the chiefs for a plot of land on which to set up a base camp on shore, for the astronomers' tents and also for the carpenters and blacksmiths who would be repairing the ship. In particular, he asked to use a half-acre patch of land in Kealakekua next to the *heiau,* the sacred stone temple, which was reserved for priests and high chiefs (and surrounded by a fence topped with human skulls). The chiefs agreed, but on condition that the ships' men be forbidden to leave their compound after sunset, and the common Hawaiians forbidden to enter at all. The chiefs set white taboo sticks around the perimeter; this was enough to keep out the thousands-strong crowd of Hawaiians, who contented themselves to sit on the low wall surrounding the tents, and observe.

As corporal of marines, Ledyard was given the thorny job of keeping the sailors and islanders apart, a task that was difficult to begin with and almost impossible once the sun went down. The officers were the first to break the rules, sneaking out to meet their mistresses on neutral ground. The sailors and marines saw what was going on, and they began stealing off, too, until the whole thing resembled a scene from a farce—officers and marines and seamen surprising one another behind practically every tree or bush. Before long, the whole agreement with the chiefs had become meaningless, and the white rods were taken down. Ledyard would later write that this breakdown "was the beginning of our subsequent misfortunes." Natives now had access to the tents, and could observe the great white men at all hours, in all conditions;

they thus "had every opportunity to form an opinion of our manners and abilities," Ledyard wrote. Ledyard would spend the rest of his life as a crosser of cultural boundaries, between West and East, "civilized" and "savage," America and England. At Kealakekua Bay, he would learn just how important those boundaries could be, and what the consequences were when they were breached.

On January 25, the high chief Kalani'opu'u (rendered by Ledyard as "Kirreaboo") swept into the bay at the head of an impressive fleet of double-hulled sailing canoes. He had been attending to business on Maui, the next island. He stopped for dinner at the *Resolution*, and the next day Cook came ashore and showed the chief around the astronomers' tents, where Ledyard was stationed. The Hawaiians were particularly fascinated by the complicated instruments, though they first mistook the telescopes for guns. An eavesdropping Ledyard came away with the impression that the Hawaiians believed that the English had come from the moon and the stars, since they seemed so concerned with the heavens.

If Cook was considered a sort of god (a point of debate among academics, still), then Kalani'opu'u was, also—despite his outward appearance. A stooped, shriveled old man, the chief was crusty-skinned and almost crippled by the effects of drinking the evidently addictive kava. His arrival had been carefully timed as part of the Makahiki. The meeting of the two gods, therefore, was an elaborate occasion. The chief removed his red feather cloak and draped it across Cook's shoulders, and they exchanged names in a formal Polynesian ceremony. Cook was now sometimes called Kalani'opu'u, while the island chief was known as Kuki, but it went deeper than that: The two men had also exchanged mana, or life force. "They seemed from that moment to conceive an uncommon attachment to each other," observes Ledyard, who witnessed their meeting. Now Cook really was associated with the gods and shared their power. He reinforced that point the following night, when the ships launched fireworks into the sky, sending the Hawaiians fleeing in terror (to the great amusement of Cook and his officers).

Ledyard had grown enchanted by the snowy, flat-topped cone of Mauna Loa, a 13,680-foot active volcano that loomed over the bay, and asked Cook for permission to climb it—an exploit reminiscent of his wintertime camping trip at Dartmouth. Setting out with four or five men, including botanist David Nelson, midshipman George Vancouver, and gunner Simeon Woodruff (like Ledyard, a Connecticut man), they set off climbing, past plantations of taro and sugar cane. They spent a chilly, dewy night with a farmer couple and their daughter, dining on roast piglet and the brandy they'd brought. The next day, they followed a path that led farther up the slope, into the forest. Along the way, Ledyard saw large trees that had been felled to make dugout canoes, which doubtless reminded him of his escape from Dartmouth. The path was "excessive miry and rough," and their Hawaiian companions refused to help carry anything, but they still made it another fifteen miles (Ledyard estimated) before making camp in a New England–style lean-to that Ledyard built against an enormous fallen log that he says measured 32 feet around. They slept under their wool blankets, and the next day they set out for the peak. The ground was rough and lava-strewn, and they did not get far before the path disappeared in a thicket and they turned around.

When they got back to the bay the following evening, they found the situation about to turn for the worse. The catalyzing event was the death by natural causes of William Watman, a quarter-gunner on the *Resolution*, who at forty-five was one of the oldest men on the ship. Even by navy standards he was regarded as a heavy drinker, which probably contributed to his death. He was only the second *Resolution* man to die, and he had requested to be buried in the *heiau*. Cook had a special liking for Watman, who had been on the second voyage as well, so he honored his friend's wishes, with the consent of the chiefs. The coffin was brought ashore in the pinnace. Ledyard marched at the front of the funeral procession along with the marine guards, but he sensed something amiss. The island was deserted, the people shut away in their houses except for the priest and two or three attendants. Watman's coffin was lowered into his grave, and a wooden cross erected on the site. That night, Ledyard saw a light in the morai, the burial place, and went to investigate. He found a dozen men sitting in a circle around the fire, and they welcomed him, recognizing him as "chief warrior at the tents." His Hawaiian name, he learned, was Ourero, and he was famous among them for having saved an elderly woman from drowning (an incident about which he does not give further details). He sat with them as they slaughtered a pig, throwing its entrails onto the fire, and the meat on Watman's grave as a kind of offering. Ledyard went away, much troubled by the solemn ritual. It seemed not a good sign.

After two and a half weeks at Hawaii, the ships began to prepare to leave. First, the crew had to reinstall the *Resolution's* rudder, which had been repaired on shore. This was no small job, for the rudder was more than twelve feet tall and so heavy that it barely fit in the ship's small boats. The crew invited some natives to assist, Ledyard says, and several of them volunteered, taking hold of the rope attached to the head of the rudder. They were not helpful, Ledyard reports, for they "pretended to pull and labor very hard, though at the same time they were in fact doing all they could to retard the business, to ridicule and make their pastime of the people." The master's mate soon had enough, and he started throwing punches. The Hawaiians jeered and threw stones in return, leading to an all-out brawl, in which the badly outnumbered

English were forced to retreat to their encampment amid a hail of stones.

The English were no longer godlike, it seemed. The islanders soon lost their fear of the strangers. "Hardly a day passed," Ledyard wrote, "that did not produce some petty disturbance," usually involving theft. The women who stayed on the ships confessed that the chiefs were planning to attack the ships and massacre the foreigners.

But theft was also a two-way street, as Ledyard points out in his journal. On February 1, Cook came ashore to purchase firewood—wood that then comprised the fence around the same sacred *heiau* where Watman had been buried. In return, he offered the insulting price of two hatchets, which the chief refused. As Ledyard tells it, Cook stuffed the hatchets into his robe and peremptorily ordered his crew (likely including Ledyard, who was there) to load the wood onto the boats. While the priests looked on in horror, the English also carried off several sacred wooden images from the temple.

On February 4, the ships pulled anchor and left, much to everyone's relief. The ships were now well supplied, though at great hardship to the Hawaiians, who had sold much of their own produce and livestock, leaving the island almost stripped bare. Cook decided first to sail over to Maui, which had a more plentiful supply of fresh water than Kealakekua Bay. But just offshore, the ships encountered strong winds, howling off the islands "in irregular and most terrible gusts, such as we had never seen," according to Ledyard. By the ninth, the gale-force winds had wrenched the *Resolution*'s foremast yet again. They had no choice but to sail back into Kealakekua Bay, and this time they found it nearly deserted. Nobody paddled out to greet them with roasted pigs and breadfruit, and there were no elaborate welcoming ceremonies. The astronomers and sailmakers cautiously set up their tents on shore, guarded by Ledyard and six marines, and the carpenters removed the foremast, carried it ashore, and went to work. Ledyard kept a wary eye on the Hawaiians. "Our return to this bay was as disagreeable to us as it was for the inhabitants, for we were reciprocally tired of each other," Ledyard wrote. "We had nothing to do but to hasten our departure to some different island where our vices were not known."

The Hawaiians began to harass the foreigners with a series of daring thefts. A boat full of chiefs visited the *Discovery*, and while some of the chiefs diverted the guards in conversation, another brazenly stole a set of armorer's tongs and then leaped into the waiting canoe, which paddled off like mad. He was captured and given forty lashes, and the tongs were retrieved, only to be stolen again, this time for good. The islanders traded only reluctantly now and demanded outrageous prices—often in the form of iron daggers and knives, to the alarm of Ledyard the marine. "Our prostituted alliance," in his words, had turned dangerous. Then, on the morning of February 14, 1779, the *Discovery*'s cutter (a small auxiliary boat with six oars) was found missing, cut from her mooring and stolen during the night.

This could not go unpunished, especially after the debacle of the tongs. As captain of the *Discovery*, Clerke was responsible for retrieving his stolen boat. But he was ill with tuberculosis that he'd caught in the London debtor's prison before the voyage (and transmitted, fatally, to his own doctor, William Anderson). So Captain Cook went ashore in his place, taking a contingent of ten well-armed marines in two boats. Meanwhile, the *Discovery* and *Resolution* positioned their smaller boats to blockade the entrance to the bay. Cook landed at about nine in the morning and marched to the house of Kalani'opu'u. The town was deserted, which was an ominous sign, "though Cook blinded by some fatal cause could not perceive it," Ledyard wrote. There were other ominous signs that Ledyard did not mention in his published *Journal.* That very night, he and his marine guards had foiled a surprise attack at the astronomers' tents.

The high chief came out of his house; he had been sleeping. His friend Captain Cook invited him to come out to the ship. They walked down to the beach, arm in arm by some accounts, followed by a crowd of several hundred men who had seemingly materialized out of nowhere. On the beach, the news reached the crowd that one of the *Discovery's* boats had fired on a sailing canoe and killed a man. As the crowd begged Kalani'opu'u to stay on shore, Cook coaxed him onward, Ledyard writes, "and led him within a rod or two of the shore, but the just fears* and conjectures of the chiefs at last interposed."

"Some of the crowd now cried out that Cook was going to take their king from them and kill him," Ledyard continued. "There was one in particular that advanced towards Cook in an attitude that alarmed one of the guard[s], who presented his bayonet and opposed him." The Hawaiians now seemed ready to attack, and Cook turned to confront his antagonist. The man did not back down, so Cook fired his pistol. In previous confrontations firearms had been the English trump card; a bit of gunfire never failed to decide matters in their favor, sending their native opponents either fleeing in terror or falling down dead. This time those tactics were worse than useless. Cook's gun was loaded with small shot (or a blank, according to Ledyard), and the charge merely bounced off the man's armored chestplate. "Manee mattoo," he shouted—"for killing birds"—and kept coming, whereupon Cook shot him in the groin with a lead ball.

---

*The "just fears": how that phrase must have rankled Cook historians. Ledyard dared to take the Hawaiians' point of view, if only for a sentence.

Cook and his men turned to retreat, scrambling for the boats while the crowd surged forward. Chaos ensued as the marines in the boats opened fire and the shore party stumbled backward into the shallows. But instead of moving in to pick up their comrades, the marines' boats paddled away from the shore, earning Lt. John Williamson, who commanded the boats, a lasting reputation for cowardice. While Cook, who could not swim, waved his hat at the boats, a spear was thrust through his back, piercing him all the way through. It was tipped with an English bayonet.

Ledyard's account of what happened on that Hawaiian beach is so vividly written that for more than a century it was taken as eyewitness truth. Generations of historians and academics have argued over Ledyard's exact role on that fateful day, the reliability of his journal, and the significance of what he saw. Ledyard was so convincing that his friend James Burney of the *Discovery*, who had watched the proceedings from a distance, definitively placed Ledyard at the scene when he wrote about the incident decades later. Jared Sparks followed Burney's lead, and the "fact" that John Ledyard "witnessed" Cook's death—and, by implication, was involved in the heroic action—became a key part of Ledyard's legend. Ledyard's version of Cook's death was even quoted in early editions of the *Encyclopaedia Britannica* as the *only* eyewitness account.

While Ledyard never explicitly says that he was there, neither does he admit that he was somewhere else. The events of that terrible day would be told and retold for the remainder of the voyage, and by the time they reached England more than eighteen months later, Ledyard had no doubt memorized the whole story (which largely came from his commanding officer, Lieutenant Molesworth Phillips). Still, it wasn't until 1936 that Cookologist Maurice Holmes raised questions about Ledyard's claim, and another three decades before the devoted Ledyard scholar Kenneth

Munford decided to address the question more carefully. A close reading of Ledyard's journal and the many other accounts of that day's events, Munford concludes, shows pretty clearly that Ledyard couldn't possibly have been on shore with Cook. The captain's marine detail consisted of six privates, one corporal, a sergeant, and two officers, lieutenants Molesworth Phillips and John Williamson. The corporal, the sergeant, and three privates were killed, but Corporal Ledyard obviously survived (the dead corporal was, in fact, James Thomas). Jared Sparks had actually received a letter from an "R.W." to the same effect. Across the bottom, Sparks wrote, unperturbed, "The above is a mistake. Ledyard was with Cook when the latter was killed by the savages at the Sandwich Islands."

More recently, as historians have begun to look anew at Cook's voyage and native perspectives on it, Ledyard's allegedly "worthless" *Journal* has taken on new importance. At times these academics have drafted Ledyard into their own quarrels. In 1992, Princeton's Gananath Obeyesekere published a slim volume titled *The Apotheosis of Captain Cook*, arguing that British and American academics—in particular, University of Chicago anthropologist Marshall Sahlins—had completely misconstrued both Cook and the native response to him. The idea that Cook was received as some sort of god, he argued, was erroneous and self-serving, allowing English-speaking scholars to portray Hawaiians as ignorant savages. This idea, he argued, reflected the historians' own need to mythologize Cook (or at least rationalize his behavior), when in fact the Hawaiians had done no such thing. He insisted that Cook was received more or less as a high chief (hence the name-exchanging ceremony), and his death was due to his own choleric temper—"unreasoning, irrational, and violent"—in short, he had gone mad, like Joseph Conrad's insane antihero Kurtz, gone feral in *Heart of Darkness*. To help make his case, Obeyesekere enlisted Ledyard. Other officers had noted Cook's sometimes tyrannical behavior, of course; his own men jokingly compared his on-deck tantrums to the stomping dances of the Polynesian heiva. Of all the scribes, though, Ledyard was most attuned to native moods. Even if he did not always understand the significance of what he recalled, his version of key events sometimes undermines the officers' (and official) versions.

A few years later, Sahlins shot back with his own book, *How "Natives" Think: About Captain Cook, For Example,* in which he vowed to "defend my honor" against Obeyesekere—eighteenth-century dueling language that Ledyard would have understood. As he makes his case, Sahlins ridicules Ledyard as "one of Obeyesekere's privileged journalists" and "not the most reliable of the Cook chroniclers." This is true enough, given that Ledyard wrote much of his account from memory, and his names and dates are off in many places (but are easily triangulated with the more-or-less correct official version). He takes issue the most with Ledyard's account of Watman's funeral, and the supposed outrage of the priests, in its aftermath, which was not mentioned in Lt. James King's official account or by anyone else. (Never mind that Ledyard had actually sat with them in their temple.) Elsewhere, however, Sahlins drafts Ledyard to his cause, too, noting instances where Obeyesekere ignored or dismissed Ledyard's version of events as ignorant or uninformed, particularly where it contradicts his thesis.

One way or the other, Ledyard's account, flawed as it may be, gives us a unique take on the events leading up to Cook's death. That day on the beach, though, Ledyard was concerned more with his own survival than with historical remembrance. Soon enough, the fighting returned to the far end of the bay, where Ledyard had been stationed throughout the ships' stay at Hawaii. As the carpenters raced to get the foremast back to the *Resolution*, Ledyard and his marines opened fire on crowds of hostile natives, who were throwing stones and rolling rocks down the hillsides at them.

The next day, Clerke assumed command of the *Resolution*, and the crews assessed the damage. Some of the dead were recovered, but not Cook; his body was gone. That night, a canoe approached the ships carrying three natives, one of whom was wearing Cook's hat. Undeterred even by a sentry's bullet, which hit one man in the leg, the trio climbed on board. Ledyard sets the scene from there: "We were extremely affected and disgusted when the other Indian produced from a bundle he had under his arm a part of Cook's thigh wrapped up in clean cloth which he said he saw himself cut from the bone in the manner we saw it, and when we enquired what had become of the remaining part of him, he gnashed his teeth and said it was to be eaten that night."

# PART THREE
## The Enterprize

# A Simple Plan

WHEN LEDYARD SAT DOWN IN HIS UNCLE'S HARTFORD
study to write his version of Cook's voyage, over the
winter of 1783, he was indeed—as J. C. Beaglehole
asserted—a man of divided loyalties and multiple agendas. Having spent eight years wearing His Majesty's red coat, he was now
among brothers, uncles, and cousins who had fought against the
Crown. So Ledyard may have felt slightly awkward at his Uncle
Tom's house, surrounded by various maimed and scarred relatives, such as his younger cousin Billy Seymour, who'd sacrificed
a leg defending Fort Griswold.

Nonetheless, Ledyard tried his best to be his old impish self.
Not long after he'd arrived in Connecticut, a letter arrived at the
Seymour house for his beloved Aunt Betsy. He snatched it from
her hand and loudly wondered which lieutenant or major might
have sent it. A playful round of teasing ensued, with Betsy
snatching Billy's crutch as a sword, and Ledyard defending himself with a flapped hat and handfuls of Indian corn. Billy and his
brother Tom Jr. joined in—they were both Yale boys, destined
for the legal profession—and the letter was extracted: It was
from John's cousin Isaac in Philadelphia, announcing his engagement to Anne McArthur of New York. The happy news led to a
mock debate on the virtues of celibacy and marriage. "How can

a Man or a Woman marry if nobody will have them?" his cousin Ned wondered, somewhat pointedly, "or if their circumstances in life will not admit of it?"

"[I]t is much better in my opinion to live as an honest batcheler," replied Ledyard, the unmarriageable thirty-one-year-old, "than a knavish brute of a Husband."

That may have helped to break the ice. At home, he steered clear of the vitriolic political debates that raged in post-Revolutionary America. "I am a violent Whig, and a violent Tory," he confided to Isaac. "Many are my acquaintances, and not one out of the pales of the family know me. I eat, and drink when I am asked; and visit when I am invited, and in short, generally do as I am bid."

A few days after that boisterous family get-together, Ledyard submitted his petition to the Connecticut Assembly requesting copyright protection for his still-to-be-published journal, describing in detail how he'd been forced into the British military and stressing that he'd avoided combat against the now-former American colonies. Ledyard had painted a somewhat different picture of his loyalties, however, in a letter he'd sent to Lord Sandwich in June 1781, eight months after returning from Cook's voyage. In his most obsequious cursive, he denied any sympathy for the rebel colonies: "I am a native of North America, of a good Family and once had considerable connections there," he wrote, "until the rupture with England in 1775 when I abandoned all and entered the Army here." He was sufficiently attached to England that he had even invested his navy pay in the London stock market (losing most of it, naturally). Would the Lord be so kind as to help him get a promotion, or perhaps an officer's commission? His friend John Gore, the American-born lieutenant, chimed in with his own cover letter, recommending Ledyard as "one who from Education and abilities is (I think)

Properly Qualified and justly merits a higher Rank Than That which he holds at present." But there is no record of Sandwich's response.

At about this same time, Ledyard appears to have sought help from the British side of the family. According to Anne Hodge, the Squire's youngest daughter (and thus Ledyard's aunt), Ledyard was in Bristol when he saw a grand carriage thunder past, emblazoned with the blue Ledyard crest, which featured the image of a lion and the fitting motto, *Per crucem ad stellas* (By the cross to heaven). He stopped the carriage, and the driver brought him to the Ledyard mansion. The master was away, but his son, who'd been in the counting room, came to the door. He seemed doubtful as well, but he admitted that John did resemble a relative who'd gone to the East Indies. If you are he, the young man said, you will be welcomed. But he still seemed skeptical and Ledyard went away in a huff. He hated when anyone questioned his integrity, as the squire and Reverend Wheelock had done. Later, the master sent a messenger to Ledyard's room, with a note and some money; Ledyard claimed to have sent the man away, with a message that "they are not Ledyards." Anne Ledyard Hodge told Sparks, "He never after called on his relations although he was several times after in England & sometimes in distress."

What he had really wanted from them, Ledyard later told relatives, was not money but help in securing his release from military service—or possibly a promotion. He didn't get it, and according to military record Ledyard deserted as a sergeant, the rank to which he had been promoted after his superior, Sergeant Samuel Gibson, died at sea in September 1780, just before the ships reached Scotland.

Although we don't know how Ledyard spent the next two years, he had proved that he could be a loyal soldier, enforcing the captain's orders even when (as he later wrote) he disagreed with them. There is no record of his having been punished during the voyage, unlike several of his fellow marines. In his letter from the British warship, he had referred to Cook as "my friend." In his journal, he took a somewhat different view, repeatedly pointing out how the captain's own behavior had led to his death.

By the time he wrote his book, Ledyard's main concern was not the war or anything else of the political moment. He had a much bigger idea in his mind, one that had been fermenting since his trip to meet the Russians on the island of Unalaska, nearly five years before. The morning after his arrival at the Russian village, he had spotted a barque of no more than thirty tons, with a rusty three-pound cannon, anchored in the cove. He was amazed to learn that the Russians braved the rough seas in such a small ship; the 462-ton *Resolution* was literally falling apart under the stress of North Pacific sailing. (Modern fishing boats, equipped with radar and satellite positioning systems, are regularly lost in the same waters, some of the most deadly on earth.) Yet this little barque, no bigger than a pleasure yacht, had sailed back and forth to Siberia, across the cold northern sea. Ledyard was even more impressed when the Russians told him it had belonged to the famed Vitus Bering himself. They were lying, but Ledyard was inspired nonetheless.

"Bheering's discoveries," he wrote later, showing his penchant for lofty sentiment (not to mention prolixity), "were those of an obscure unassisted genius who has every difficulty to surmount that can be thought incident to a man illiberally educated, and to such a vast undertaking." The Danish-born explorer's feats compared favorably in his mind to Cook's accomplishments, which were "those of a person whose fame had already been established, whose genius had all the assistance of art, and whose equipments in other respects were the studied accommo-

dations of the greatest nautical kingdom on earth." Ledyard was
unaware that Bering's ship, the *St. Peter*, had actually been wrecked
on the island of St. Elias in 1741, and that Bering and many of
his men had perished of scurvy. "I was determined to go on
board of her," he wrote, "and indulge the generous feelings the
occasion required."

The idea Ledyard formed of Bering, of a lone explorer in a
small craft, independent and unbeholden to anyone, had excited
his imagination. He saw himself as more like Bering than Cook,
and he trained his sights on the same part of the world that the
Dane had explored. He had also taken note of the Russians' fur-
trading station on Unalaska. The "factory," as he called it, had
been established about five years before Cook arrived, to purchase furs from native trappers (in addition to those exacted as
tribute), and prepare them for shipment home. Once a year, the
little barque sailed to Kamchatka with a cargo of furs, returning
with fresh supplies for the next season. Only later, when they
reached China, had Ledyard and his shipmates realized the enormous profits that were involved. "Skins which did not cost the
purchaser sixpence sterling sold in China for 100 dollars," Ledyard bragged in his journal—and for once in his life, he was not
exaggerating.

John Ledyard hadn't written his *Journal of Captain Cook's Last
Voyage to the Pacific Ocean* simply for the sake of writing a book,
though it did bring him a little fame. It was really intended to be
a promotional piece: He was serving notice to the merchants of
America of the huge profits waiting for them on the far side of
their own continent. Somewhere between his landing at Nootka
Sound and his escape from the British at Long Island, he had
seen the future of America, and it lay to the west. For the first
time in his life, John Ledyard had something like a plan, and it
was both simple and visionary. He would return to Nootka

Sound with a small group of traders and soldiers and establish a fur-trading station like the Russians' in Alaska. Nootka Sound appeared to be well south of the Russians' reach, so he needed not fear their competition or their impact on prices. At Nootka, he and his men would load up on cheap furs, then sail over to sell them in China. The only potential danger in this enterprise, barring gross incompetence or disaster at sea, was that the ships might sink on the way home, under the weight of the profits.

Had things gone in his favor, perhaps, John Ledyard might be as famous now as John Jacob Astor, who made his fortune in the fur trade. In the war-shattered United States of 1783, though, he found his sure-fire scheme was difficult to sell. Even his own uncles, Benjamin and Ebenezer Ledyard, who were established merchants in New York, were unable to help; the continuing British occupation had decimated their business, creating huge uncertainty. In November 1783 Ebenezer wrote to Tom Seymour (who sought a job for his son Henry), saying, "There is no knowing who will be principle merchants Six Weeks hence or in the Spring."

Ledyard hoped that his book might allay investors' doubts, but it didn't appear until June 1783. Nathaniel Patten's cracked and worn printer's type seemed to symbolize the threadbare state of the young American economy, but Ledyard was already hard at work on his scheme. As usual, he was a few steps ahead of himself. Leaving the unfinished manuscript with Patten and collecting his twenty-guinea advance, he headed for Philadelphia sometime in early May. Traveling via Bordentown, New Jersey, Ledyard hopped a boat down the Delaware River and in Philadelphia ensconced himself at the Crooked Billet on Chestnut Street, where six decades earlier a teenage runaway from Boston named Benjamin Franklin had also spent his first nights in the city. Dressed in a fine shirt, he went off to meet with the merchants of Philadelphia. His first stop was Blair McClenachan's large shipping house by the Delaware River. McClenachan wasn't interested in his proposition, nor were two other merchants that he visited. Strolling around the docks, he could see why. Although "sixteen sail of seven different maritime powers arrived here a few days ago," as he reported in a letter to Isaac, the docks were teeming with out-of-work American sailors. Britain had lifted her blockade of the Delaware only a month before, but her own ports remained closed to American vessels. "I doubt that I should even be put to it to get to Sea before the mast," Ledyard lamented.

He returned to his lodgings, "went up and counted my cash—and turned it over—and looked at it, shook it in my hand, recounted and found two French crowns, half a crown, one fourth of a dollar one eighth of a dollar and lastly twelve coppers." Not much remained of Nathaniel Patten's twenty guineas, but then, money tended to fly out of Ledyard's pockets. He had relatives in Philadelphia—his aunt Anne Ledyard Hodge, the Squire's youngest daughter, and her husband, Andrew Hodge Jr.—but he hesitated to ask them for anything, perhaps out of pride. "Shall I visit H——s?" he wonders in his note to Isaac. "I looked at my stockings, my Breeches—they will do—my shoes—if I look that way—my two crowns and I shall part— we did part—I put my new pumps on, washed, shaved, and walked to H——s where I had determined not to go." Swallowing his pride, he asked Andrew Hodge for a small loan, generously promising that Isaac would pay it back. Rather shamelessly, he closed that same letter with a request that would become familiar to his friends and relatives: "Send me," he pleaded, "either by Mr. H or at the first conveyance some Cash."

A few weeks later, things began looking up. In late May or early June Ledyard arranged a meeting with the powerful

Robert Morris, the financier of the American Revolution and probably the only man in America who could help him. Morris owned a shipping firm whose monopoly on the tobacco trade with France had helped make him one of the wealthiest men in America. At the same time, Morris had helped shepherd the new republic through the difficult war years, during which she had teetered on the edge of bankruptcy. In January of 1783, Morris had announced his intention to resign as the new republic's superintendent of finance, and was seeking new private ventures when Ledyard walked through the doors of the office of finance.

Dressed up once again in his finest costume and his brand-new pumps, Ledyard made his pitch to the financier himself: a shortish, orotund man with twinkling blue eyes like his own. Morris was intrigued by Ledyard's idea. Other people had approached him about sending vessels to China, but Morris had demurred because of his government responsibilities and the uncertain state of the States. Ledyard's plan piqued his interest, and after a second meeting Morris became a convert. This was a revolutionary approach to the China trade. While American merchants well knew the profitability of tea, they had little to offer the Chinese in return except for ginseng root, gathered in the backwoods from New Hampshire to Virginia. So the notion of a fur trade, based on the West Coast and reaching over to China, was big news. The silky black pelts of the American sea otter were almost mythically soft, a fantastically profitable, and plentiful, cargo.

"What a noble hold he instantaneously took of the Enterprize!" Ledyard exclaimed, in a letter to Isaac. "I have been two days at his request drawing up a minute detail of a Plan and an Estimate of the outfits; which I shall present him with tomorrow and am pleased to find it will be two thousand pounds less than one of his own. For tomorrow is a day big with the fate of Josephus and America as it respects her trade. I take the lead of the greatest commercial Enterprize ever embarked on in this Country." (Beginning as early as 1774, Ledyard almost always signed his letters to Isaac as "Josephus," after the first-century Jewish historian Flavius Josephus, who famously served both his own people and Caesar—rather like Ledyard the red-coat-wearing Yankee.) "For God's sake send me some money," he concluded, "lest the Laurel now suspended over the Brow of thy Friend fall irrecoverably into the mier."

Morris urged his business partners to adopt Ledyard's plan. The Continental Army contractor Daniel Parker and his partner William Duer were assigned the job of finding a ship, or ships, for the voyage. In July, Parker went to Boston, where a new ship was being built, to be called the *Empress of China.* Ledyard was also dispatched to Boston in search of crewmen. (Morris, he complained, was "wrapt up in the Idea of Yanky Sailors.") By late summer, word of the venture had leaked into the *Salem Gazette,* which reported on August 21 that a ship was fitting out in Boston for a voyage to China, with a cargo worth £150,000, and that further, "many eminent merchants, in different parts of the continent, are said to be interested in this first adventure from the New World to the Old."

The New England merchants were already intrigued about trade with China. American independence meant that they no longer had to worry about running afoul of British monopolies or the British revenue cutters that protected them. But the British were also interested in the Northwest fur trade, and someone (probably Parker, who had contracts to serve the evacuating British forces as well) spilled the beans to Guy Carleton, the gossipy British commander at New York. Carleton immediately saw the threat to Britain's own ambitions, and his alarmed letters gave details of the plan as it stood, complete with vessel tonnages and itineraries: According to Carleton, the *Empress* was headed around Cape Horn for California, on a "voyage of discovery," probably with Ledyard aboard. Another ship laden with cash and ginseng would proceed via the Cape of Good Hope to Canton, following the conventional route that European ships used.

By late September the plan had expanded to include at least six ships, and two possible approaches to China. In October, Carleton updated the British: Now the *Empress* would sail to Canton via the Society Islands, while a second ship, probably the *Columbia,* would leave Boston in November for the western coast of North America, with Ledyard on board. A third ship would take the traditional route via the Cape of Good Hope.

Ledyard felt confident enough that September to write a letter to his mother from New London, where he was inspecting ships for his voyage. He had seen little of her since surprising her at the boardinghouse, and he hadn't written; he rarely wrote unless he had good news to report. Now he did, but he also realized that he might never return, so the letter is part boast and part bittersweet farewell. It was his duty, he declared, "as the leading descendant of a broken & distressed family," to engage in risky speculative ventures. "Sometimes I have been elated with hope: sometimes depressed with disappointment & distress," he wrote. "My prospects at present are a Voyage to the East Indies & eventually round the World: It will be of about 2 or 3 years duration. If I am successfull I shall not have occasion to absent myself any more from my friends: but above all, hope to have it in my power to administer to the wants of a beloved Parent & others who languish & fade in obscurity."

But the plans were less solid than either Carleton or Ledyard had believed. In New London Ledyard had seen several suitable ships, including the *Comte d'Artois* and the old Continental frigate *Bourbon*, which had been put up for sale on behalf of the government by none other than Robert Morris, superintendent of finance. The voyage still needed a captain, so Ledyard tried his luck with his old shipmate and friend Daniel Deshon, the nephew of his father's old colleague John Deshon (the one who'd rescued him from his first attempt to enlist with the British, at Gibraltar). Daniel was now a captain himself, with a fine new ship in New London Harbor. But this Captain Deshon didn't believe the wild tales Ledyard told, much to his later regret. "He was afterwards heard to say," wrote Jared Sparks, "that Ledyard's account, in its minutest details, was verified by the first voyages of its kind from the United States, and that he had often regretted his not having listened to him." (Not eager to miss another golden opportunity, Daniel Deshon later became the first New London captain to enter the whaling industry, the mainstay of that port during the nineteenth century.)

Almost inevitably, the venture began to collapse under the weight of its own complexity. Moving on to New York, Ledyard and his partners secured a 300-ton ship that even after extensive repairs was declared unseaworthy for such a voyage. Meanwhile, the partners began to bicker among themselves. William Duer became miffed at Morris, and Ledyard seems to have been part of the reason. In an October letter to a third partner, the French-born merchant John Holker, Duer expressed doubts about the viability of the fur voyage, and blames Morris for giving so much responsibility to "a Person with whom he had a Short Acquaintance," clearly meaning Ledyard. As a father with a young family, Duer declared that he was not about to undertake such a "dangerous experiment in navigation." Morris was upset with Parker, too, over delays in the voyage that Parker in turn attributed to "a fault in the first plan given by Mr. Led-yard." Parker was having difficulty finding a captain to pilot Ledyard to the West Coast. It just seemed too risky.

Ledyard was living on tenterhooks. As his plan collapsed, piece by piece, he began to despair anew. His money had run out, and he was living off of the small allowance that Morris was ev-idently paying him, and the generosity of friends such as Com-fort Sands, the New York merchant and patriot. In a November letter to his mother, Ledyard tried to sound upbeat: "The Chris-tian that had been shipwrecked and buried in sin has tenfold more matter for joy, than one that has suffered but little.... Never May I forget that the hardest flight is highest crowned." In truth he was miserable in New York. As Comfort Sands wrote to Jared Sparks, "He was there anxiously awaiting the event & was without money or friends." Sands advanced him money from time to time, apparently believing he was investing in Ledyard's voyage, and forty years later, he was still complaining (to Sparks) that he'd never been repaid a penny of it.

Ledyard, unfortunately, was destined to sail in the opposite direction from the one he desired. The squabbling between the partners had put the whole enterprise in doubt; by December, William Duer had pulled out of the venture for good. Daniel Parker was headed for bankruptcy, and ended up fleeing the country and his creditors in the spring of 1784. The remaining partners could afford to send only one vessel, and the *Empress of China* ultimately sailed directly for China in February of 1784—without Ledyard. He was bound for Europe instead, embarking for Cadiz in the summer of 1784, probably aboard the *Bourbon*—ironically, under Captain Deshon. "The flame of Enterprize, that I excited in America, terminated in a flash," an embittered Led-yard wrote Isaac from Europe, "that equally bespoke the inebri-ety of head, and pusillanimity of heart, of my Patrons."

# The Sport of Fortune

ONCE AGAIN, JOHN LEDYARD HAD STRUCK OUT IN AMERICA, heading abroad to make a fresh start. "It seems decreed," he declared shortly after he arrived in Cadiz, "that I John Ledyard shall hop, skip, and jump about on this world of ours, in such an untraversable way, that it can hardly be asserted, whether he moveth in the general circle, his own circle, or any circle at all." He had only three French crowns in his pocket (the equivalent of about $450) when he sailed from New London, "which is a circumstance that strikes my imagination . . . agreeably," he wrote to Isaac. "O be thou blest my early Friend and most pleasing companion amidst the Labyrinths that surround me. Be assured that you hold the place of Brother and will ever deserve to do about the heart of the hitherto unfortunate Josephus."

For all of his life, Isaac had been John's best friend and confidant, his touchstone. They had grown up together, sharing the same tragedy in their childhood, when their sea-captain fathers had died just weeks apart. Exiled to their grandfather's chilly attic in Hartford, they had united: It was them against the world. Isaac had been seven years old at the time of their fathers' deaths, and was three years younger than John, but he would become his older cousin's protector and champion. The affection was mutual. When a cache of Ledyard's letters was discovered in a

Seymour family desk drawer in Hartford in the 1930s, addressed to someone named Monecca, they were at first thought to have been written to a woman. "Kiss me my Cousin my friend, my Monecca," begins one missive, "for while I live I will love thee— let us embrace."

Monecca was not a woman, but John's old pet name for Isaac, and he left no hint of what it meant. Ledyard never explained why he called himself Josephus, either, but perhaps it was because his namesake, too, had witnessed a period of rebellion and transformation (including the birth of Christianity). Josephus's letters to Isaac form a kind of running journal of the next few years of his life. In them, he reports on his latest successes and disappointments, forwards his observations of the places and people he's met, and sometimes simply unburdens his romantic soul.

Isaac Ledyard led his own full and accomplished life. While he had grown up with John, first in the Squire's household and then with Tom Seymour, Isaac had followed a more conventional path, studying medicine with a physician named John Bard in New York. He had then served in the medical corps of the Continental Army as assistant purveyor to its Medical Department, based at the military hospital at Fishkill, New York. This was no easy assignment. Given the chronic shortages of bandages and other supplies, he would have had to rely on his own resources. Toward the end of the war, Isaac got caught up in some official dispute that caused him to resign his commission pending a court-martial, not long before John returned home. ("I rejoice that you have quit the army," Ledyard reassured him in a letter, "you are by nature too good & generous to be a slave.") The case was dropped, and Isaac eventually settled in New York and married Ann McArthur in 1785. The couple moved into the Morris-Jumel Mansion, whose Loyalist owner had quitted it for England. Located in what was then countryside, the house still stands at

162nd Street and Amsterdam Avenue in Harlem Heights. (Built in 1765, Morris-Jumel is Manhattan's oldest house.) After the Revolution, Isaac carried on a spirited pamphlet debate with his acquaintance Alexander Hamilton. Calling himself "Mentor," to Hamilton's "Phocion," he argued against Hamilton's plea for détente with England and an amnesty for Tory sympathizers (cousins who'd served the British unwillingly were presumably exempt). He also authored an anonymous "Essay on Matter" that struck at least one stern minister as "a sly attack on the Christian religion."

What the serious-minded Isaac thought of his wayward cousin, we simply don't know. None of Monecca's responses have survived; judging from Ledyard's oft-expressed frustration, they were few and far between. He doesn't seem to have sent very much cash, either, despite frequent requests. But Isaac safeguarded his cousin's letters, and later, after John's death, he assembled them in a lovingly prepared biography that was still unpublished when Isaac died in 1803, aged forty-eight. He had been John's only life-long friend, his one link to the road behind him.

Ledyard's first stop in Europe, the Spanish port of Cadiz, was already ancient when Christopher Columbus had set sail from there in 1492. Founded around 1100 B.C. by Phoenicians, Cadiz was enjoying renewed prosperity thanks to a thriving trade with an America in dire need of alternatives to English ports. Cadiz soon became America's largest trading partner, with brand-new city walls and plenty of American flags in its harbor. Within a week or two of his arrival, Ledyard was literally swept off his feet by General Alexander "Alejandro" O'Reilly, the local governor, who passed him one day in his carriage—"as clumsy and Gothic as the devil"—and took him to see a bullfight. Ledyard found it a "barbarous amusement" (he preferred the opera) but he was quite taken by the figure of O'Reilly, "a poor mi-grating Irish cadet" who governed with authority and panache.

Ledyard always admired such bold, larger-than-life characters. Like Ledyard, O'Reilly was a peripatetic figure who had put himself in the service of a foreign king, though on a grander scale. He had somehow landed at the Spanish court, and in 1769 had been dispatched to New Orleans, during the brief Spanish occupation of that city, to put down a rebellion there. He was later sent to quell the irksome Barbary pirates, off the coast of Algeria, but they had handed him a humiliating defeat in 1775, and now he had retired to Cadiz, where he ruled imperiously over the city and the region. "Riley is to Cadiz and all within his jurisdiction . . . what Czar Peter the Great was to Russia," Ledyard wrote Isaac.

In Cadiz, Ledyard was initiated into expatriate life, dining in a circle of Irish and American merchants, with the odd Spaniard and Russian thrown in. Like many another American abroad, he adopted a condescending pose toward his native land. This must have irked his war-veteran cousin to no end. "Here I am told you err in politics," he lectured Isaac, "by which I mean those Politics your independence has given birth to." (The Europeans were having difficulty with the concept of Congress, and their kings were understandably slow to recognize American independence.) As if to bolster his own sophistication, he took care to note that he wrote "with a glass of Red Wine now in my left hand."

Ledyard had not given up his dreams of the fur trade; he'd merely transferred them to Europe. His scheme found no traction in Cadiz, though, and he lingered there only a month before setting off to France and the key port of L'Orient, located on the Breton coast. Already he had evidence that he was on the right track. The official account of Cook's last voyage had been published in 1784, confirming his own stories of the profits to be made in American furs. But the book had also inspired European competition. While still in Cadiz, he had heard garbled reports of a large Russian ship fitting out in London for a voyage to the Northwest coast of America, with some of Cook's men serving as her officers. He was heartened and agitated at the same time; he might be on the right track, but he was no longer the only one. He blamed his American partners for the delay. "And hadst thou Morris not ingloriously shrunk behind a trifling obstruction," he railed to Isaac in a later letter, "I [would have] been happy and America this moment triumphantly displaying her flag in the most remote and beneficial regions of Commerce. Faith I am tired of my vexations."

Morris deserved more credit than that. He had not only paid Ledyard for his time and supported him while in Philadelphia, but the influential merchant had sent Ledyard off with letters of recommendation to his French business contacts, as well as to the American consul Thomas Barclay in Paris. Within two weeks of his arrival in L'Orient, in late September 1784, Ledyard was already claiming to have formed "a most respectable company" with some of the local merchants, including Simon Bérard and the house of le Coulteux. The company had already purchased a fine ship for his proposed voyage, he wrote to Isaac; even Ledyard couldn't believe his good luck. "I have been so much the sport of accident, that I am exceedingly jealous," he wrote. "But—here comes a but—pray heaven they may not butt the modicum of brains out of my Head which Morris hath left there—the but is this, I have arrived so late in the season in this Country that the Merchants have procrastinated the Equipment until the next summer and have requested me to stay here until then, allowing me genteely for that purpose."

There was, it seems, always a "but" in Ledyard's plans. His imagination tended to run a little ahead of reality, as did his letters home, eager as he was to report good news. "I keep the grandest company in L'Orient, & am universally respected," he boasted to his younger brothers, Thomas and George, in February 1785. "I have a fine ship of 400 tons, and in August next expect to sail on another voyage round the world," he went on. "If I never see you more, it shall be well; If I do, it shall be well."

In truth, Ledyard was living on an emotional roller coaster. "This head I wear is so much a dupe to my heart—and at other times, my heart is so bedeviled by my head that I have not much confidence in matters of business, in either." He was plagued by a touch of "Cook's rheumatism in my bones," perhaps the result of some sort of tropical fever. He also seems to have suffered from what we now recognize as bipolar syndrome. When he was high, he was the wittiest, most glib, and urbane dinner companion; he wrote chatty letters to Isaac, full of inside jokes and ribbing. ("Pray how is thy Liver?" he inquired in September. "Does it decay fast?") When things went wrong, Ledyard would plunge into silent, black depressions that sometimes lasted for months. He'd arrived in L'Orient in the grip of some fever, he told Isaac, which he admitted was "heightened by a fit of uncommon melancholy."

He tended not to write when he was depressed, and his letters home seem to have stopped in February 1785. He remained quiet until the following July, when he turned up in Paris. The L'Orient ship had apparently never sailed. "The Devil is in it, said I, if this negotiation falls through," he wrote. "And yet, it did fall through, as easy as a needle would pass through the eye of a camel." He had three crowns in his pocket, he said, the same amount of money with which he'd arrived in Spain over a year earlier. "The L'Orient failure must have had more bitterness in it than almost anything which he endured in his travels," his cousins later observed, in their notes accompanying his letters, "and, it is expected, must have caused some debate in himself of persevering in his designs. For he seems on his arrival in Paris to have retired within himself, and to have shut out comfort—at least if not hope."

Though he was quite sociable and loved a good party, Ledyard was emotionally self-reliant. He endured his frequent melancholy periods by digging deep into his own reserves, like the Alaskan native people who dug their houses into the earth itself, to escape the wind and the cold and the endless darkness of winter. When he did reveal his misfortunes, he would cloak them in a comic style that his relatives later called "Shandian," after the hapless, grammatically challenged protagonist of his favorite book.

Published between 1759 and 1767, Laurence Sterne's *The Life and Opinions of Tristram Shandy, Gentleman* caused a huge sensation when it appeared, and Ledyard was always drawn to the newest new thing. In his letters, especially the famous one to Wheelock, he tried to emulate Sterne's wildly digressive writing style, stretching the rules of English syntax to the breaking point and beyond. Like Sterne, Ledyard wrote headlong, using long dashes to link one thought to the next, rarely interrupting the flow with anything so pedestrian as a period. But the connection goes much deeper than style. He reveled in Sterne's absurd and often raunchy humor, which observed few moral or social taboos. Like Sterne, he was a radical change agent, who operated outside the norms and forms of his time; he also liked to make people laugh. In his letter-writing, he adopted a self-consciously autobiographical voice, much different from the detachment of his Cook journal. He particularly identified with Yorick, Sterne's fictional stand-in, a perceptive country parson who appears in *Shandy* and who also narrates his surreal 1768 classic, *A Sentimental Journey through France and Italy.* Yorick's theory of travel might well have been Ledyard's own: "What a large volume of adventures may be grasped within his little span of life," he declared, "by him who interests his heart in every thing."

As he entered his middle thirties, an age when most of his peers were married, settled, and accomplished, Ledyard's life was starting to seem like something out of the pages of Sterne. He floated along, dependent on the faith and sometimes charity of others, with his own dreams always unattainable thanks to a series of not-to-be-believed misfortunes. In his own letters, he began to portray his life as a kind of absurd comic novel, "with myself the jest & riddle of the drama." Like Sterne's Uncle Toby character, who was consumed (and defined) by his "hobby-horses," Ledyard was burdened by his own obsession with the Northwest fur trade, which he dubbed "My Ass." In a long letter to Isaac, he explains his move to Paris by means of a distinctly Shandyesque dialogue with the imaginary beast. "Will you go to Paris said my Ass?" he writes, "I fear I have not money enough said I: I will eat thistles said my Ass: but what shall we do when there said I—tho I put the question wrong & so my Ass was silent: I too shall be forced to eat thistles myself said I, answering myself." A few lines later, his real despair pokes through, as the Ass tells him: "At Paris you will be unknown, & should you at the worst perish there you will be insured the advantage of dying unknown which many I assure you have wished to do & could not."

Forty-eight hours after leaving L'Orient, Ledyard was standing in front of the palace of the Louvre. But he was not the sort to remain unnoticed for long. While wintering over at L'Orient, he traveled to Normandy with an English acquaintance, and they had stopped at a country tavern for the night. The tavern was small, so they had to cook their own dinner, and while Ledyard was in the kitchen the house servants noticed the tattoos on his hands and arms. The Englishman's servants then said that Ledyard had sailed around the world with the celebrated Captain Cook. It wasn't long before an invitation arrived from the local grandee, the Marquis de Conflans, inviting them to dinner at his château. "It was too late," Ledyard reported. "The Englishman & I had begun pell mell upon a joint of roast." So they visited the marquis in the evening, and "could not but be honored with the reception we met." Loneliness and poverty were not to be his fate in Paris. "So curiously wretched have I been," he wrote home later, "that without anything but a clean shirt, was I invited from a gloomy garret to the splendid tables, of the first characters, of this kingdom."

His "Ass" would ride again. Before long, Ledyard acquired a new partner: John Paul Jones, the celebrated naval commander and hero of the Revolutionary War. The son of a Scottish gardener, Jones had played a decisive role in the war against Britain, where the press still called him Pirate Jones, for his depredations against the British fleet. Jones had replied that he fought "in defense of the violated rights of mankind," a sentiment that Ledyard would have admired. After the end of his service to the Continental Navy in 1784, Jones had come to France to collect the huge sum of prize money owed him and his men by the French government for taking several British warships, including his most famous kill, the man-o'-war *Serapis*. Jones was a hero in France, his statue already displayed at Versailles, but the collection effort was going slowly, impeded by French red tape. Undeterred, Jones was already looking for ways to spend his money. He had approached Morris while in Philadelphia during 1783, and Morris likely put him in touch with Ledyard.

Like Ledyard and General O'Reilly, John Paul Jones was a "migrant cadet," a warrior for hire, only on a grander scale. Unlike them he had made himself a hero. Four years older than Ledyard, Jones was a romantic character with a huge ego, a man who always seemed to be hungering for the next adventure, either amorous or exploratory. The idea of a voyage to the Northwest would have struck Jones's imagination, and his ambition, quite agreeably. "My desire for fame is infinite," he'd confided to a friend, and in Ledyard he met his match. Together they drew up a business plan, in French, the language of their potential investors. They would purchase a vessel of 250 tons, hire forty-five French officers and men, and sail on October 1st, 1785. Passing around Cape Horn to Hawaii, they would take on more provisions and then continue to the Northwest coast by early April. There they would stay for six months, establishing a camp for the purpose of collecting furs, which the plan claimed "could be bought for a bagatelle, and sold at a market where the venders might fix their own price." After deducting the cost of the vessel, equipment, provisions, and wages, Ledyard and Jones estimated a profit of £36,250, more than $5 million in today's money.

Ledyard was so confident in his plan that in his letters home, the one ship became two. "My affairs stand exactly thus," Ledyard wrote Isaac, in July of 1785: "The celebrated Captain Paul Jones has embarked with me in my expedition: he advances all the outfits himself except the two ships, one or both of which he is now at L'Orient endeavouring to procure as lent or chartered by the King of France; he tells me he thinks he shall succeed, & his character is to speak & act with great caution." If the king did not come through, Ledyard said, Jones had promised to finance the voyage out of his own personal fortune. "Two or three weeks will determine the matter & I will inform you," he wrote. "Whatever depends on Jones's stability, perseverance, & wishes may be firmly relied upon."

Using Jones's cash, Ledyard had already begun procuring the supplies necessary for the voyage and for the factory and garrison he hoped to establish on the Northwest coast. Rather than risk everything on a single voyage, Ledyard and Jones hoped to launch an ongoing, self-sustaining enterprise. They would set up a stockade and a factory and spend six months acquiring furs.

When Jones's ship left for China, hopefully laden with pelts, Ledyard would stay behind in his little fort, with a surgeon, an assistant, and twenty soldiers, but effectively alone on the far side of the world. When the expedition returned to New York, Ledyard promised, Isaac could read his letters, "& perhaps the history of Ben Uncus."

This curious line, tacked on to the end of a letter, gives the first hint that something motivated Ledyard besides money. Ben Uncas had been a powerful Mohegan chief in Connecticut in the early 1700s; Ledyard used the name as his pet term for all Native Americans. Ledyard was of course interested in the venture's profits, but he was also eager to get another look at the Pacific Coast people who'd so captivated him at Nootka Sound with Cook. There was a reason the Jones plan did not call for Ledyard to return with the ships. He had a greater journey in mind, and the commercial venture was but a means to that end. From Nootka Sound, he intended to return home on foot, retracing the native peoples' trading routes—all the way across the continent to New York.

There was some unexplained delay with the Jones project. Robert Morris had promised help, but was dragging his feet—burned once, he seemed unwilling to attempt another Northwest voyage. Worse, French ships turned out to be three times as expensive as Ledyard had estimated. They were having trouble, as well, obtaining French government permission for the venture, perhaps because the Spanish had already claimed most of the West Coast of North America. Meanwhile, it was beginning to look like their buyer's market for Northwest furs would soon be spoiled by competition. Two English ships had already departed for the Pacific, and Ledyard knew from experience the damage they would inflict on native goodwill. "They are the worst people in the world to follow in commerce or colonization among an uncivilized people," he moaned to Isaac. To make matters worse, the French explorer La Pérouse was fitting out in L'Orient for what appeared to be a major expedition to the Pacific. Ledyard took this as confirmation that he was on the right track: "You see what honorable testimonies daily transpire," he wrote home, "to evince, that I am no otherwise the mad, romantic, dreaming Ledyard, than in the estimation of those who were themselves so."

In Paris, Thomas Jefferson was also intensely curious about La Pérouse: "What number of men, and of what conditions and vocations, had he on board?" he wrote to Jones in L'Orient. "What animals, their species and number? What trees, plants or seeds? What utensils? What merchandise or other necessaries?" He cautioned, "This enquiry should be made with as little appearance of interest in it, as possible." In October Jones informed Jefferson that two 600-ton ships had set sail from Brest in August, bound for the Pacific. They were supplied with French trees and plants, as well as linen, wool, iron and copper and tools, agricultural implements, and a million French livres in cash. In short, he believed, the French seemed to be planning to establish some sort of trading colony—complete with farm fields and formal gardens, it appears. The ships were likely bound for the South Seas, Jones wrote. (In fact, La Pérouse headed for Hawaii, then Alaska. He eventually made his way to Australia, where he ultimately died.) "It is not difficult to perceive that he has other [objects]," Jones added, "equally worth of the attention of a great Prince: one of which may be, to extend the Commerce of his Subjects, by establishing Factory's, at a future day, for the fur trade on the North-West Coast of America."

With that, John Ledyard's "mad, romantic" fur-factory scheme gained a new and influential supporter: the American minister to the court of France.

# Man of Genius

SPRAWLING CENTER OF SPECTACLE AND SIN, PARIS IN 1785 was like a combination of present-day Las Vegas and ancient Athens. What had been a sleepy backwater in the 1750s was now an eighteenth-century boomtown, a financial and intellectual capital of Europe. Rents were astronomical and speculation was rampant; much of the city was quite literally new, having been built in the preceding two decades. The nouveau riche merchant class was unafraid of flaunting their wealth, erecting ever-more-gaudy mansions in housing developments on the edge of the sprawling city. In the alleys and back streets, the poorer classes starved, and fought, and murdered each other at a rate of more than one a day. "The laws are severe," observed Ledyard, after a visit to the city morgue; therefore "no person commits a capital crime ... but murders in order to hide the offence."

French society itself was on the cusp of radical transformation. The French Revolution was still a few years away, but the signs of democratic change were everywhere. The crushing poverty of the majority of the population and the frivolous opulence personified by Marie Antoinette could not both be sustained. In the libraries and salons of the merchants and intellectuals, in conversation and in pamphlets, dangerous ideas were being exchanged; among the most dangerous were those expressed by the recently arrived American minister, Thomas Jefferson, whose Declaration of Independence the French revered. (They also admired the out-going minister, Benjamin Franklin, whom Ledyard happened to meet before he left Paris in July 1785.)

Amid all this splendor and wealth, the Americans were a threadbare lot, hovering around the Hôtel Langéac, Jefferson's rented mansion in a suburb that had once been a royal nursery. Jefferson's table attracted artists, scientists, literary types, and other misfits, as well as bankrupt tobacco planters, drunken merchants, liberal priests, and self-styled "men of genius," with some claim to literary or scientific accomplishment. "Such a set of moniless rascals have never appeared since the epoch of the happy villain Falstaff," wrote Ledyard, who was living relatively comfortably on his allowance from John Paul Jones. (His cash reserves now totaled five crowns, up from three.) One muddy spring day, Ledyard and his friends Thomas Barclay and David Franks were denied admission to the palace of Versailles because they'd committed the fashion crime of wearing boots. Jefferson was putting himself into debt to maintain his Parisian lifestyle, and rued his status as "the lowest and most obscure of the whole diplomatic tribe."

Looking back, it seems inevitable that the two men would meet, but Ledyard was likely introduced to Jefferson by Colonel David Humphreys, an old acquaintance of Ledyard's from Hartford. More of a poet than a military man, Humphreys had been one of the Hartford Wits, a group of literary fops slightly older than Ledyard that also included the painter John Trumbull. Humphreys had published a number of popular poems before and after the American Revolution, and he was a man after Ledyard's own heart. "He is a voluptuous animal," Ledyard wrote home, "... and is devoutly fond of women, wine, and religion, provided they are each of good quality." A former aide-de-camp for George Washington, Humphreys was also quite attentive to matters of status and had made sure to attach himself to Jefferson's rising star. (Jefferson biographer Dumas Malone found him "a pretentious young man.") In Paris, Humphreys served as secretary of the American legation. One night over dinner (and over Ledyard's protests), Humphreys told the story of his friend's canoe trip down the Connecticut River; it must have been quite the legend in Hartford, but Jefferson had not heard it. He laughed and remarked that "I had observed a great consistency of character from that moment to this," Ledyard wrote.

Ledyard and Jefferson—the unemployed Connecticut dreamer and the learned Virginia diplomat—actually had much in common, not least of which was a love of Laurence Sterne. (*A Sentimental Journey* was one of Jefferson's favorite books.) "My friend, my brother, my Father," Ledyard wrote Jefferson, who was eight years his senior, "I know not by what title to address you." To Ledyard, Jefferson personified the new American republic and its spirit of freedom, a marked contrast to Europe's dukes and lords, whom he saw as mere "lacquies of Ministers and kings." "Your worthy Virginian," he wrote home, "is in public & private, in every word & every action the representative of a young, politic, vigorous & determined state." Sooner or later, a copy of Ledyard's *Journal* found its way into Jefferson's hands. It didn't stay there for long, as he lent it to Madame Lafayette, who passed it along to her circle of friends, who passed it from hand to hand until Jefferson lost track of it. He was intrigued by Ledyard's rambling spirit and perhaps even a little envious of his freedom. Though heavily encumbered by his diplomatic and social duties, Jefferson still considered himself, as he wrote, a "savage of the mountains." Having no legitimate son of his own, and being a widower, he went out of his way to befriend and mentor young Americans in

Paris. Ledyard, who was both a man of genius and an *homme de bois,* a man of the woods, made a welcome addition to Jefferson's table.

Jefferson saw Ledyard as more than an entertaining dinner guest, however. He had closely followed Ledyard's proposed venture with John Paul Jones and was not blind to its strategic importance. The other major powers, including Britain, Russia, and Spain, were eyeing the Northwest coast of North America. Jefferson was most worried about France, however, and he suspected that the La Pérouse expedition was more ambitious than it seemed. The loading of the ships, as he wrote to John Jay, the secretary of foreign affairs, in August 1785 (after he'd heard from Jones), "appeared to me to indicate some other design: perhaps that of colonising on the western Coast of America; or, it may be, only to establish one or more factories there, for the fur trade. Perhaps we may be little interested in either one of these objects. But we are interested in another, that is, to know whether they are perfectly weaned from the desire of possessing continental colonies in America."

If anybody was going to possess North American colonies, Jefferson had decided, it would be the United States herself. He had long been intrigued by the vast unknown America west of the Blue Ridge; his father had invested in a western land company as far back in 1750. Now he had met somebody who had actually stood on the far West Coast of the continent. He was fascinated by Ledyard's tales of Nootka Sound and the copper-wearing native people there. At last he had met someone as obsessed as he was, and quite possibly mad enough to attempt the impossible.

Jefferson had already begun to think about linking the West Coast and the East. As early as 1783 he had written to General George Rogers Clark suggesting that he lead an expedition across the continent. Clark agreed that the idea was a good one, but regretted that he was too busy (two decades later, his younger brother William Clark would not be, and would join Meriwether Lewis on his epic journey). Clark also made a key suggestion: A small party of three or four men might pass more easily through Native American domains, he believed, than a large, heavily equipped and armed force.

Ledyard was still counting on John Paul Jones. He spent the late summer and autumn of 1785 waiting, as he put it, "with an anxiety not very philosophical" for the final word from the French government. When the answer finally came, it was no: The French were unwilling to trespass on Spanish claims in the New World, and had denied official sanction to the voyage. Jones himself was too preoccupied trying to pry loose his prize money from the bureaucrats in the French navy, a never-ending struggle, and his interest in Ledyard's plan had waned. "Upon the whole I may venture to say that my enterprise with Paul Jones is no more— that I shall inter this hobby at Paris," he wrote to Isaac.

It was Ledyard's third helping of failure in just two years, and he was forced to turn his attention to other things. He briefly contemplated going to Africa with Colonel John Lamb, another family friend from Connecticut who had been appointed to negotiate with the Barbary states for the return of American sailors held hostage by Muslim pirates (who were demanding outrageous ransoms). The Barbary pirates were not merely a thorn in the new nation's side; they posed a serious threat to American commerce. Other European nations had successfully negotiated their own truces, but the new United States had not yet done so. There was one British mercenary officer, working for the king of Morocco, who held a particular dislike for American crews. As Ledyard put it, "[He] expresses it as his utmost wish to enslave a cargo of Americans and crucify the thirteen stripes." Lamb was bound for Algiers to negotiate with the ruling Bey there, but he seemed an unpromising candidate for the job. When Ledyard met him, he had a black eye and a broken leg, incurred during the crossing from England. He was often drunk, usually disheveled, and generally "not a proper agent," in Jefferson's opinion. Ledyard ultimately decided to stay in Paris, the first place since the Groton of his youth where he felt fully at home.

Generations of Americans have gone to Paris to reinvent themselves, but John Ledyard's was the first. At Jefferson's table, he was no longer the Dartmouth dropout and failed entrepreneur whom his family saw. As the wine flowed, he became one of the men of genius whose learning and wit made the City of Light sparkle (along with the gas lanterns that had been installed in the 1740s). The expatriates in Paris, even the ones from Connecticut, were far more tolerant of Ledyard's eccentricities and his libertinism than his own family had been. His Tahitian tattoos were an automatic conversation starter, and he had plenty of stories about Cook's voyage, but they were hardly the least quirky thing about him. Tom Barclay told Ledyard he'd never seen such a "medley" of conflicting traits as he. In the limestone yellow light of Paris, Ledyard could become his own person, at last. "Paris is like a strong whirlpool," he wrote Isaac: "It collects a parcel of light rubbish within its vortex which very seldom returns by the way it entered to the surface of the stream of life, & if I ever do it will not be according to the general course of things I assure you for I bid defiance to them when I left America."

Like Jefferson, Ledyard loved to ramble around the city, absorbing its creative energy and its harsh social contrasts. All of the currents in that turbulent society converged on one place, the Palais-Royal, which fascinated Jefferson and Ledyard alike. Built in 1784 by the duc d'Orléans, just a short distance from the king's seat at the Louvre, the Palais-Royal was what today's urban planners would call a mixed-use development. A palace in name only, it was more like a shopping mall with apartments attached to it. Its arcades housed cafés, bars, bookshops and other businesses; freshly printed and semiscandalous newspapers circulated in its public gardens, which attracted everyone from foreign diplomats to minor noblemen to dark characters from the Parisian demi-monde. All of Paris, it seemed, gravitated to the Palais-Royal, in a great democratic spectacle unrivalled anywhere else in Europe.

Ledyard was appalled—and enthralled. Like a good American tourist, he had visited the Louvre, whose paintings had reminded him "of the greatness of the human mind which seems capable of infinite improvement." The adjacent Tuileries gardens, however, were "a resort to the most sickening vices." But the Palais-Royal exceeded even those sodomitic groves. Ledyard found it "a vile cinque of pollution, and contaminated not only by bawds, and pimps, and procuresses." Never content to say something once, he went on: "[W]hen I report the absolute fact that the Father, the Mother, and the daughters are here together for the sole and professed purpose of mutual prostitution, you will wish me to say no more tho' with equal truth I could enlarge." Late one night, after dinner with Barclay and Franks, he encountered a group of demimondaines in the gardens of the Palais:

> I was called by name as I was traversing the walks by a lady who composed a considerable part in a group of married & unmarried whores & who had before seen me at tea in the chamber of an English sea lieutenant, a friend of mine who has superb lodgings in the Palais Royal. External decorum is the greatest & the least requisite here. The lady who called to me had her little old four feet 5 inches husband with her—& a true Parisian husband is he—an inch more in his stature, a year less in his age, or

a scruple more of virtue or understanding in him would have disqualified him. I took a chair & made use of the words superieurement, superb, magnifique, charmant, beau, belle, infinement &c. I placed it between the happy pair & seized the hand of the lady the husband found himself deranged & withdrew his chair behind the group where he very complaisantly sat while I had an appointment made by his lady & sealed with a thousand rhapsodical kisses & protestations of eager desire and eternal passion. It will not be her fault if I never see her again, nor will it occasion in her more than 5 minutes pain or pleasure whether I do or not.

Someone has drawn a large X through this entire paragraph; the passage does not appear at all in the transcript of this letter in John Ledyard's collected papers. An appointment with a married prostitute was apparently not something that posterity needed to know about John Ledyard, in his relatives' opinion. (In the edited Papers, Ledyard's take on the Palais is: "No friend to France should ever see it.") Jared Sparks, for his part, boils Ledyard's entire eighteen-month Paris stay down to a few tidy paragraphs, with no mention of the Palais or prostitutes at all. His Ledyard would never pull up a chair to flirt with a lady of pleasure.

This letter is one of the few Ledyard documents written in his own hand to survive; most were copied by relatives, as were his journals. The originals, in most cases, have been lost or destroyed— whether by accident or on purpose—leaving only their bowdlerized transcriptions, which Jared Sparks used as the basis for his biography. But as this letter shows, there was a big difference between the edited John Ledyard and the real thing. The censorious relatives not only crossed out John's racy passages, but most references to actual people, such as his sister Fanny ("a solitary wandering girl") and brother Tom ("as grievously flagellated by disease as Job himself").

Another curious fact that his relatives concealed was that the celebrated Ledyard liked to write his letters in the nude. "At this moment that I am scribbling [I am] sitting with my pipe in my mouth & a glass of plain burgundy & nothing on but my shirt," goes one crossed-out passage. "It is an indulgence that I have somehow happened into to sit ~~bare-arsed~~ naked some two or three hours before I sleep, & in the same unconstrained situation I think & occasionally write my friends, which is certainly a proof that I write without disguise." His relatives preferred disguise, primly pulling the curtains whenever he revealed too much of himself or anyone else. The world did not need to know that he flirted with whores, wrote in the nude, and drank the nights away with their Connecticut friend John Lamb, who he'd once had to "put to bed drunk as a Lord, & nobody will ever know it but you and those he got drunk with." But try as they might, his relatives couldn't completely hide the real Ledyard, or his nakedness, which is why he still speaks to us, two centuries later.

In this long letter, a dozen pages written over a period of weeks in the summer of 1785, we see Ledyard honing his skills as an observer, quirky and keen-eyed. On seeing the king for the first time, shooting partridges in the countryside, he says, "I should have taken him for the captain of a merchant ship amusing himself in the fields, he has the lounging swaggering salt water gait in the greatest perfection, though I suppose he never saw salt water in his life." Jefferson didn't need to read Ledyard's *Journal* to know what a terrific observer he could be. He began persuading his young friend to resurrect his "Ass." Rather than try to mount a full-scale commercial expedition, which would require investors and ships and crew and supplies, Jefferson suggested, why not simply go it alone—the way General Clark had suggested, with one or two companions, or perhaps none at all?

Ledyard seemed like the right man for the job. "He has genius, an education better than the common, and a talent for useful & interesting observation," Jefferson wrote to the Marquis de Lafayette in February 1786. "I believe him to be an honest man, and a man of truth." He added, "To all this he adds just as much singularity of character, and of that particular kind too, as was necessary to make him undertake the journey he proposes."

In his autobiography, written more than three decades later, Jefferson claimed that he was the one who proposed Ledyard's next journey. "Being out of business, and of a roaming restless character," Jefferson wrote, "I suggested to him the enterprise of exploring the Western part of our continent, by passing through St. Petersburg to Kamschatka, and procuring a passage thence in some of the Russian vessels to Nootka Sound, whence he might make his way across the continent to the United States." It was not only Jefferson's idea, however. Ledyard had been contemplating the transcontinental journey since his return from Cook's voyage, and probably before that. He had told Tom Seymour that he planned to return to the Northwest coast, and from there "perform a journey, which would astonish his countrymen," Jared Sparks wrote in his notes, after interviewing Seymour. At the time, Jefferson clearly regarded the idea—and possibly the man who would attempt it— as slightly, singularly mad. In sum, Ledyard planned to walk around the world. "Should he get safe through it," Jefferson wrote to Lafayette in February 1786, "I think he will give an interesting account of what he shall have seen."

That same month, Ledyard wrote Isaac excitedly: "In about fourteen days I leave Paris for Brussells, Cologne, Vienne, Dresdon, Berlin, Varsovie, Petersburg, Moscow, Kamchatka Sea of Anadivy, Coast of America, from whence if I find any more cities to New York, when I get there I will name them to you in propria persona." He added breezily, "I will write to you from Petersburg, after I have seen Kate, of the North," by whom he meant Empress Catherine the Great of Russia, now the sole obstacle to his plans.

As usual, Ledyard's dreams were getting a little ahead of his feet. He would need a passport to travel through Russia. Jefferson went to work on his behalf, turning the heavy wheels of diplomacy, starting with Lafayette. Always eager to help Americans, Lafayette laid Ledyard's proposal before Baron von Grimm, the well-connected man of the world who represented Kate of the North at the French court. Grimm found the idea novel enough to convey a written appeal to St. Petersburg. In the meantime, he offered to sponsor Ledyard with 600 francs of the empress's money. The proposal itself, which Ledyard drafted, was brief and full of confidence:

> Mr. Ledyard's proposals to Her Imperial Majesty of All the Russias are: to go from Petersburg to Kamchatka by crossing Siberia, to embark at some point of this coast on one of the galliots of Her Imperial Majesty for the settlement on the Island of Unalaska, and from there to push on to the coast of America between the aforesaid parallels to the eastern coast of the continent of America, and once there to seize the first opportunity to proceed to St. Petersburg with the details of the discoveries made during this trip.
>
> He proposes to take a scientist with him, as well as two strong and robust domestics. He reckons that the trip will take no more than two years starting from his departure from Petersburg, and that expenses will not exceed the sum of 500 golden Louis.

Ledyard was being more than a tad disingenuous: He had no intention of returning to St. Petersburg to report his findings. By April, he still had no reply, yet felt confident enough to write to his mother for the first time in many months. "I steal a moment from Ministers and Kings," he began grandly, "to kneel before the woman who gave me existence." He spared her the details of his plan, perhaps realizing how mad it all must have sounded. He informed her only that he was leaving on another tour around the world, and that he expected to be gone two years. (In a letter written to Isaac the next day, he estimated that he would be away five years, "or perhaps 6 or 7.") His new project, he assured her, would not only make him famous and bring honor and riches, it would take him where he really wanted to go, to the one place on which all his wanderlust was focused—home.

In the meantime, he could do nothing but wait, although he was yearning to leave. "I die with anxiety to be on the back of the American states, after having either come from or penetrated to the Pacific Ocean," he wrote Isaac. "There is an extensive field for the acquirement of honest fame. A blush of generous regret sits on my Cheek to hear of any discovery there that I have not part in, & particularly at this auspicious period: the American Revolution invites to a thorough discovery of the Continent and the honor of doing it would become a foreigner. But a Native only could feel the pleasure of the Atchievement." While waiting, he amused himself in various ways. He went to see a mad inventor attempt to walk on water, apparently using some kind of pontoon shoes. Unfortunately the man ended up capsized, heels-over-head. "The thing is sillily imagined and even worse executed," Ledyard remarked.

The seedy side of Parisian life exerted a continuing fascination on him. He paid a visit to an orphanage and the Bicêtre prison, as well as a hospital for fallen women, run by nuns. He was so moved that he donated six livres on the spot, at a time when his total net worth consisted of a small pile of coins on his dresser. As he stood by, one of the young woman patients gasped and expired, and the nuns gathered to give her last rites. In a letter to Isaac, he raged, "Where is the wretch—the villain—the monster?" He was subject, over the years, to these periodic fits of moral outrage. He had certainly suffered from venereal diseases on the voyage with Cook; he may even have suffered from syphilis, like many of the crew, so perhaps his outbursts coincided with some sort of recurring venereal complaint. But he was certainly no fan of celibacy, either, and on the way out of the hospital, he caught the eye of a comely young nun, "who was as debonair, gay, and even lascivious as if she had been in the Palais Royal," he wrote lecherously, "and seemed as ready to become a sacrafice to pleasure as the unfortunate victim she had been dismissing with her Benediction had been."

Ledyard spent the spring and summer of 1786 living at Saint-Germain-en-Laye, a small village outside Paris where the king maintained a terraced garden with a magnificent view of the valley of the Seine. Ledyard would run the length of the nearby royal forest and back every day, a total of four miles, training for his upcoming trek. He thought nothing of walking the twelve miles into Paris, often for some trivial errand like mailing a letter, and then returning home in time for dinner. "I am like one of Swift's Hughhainums [Houyhnhnms]," bragged the first American to dare go jogging in Paris. Walking suited Ledyard, as it did Jefferson; he was a restless but not rapid traveler. Much of the pleasure, for him, was not in traveling but in stopping. Alone, on foot, he was open to experience, and he relished every chance encounter along the way—not just with the women of the Palais-Royal. In the forest of Saint-Germain one morning, he came upon a man who'd fallen off his horse and lay trapped beneath it. Ledyard helped free the man, pulling a muscle in his own groin in the process, but it felt good to be able to aid someone else for a change. "The man was much hurt," he wrote.

More often, other people were coming to Ledyard's rescue. He was chronically short of funds and dependent on various patrons. "Vice consuls, consuls, plenipotentiaries, ministers, and whores of fortune, all . . . have had the honor to be tributary to me," he wrote Isaac. He'd even petitioned the king of France: "He read my Bull after he had eat a large Poulard which he does at every meal," Ledyard wrote, but the king had been dissuaded by wary courtiers. ("The Devil take their Genius for Intrigue—it is as universal a talent among the French as basketmaking is among our American Indians and much resembles it.") Jefferson, too, was lending Ledyard money periodically, his account books show: fifty francs here, 132 francs there. In the spring and summer of 1786, Ledyard often dined with Madame Barclay, wife of Consul Tom Barclay, who had by then embarked on his long mission to North Africa; he may even have lodged with the couple in Saint-Germain (how we yearn for the uncensored versions of his letters from there).

Ledyard was then in his thirty-fifth year, the same age at which his father had died, and feeling "healthy, active, vigorous & strong," as he put it in a letter, quoting his father's epitaph. Despite his reputation as a great adventurer and the exalted company he kept, Ledyard was beginning to feel rather like a failure. The project he had set for himself was daunting and perhaps undoable. One look at the latest globe, like the one on display at Versailles, could have told him how difficult the task he had set for himself was. Russia and Siberia (the Royaume d'Irkoutsk) seemed to stretch halfway around the world, an impossibly vast sweep of land. On the other hand, at least Siberia belonged to the known world, having been settled for more than 150 years. Ledyard and Jefferson knew it was possible to cross the continent: On Cook's voyage in 1779, a letter from Captain Clerke had traveled from Kamchatka to London in just six months, informing the world of

Captain Cook's death—well ahead of the returning ships. If successful, Ledyard would be the first man to walk around the world, the first circumambulator. Failure was just not an option.

He hadn't heard from home in more than a year. Isaac had gotten married in the summer of 1785 and was much busier than he had ever been. "If matrimony is the cause of that frigidity of heart which contaminates thy epistles—why, the devil take conjugality," Ledyard scolded him in a July letter, before adding, "my humble service tho to Ann thy spouse, & kiss her for me." Ledyard's letters now served more as confessionals than communiqués. "The villainous unprofitable life I have led goads me," he mused, more to himself than to Isaac, "& I would willingly crowd as much merit as possible into the Autumn & Winter of it. Like Milton's hero in Paradise Lost (who happens to be the Devil himself) it behoves me now to use both Oar, & Sail to gain my Port."

In August, Ledyard finally heard the empress's verdict: She refused him permission to cross Siberia. The news came via Jefferson, who had spoken to Baron von Grimm at Versailles. ("In the future," Catherine had scolded Grimm, "don't throw any more of my money out the window.") Jefferson was more diplomatic. "She thinks it chimaerical," he wrote gently to Ledyard on August 16, adding an encouraging suggestion: "I am in hopes that your execution of it from our side of the continent will prove the contrary." It was an eminently sensible idea: Start in Virginia, or Philadelphia, or New York, and head west. Settlers had been pouring into the Ohio River Valley since the end of the French and Indian War in 1763, more than two decades earlier, while land speculators (including George Washington) had extended their claims as far west as Indiana. The retreat of the French and the defeat of the British had left a kind of power vacuum west of the Appalachians. Ledyard had already devoured Jonathan Carver's account of his travels to the Upper Mississippi Valley in the

1760s. And he certainly knew of the Canadian fur trader Peter Pond, who had reached the Athabasca River, in present-day Alberta, within sight of the Rockies, in 1778.

For Ledyard's purposes, however, a westward journey would absolutely not do. The frontier natives tended to be more hostile than the coastal ones, for one thing, and even if he did make it past them and all the way to the Pacific Ocean, there would be nobody there to greet him other than the eagles and the otters, and perhaps a few of the wild, mud-smeared West Coast natives. He would be alone, nearly 3,000 miles from home, with no choice but to turn around and cross the continent again. He would have to be doubly lucky to survive that. But Ledyard needed to travel from west to east, Pacific to Atlantic, for another reason: Only that way could he make his grand return to the former colonies, the great homecoming that would finally redeem him.

The celebrated Traveller really only cared about one destination, which was his home: the shore of Long Island Sound, from Groton down to New York and back out to Southold, an elongated triangle in which his family and his friends were clustered. His whole life was a sort of self-imposed exile, but he never regarded it as a permanent one. There was a part of the Traveller that hated traveling. His impending absence, he wrote Isaac, seemed "as bad as the gallows." But he had needed to leave America in order to return, transformed. And when he did come home, triumphant and successful, he planned to make everything right. He would present his young half-sister Julia with a lock of her hair, which he had kept throughout his travels. He would, finally, support his aging widowed mother. Perhaps he would even get married. "For this is not the work of Nature," he had written from Paris, briefly regretting the rootless life he'd led: "She made me a voluptuous, pensive animal and intended me for the tranquil scenes of domestic life; for ease and contemplation; and a thous'd other fine soft matters that I have thought nothing about since I was in Love with R[ebecca] E[ells] of Stonington."

But even as Jefferson set pen to paper with the bad news, in mid-August of 1786, Ledyard was already in London, bent on a different and, typically, more complicated version of his scheme. He'd heard that a British merchant ship was preparing to leave for Nootka Sound, and he was determined to hitch a ride aboard her. "Farewell old Ass," he declared to Isaac, "& welcome new Ass."

# Honest Fame

THAT SUMMER, LEDYARD'S LIFE CHANGED WITH AN EARLY-morning knock on his door in Saint-Germain. It was barely six in the morning. Shaking off the night's burgundy, Ledyard flung on his *robe de chambre* and found a young gentleman waiting at the door. It was his friend Sir James Hall, a twenty-five-year-old Scotsman who had come to Paris at the tail end of his own grand tour of Europe, which was then obligatory for young English noblemen. Hall, who would go on to become an important geologist and physicist, had taken a liking to Ledyard—another in Ledyard's long series of affectionate relationships with wealthy and powerful men. The two had met at Jefferson's, and Hall later invited him to dinner at his own posh lodgings, where Ledyard found "two Members of the English house of Commons, two Lords Beaumarchais, and several Members of the Royal Academy at Paris at his Table."

"I was glad to see him, but surprised," Ledyard wrote of his unexpected visitor, who was en route from Paris to Cherbourg, and then London.

He observed, that he had endeavoured to make up his opinion of me with as much exactness as possible, and concluded that no kind of visit whatever would surprise me. I could do no otherwise than remark that his opinion surprised me at least, and the conversation took another turn. In walking across the chamber, he laughingly put his hand on a six livre piece, and a Louis d'or that lay on my table, and with a half stifled blush, asked me how I was in the money way. Blushes commonly beget blushes, and I blushed partly because he did, and partly on other accounts. 'If fifteen guineas,' said he, interrupting the answer he had demanded, 'will be of any service to you, there they are,' and he put them on the table. 'I am a traveller myself, and though I have some fortune to support my travels, yet I have been so situated as to want money, which you ought not to do—you have my address in London.' He then wished me a good morning and left me.

Despite all the blushing, on whatever account (did Ledyard have company in his bedroom?), Hall's visit proved pivotal. He told Ledyard about the Nootka-bound ship in the Thames. Within days, Ledyard himself left Paris and crossed the English Channel, a difficult trip that then took five or six days, to join the vessel. The ship's company included at least one of Cook's ex-officers, whom Ledyard does not name perhaps, and other gentlemen, "among whom are some of science," he wrote Isaac in a short, excited note that he apparently penned aboard the ship *Harriot* on August 18. His great expedition, dreamed of for so long, was about to become a reality.

Using Hall's money, Ledyard had set about equipping himself for the long journey. He did not buy very much. Rather than purchasing a musket and food supplies, extra clothing, and perhaps a horse, he instead clambered aboard the ship with just "two Great Dogs, an Indian pipe and a hatchet," as he wrote Jefferson, who was no doubt alarmed. His funds did not allow more substantial equipment, he explained, but he actually preferred traveling lightly.

As one of Cook's marine guards, he'd seen firsthand how a heavily armed force could upset native people and put them on the defensive. When he met native people individually, on their own terms, as in his kayak expedition on Unalaska and his evening with the Tongan chief Paulaho, he had been treated with courtesy and respect. He believed that it was actually safer to travel alone and unarmed. He could move quickly across the landscape, using the dogs to help him hunt, the hatchet for chopping wood, and the pipe to facilitate his negotiations with native people—whom he hoped would help convey him across the continent. (His fast-and-light approach, it's worth noting, is almost the complete opposite of Lewis and Clark's heavily equipped and well-manned expedition.)

On the other hand, Ledyard may simply have been naïve. The fierce, spear-brandishing Nootka natives might easily have slaughtered any lone voyager lacking the protection of a ship's cannon and marines with muskets. And even if they did not kill him, their own enemies might have done so; while Cook's ships sat anchored in Nootka Sound, in fact, the natives had repelled an attack from a neighboring tribe. But Ledyard seems not to have cared whether he returned or not. "If I live to see you it will be in two or three years," he wrote Isaac (who by now was probably a little tired of these dramatic farewells). He bid adieu to Thomas Jefferson, thanking him for his help, and to Lafayette as well. "If I find in my Travels a mountain as much above the Mountains as he is above ordinary men I will name it La Fayette," he promised. He sent a few treasured possessions to Isaac, discarded the rest of his belongings, and then he was off.

"It is a daring, wild attempt," wrote Ledyard's friend William Stephens Smith, the secretary of the American legation in London, to John Jay. "He is perfectly calculated for the attempt—he is robust and healthy—& has an immense passion to make some discoveries which will benefit society and insure him, agreeable to his own expression, 'a small degree of honest fame.'" Smith continued, "If he succeeds, and in the Course of 2 or 3 years, should visit our Country by this amaizing Circuit, he may bring with him some interesting information—if he fails, and is never heard of—which I think most probable, there is no harm done—he dies in an unknown Country, and if he composes himself in his last moments with this reflection, that his project was great, and the undertaking, what few men are capable of—it will, to his mind, smooth the passage."

Ledyard didn't get far, at least not on that first try. One month later, on September 18, we find him still at Deptford, on the Thames outside London, writing to Smith that the *Harriot* was finally about to leave, bound for Ireland, the Canaries, and onward via the dread Cape Horn. But the *Harriot* never sailed. According to Ledyard's letter to Jefferson of November 25, 1786, the ship was "seized by the Custom house & is this day exchequered," perhaps because of back taxes, and perhaps because its planned voyage would infringe on the monopolies enjoyed by the British East India Company. "I am still the slave of Fortune and the son of care," he sighed to Jefferson, who by now had done all he could. "I am indeed a very plain man, but do not think that mountains or oceans shall oppose my passage to glory while I have such friends in remembrance—I have pledged myself—difficulties have intervened—my heart is on fire—ye stimulate, & I shall gain the victory."

Three months after leaving Paris, Ledyard had gotten no farther than London. His possessions had also been seized: "shield Buckler lance Dogs—Squire & all gone," he wrote Isaac. "Am here without funds or friends sufficient for the purpose—may in a few days want Bread—or may lie on the road to fame or be d——d to fame." He continued: "I am a Deserter in this country, dine with Sir this & Sir that, on board a Ship one moment in a proud insolent stiff English Tavern the next." Judging from the sloppy syntax, the letter was probably written after a visit to the latter locale. He was so frustrated that he found himself getting into fistfights, and in that November letter he brags of "boxing some Puppy at the Theatre a la mode d'anglais—in the museum and the Lord knows where." To Jefferson he was more explicit, claiming that he'd "literaly been obliged to thrash 5 or 6 of those haughty turbulent & very insolent people: one of them at the theatre where I assure you one is still more liable to insult than in the streets even."

Ledyard was eager to leave England, and Jefferson would have understood. He'd been quite rudely treated on his own visit to London in April 1786, when King George III had pointedly turned his back on the author of the Declaration of Independence. But he would have been nonplussed to learn that Ledyard now sought British sponsors for his trip. With his money running out, Ledyard turned to the most generous man in London: Sir Joseph Banks, whom he'd met through Hall. Now the wealthy, lordly, and autocratic head of the Royal Society, Banks in his youth had been quite a traveler—adventuresome and curious, with a fortune to support his own travels as well as others'. As a young man of twenty-six, romantically attached to Miss Harriet Blosset, Banks had sailed with Cook on the first voyage of the *Endeavour*, and the ensuing scandal in London put an end to his engagement (to his likely relief). His reputation had recovered, however, and he had been elected to the exclusive Literary Club by the likes of Samuel Johnson and Sir Joshua Reynolds, who also painted a famous portrait of Banks the traveler leaning louchely against a table strewn with maps, his red coat unbuttoned.

Banks and Ledyard clearly got on well, despite Banks having been responsible for taking Ledyard's old nemesis Omai to England.

It was nothing that some good port couldn't smooth over, and within a few days after they'd met Ledyard was claiming Banks, a bibulous bon vivant like himself, as "my friend." They had both been with Cook, after all, and they both had tattoos. (Sadly, none of their letters survive.) By this point, the well-connected Banks had given up his own travels on account of his gout and also because he had finally gotten married. He had become a kind of impresario of exploration, running a network of wealthy sponsors and adventurers from his sprawling mansion on Soho Square. He had the ear of the king, and he could make anything happen. Now he tapped his network of gentleman friends to subsidize Ledyard's journey—whichever way he chose to attempt it. "The Enterprize is to cross the continent of north America from Nootka to New York," these worthies declared in their commission to Ledyard, "to be done either by sailing from London to Nootka [a journey Ledyard had tried and failed to arrange at least three times now] or by passing east from London to Petersbourg, Moscow Kamchatka & thence across the northern Pacific ocean to Nootka from New York to London."

Among the subscribers were Banks, Hall, the pioneering physician Dr. John Hunter, and one American, William Stephens Smith, acting consul to Britain, who scribbled a note beside his own signature: "Wishing Mr. Ledyard not to confine himself to the particular views of any Gentlemen in England and that he should not be under the necessity of reporting to them the discoveries he may make in America," Smith promised that he "will make such advances of Cash as will enable him to move upon principles of economy free from those shackles which they appear disposed to confine him with." The exact amount of Smith's donation is not specified, but it seems unlikely that Ledyard felt at all constrained by the seven-odd pounds sterling that his English sponsors had bestowed on him. Ledyard also carried letters of introduction and letters of credit from Banks, which might or might not prove useful in the wilds of Russia (though certainly not in North America). He'd gotten his "two Great Dogs" back, as well as some other equipment, but he still insisted on traveling without a firearm—or permission from the empress. The only sort of official document he carried was a two-page letter of introduction from Smith, explaining to all and sundry that "Mr. Ledyard's object is to enquire into the natural History of the Countrys through which he may pass for the Extension of Science and the Benefit of Mankind." Smith further requested "that he may be protected from every delay or detention, not Justified by the Laws of the place where he may be."

With this makeshift passport, Ledyard was headed around the world. His first stop would be St. Petersburg, where he hoped to apply to the empress in person, which seemed doubtful. "Speak to me no more of this Ledyard," she'd snapped to Baron von Grimm, ending what was apparently a two-month lobbying effort by Lafayette and Grimm in Ledyard's behalf. Not even the empress's final rejection could persuade Ledyard to do otherwise. "I dare not write you any more": Ledyard concluded cryptically in a December note to Isaac, written just before he left. "To introduce you to the real State of my affairs would confound you."

# PART FOUR
# Kicked Round the World

Ledyard hitchhiked and walked from Copenhagen to St. Petersburg by going north around the Gulf of Bothnia ("Bottnischer Meer Busen"), a 1,200-mile journey through Sweden and Finland in the dead of winter.

# Aurora Borealis

B Y CHRISTMAS LEDYARD WAS IN HAMBURG, WRITING TO William Stephens Smith. He had already lost one of his dogs in a sudden snow squall on the Elbe River, during a forty-hour passage in an open boat. "My other faithful companion is under the Table," he wrote on December 20, 1786. He was down to his last ten guineas, but he was living well: "I dined to day (having just come to town) with Madam Parish Lady to the Gentleman I mentioned to you."

The gentleman was John Parish, a Scottish merchant based in Hamburg, one of a handful of men who had grown wealthy by supplying both sides in the American Revolution from neutral countries such as Germany. Ledyard was less interested in the rich man than in his wife, with whom he seemed smitten. "I could go to heaven with Madam Parish," he confessed to Smith, "but she had some Englishmen at her Table that I could not go to heaven with—I cannot submit to a haughty eccentricity of manners so prevalent among the English. They have millions of Virtues, but damn their vices, they are enormous." (The insolent "Puppies" of London still irked him.) The rest of the company was no better, including a "stiff rumped Calvinistical Chaplain and his mummy of a Wife." But in the end Ledyard's persistence was rewarded, as Madame Parish made sure he was "happily compensated" with an hour of her undivided attention. "You see I take a sup from the cup of pleasure on the road," he wrote slyly. "I wish I had established a little Fame and Fortune that I might take some larger draught and even be intoxicated without Danger."

Ledyard was on the trail of the mysterious Major Langborn, a fellow American who also happened to be on his way to St. Petersburg. Bearing a striking similarity to Ledyard, William Langborn always traveled on foot, carrying but a single clean shirt, while his luggage was sent by carriage from place to place. He had passed through Hamburg three weeks earlier, staying at the same tavern as Ledyard, and was now stranded in Copenhagen with his one shirt, his luggage having been lost along the way. Although Ledyard had just ten guineas to take him around the world, the ever-generous Yankee vowed to track down his countryman and help him out in any way he could. "I will fly to him with my little all and some clothes and lay them at his feet," he wrote, hoping that Langborn might join him on the road to Russia.

They would have been well matched. The thirty-one-year-old Langborn had been an officer in the Continental Army, serving (with Humphreys and Smith) as an aide to General Washington. As eccentric as Ledyard in many ways, he had made his own contribution to the cause of freedom. Upon inheriting his family's Tidewater plantation, Langborn had summoned the overseer and ordered him to keep track of the number of lashes he inflicted on the slaves—so that the overseer might receive the same number in return. When the British came through the area, all the slaves would scatter, which was not unusual; when the redcoats left, however, the slaves would return, which was. As a young man, he'd been in love (once more, like Ledyard) with a cousin named Anne, but she had married another cousin. Heartbroken, Langborn had left his properties and sailed for Europe, where he was to spend a full thirteen years wandering alone, accompanied only by his dog.

Langborn liked to travel as cheaply and anonymously as possible, dressed in rough clothes like an ordinary traveler. On arriving in cities, he would generally resume his identity as a Virginia gentleman, though not always. He spent several months in Paris, living in a cheap room, before his friend Lafayette learned of his presence there. When Lafayette chided him, Langborn replied, "You are in high power here, surrounded by a multitude of officers and dignitaries, and encumbered with ceremonies, which I could never endure. I cannot live under restraint; I value your friendship but I cannot part with my freedom."

In essence, this was the same reply he gave Ledyard, who finally reached Copenhagen in early January. Langborn had been living there for two weeks, and his sole shirt had gotten so filthy that he was now too embarrassed to leave his room. The Danes were suspicious of him and made threatening noises about having him arrested. Ledyard arrived just in time to rescue him from that fate, with money he drew on William Smith's credit via a local business partner of John Parish. (How Ledyard had managed to spend nearly all his money in barely six weeks is another mystery.) He shared the money with Langborn, with whom he now lived "with the strictest Friendship." But Langborn—whom Ledyard found "Singular"—had his own plans, which involved more wandering and less haste, and so they parted. "I esteem you," the fellow told Ledyard, "but I can travel in the manner I do with no man on Earth." Although he'd given the man his last few guineas, Ledyard took the rebuff with as much good cheer as he could and pressed on, alone and nearly penniless once again. "I shall be at Petersburg before you read this," he promised Smith on January 5, 1787. He predicted he'd reach the Russian capital "comfortably," but as usual, he was overly optimistic.

Only the most determined man could have attempted Ledyard's next feat. Over the following two months he completed the most difficult and least well-documented journey of his life. He left Copenhagen a week after his letter to Smith, around January 10,

1787. He planned to head north to Stockholm, where it was possible in winter to cross over the frozen Gulf of Bothnia by horse-drawn sledge. But the winter of 1786–87 had been unusually warm, and the forty-three-mile-wide strait separating Sweden from Finland's Åland archipelago had not completely frozen. So Ledyard would have had no choice but to continue north, traveling all the way around the Gulf of Bothnia, which reaches almost to the Arctic Circle, a journey of more than 1,400 miles in the dead of Scandinavian winter.

He covered the distance in just ten weeks. On March 19, 1787, merely seventy-three days after he'd written Smith from Copenhagen, he addressed a letter to Jefferson from St. Petersburg, Russia. Ledyard barely wrote anything about what must have been an arduous journey except for a few tantalizing lines: "I cannot give you a history of myself since I saw you," he wrote, "or since I wrote you last: However abridged, it would be too long." He had traveled more than 1,200 miles on foot through Scandinavia in winter: "thro Denmark, thro Sweeden, thro Sweedish Lapland, Sweedish finland & the most unfrequented parts of Russian finland," he wrote Jefferson.

Though Scandinavia belongs to Western Europe, few travelers ventured so far north during the winter, and those who did were always stunned by the severity of the cold. Reaching Stockholm a dozen years after Ledyard, for example, the Italian traveler Giuseppe Acerbi watched a fire consume several fine buildings in the city because it was so cold that water froze in the firemen's buckets. Traveling in the 1730s, the French scientist Pierre Louis de Maupertuis made it as far as Tornio, at the north end of the Gulf of Bothnia, where a horrifying sight greeted his party:

> From the solitude that reigned in the streets, one would have supposed all the inhabitants to be dead: ... at Tornea

there were to be seen persons who had been mutilated by the frost: some had lost their legs and arms. The cold, always very great in those parts, was often so severe as to prove fatal to those who were exposed to it. A sudden tempest of snow at times menaced still greater danger. The wind seemed to blow at once from every quarter of heaven, and with such violence, as to throw down the chimneys of the houses. Any one who should be caught in such a storm in the country, would in vain endeavour to find his way back by means of his acquaintance with places, or marks made by trees. He is blinded by the snow, and plunges into some abyss if he move a step.

Even a relatively warm Scandinavian winter would have seemed frigid to Ledyard, who had left London with only a thin woolen cloak for protection. "In opulence & poverty I have kept it slept in it, eat in it, drank in it, fought in it, negociated in it," he wrote his cousin Isaac, when he sent the cloak home nearly two years later: "It has been thro every scene my constant & faithfull servant." With minimal clothing and funds, Ledyard would have had to rely—as he always did—on the hospitality of the locals. It was his preferred mode of travel, ever since Unalaska. "Upon the whole," Ledyard remarked to Jefferson, at the end of it all, "mankind have used me well."

Acerbi had also found the Scandinavians to be generous and friendly, noting that "the stranger is greeted as a person of the first distinction." He certainly had been. One night, he writes, he was preparing to sleep when he heard someone tapping at the window. Fearing an intruder, he grabbed his pistols. "But how great was my surprise!" he wrote. "It was a fine girl who wanted a corner of a bed. I immediately uncocked and laid aside the pistols, for fear of doing mischief. What happened afterwards? . . . . Let the reader conjecture what might have happened to himself in similar circumstances."

Ledyard would not have had time to linger, since he averaged about twenty miles per day between Copenhagen and St. Petersburg. How had he managed it? "He set out for Tornea in the heart of winter, afoot and alone," Sparks wrote, "without money or friends, on a road almost unfrequented at that frightful season, and with the gloomy certainty resting on his mind, that he must travel northward six hundred miles, before he could turn his steps toward a milder climate, and then six or seven hundred more in descending to Petersburg."

A few years ago, two intrepid college students tried to retrace Ledyard's trek around the Gulf of Bothnia. Peter Bohler and Peter Brewitt were Dartmouth juniors who had persuaded the college's Institute for Arctic Studies to sponsor a three-month trip to Scandinavia. They were both active in the Dartmouth Outing Club, which had been founded in 1909, but which was really an outgrowth of Ledyard's famous winter camping excursion in 1773. Arriving in mid-March, as southern Sweden was just emerging from winter, they saw at once that their cross-country skis would be useless—it had been another warm winter. Then as now, snow and ice are the winter traveler's friend, enabling sledges to travel easily over rugged terrain and solidifying roads that in spring turn to rivers of mud. Traveling on foot, they soon realized that Ledyard could never have covered twenty miles per day by himself. More likely, he had hitchhiked, catching rides on the sledges that carried mail between post houses along the Swedish coast, following a road called the Norrstigen. This road had existed since the 1200s and was maintained by the king; fragments of it still exist, they found, running parallel to the E4 highway.

But this was pure conjecture: None of the town archives they checked contained any mention of an American traveler passing through in 1787. There were few records of any sort, since the all-wood towns had burned down regularly since then. And Ledyard's name does not appear in the guest register of the famous little church at Jukkasjarvi, a little hamlet just above the Arctic Circle, north of Tornio, where travelers had been signing their names since the French traveler and writer Jean-François Regnard had passed through in the seventeenth century. Maupertuis signed in 1736, and Langborn wandered through in July 1787, having reached the head of the Gulf of Bothnia at a more leisurely pace and in a more agreeable season than Ledyard, who was in too much of a hurry to detour even a little bit out of his way.

Once he entered Finland, Ledyard would have found roads and accommodations scarce. The Norrstigen clung to the coast, leaving him to make his own way across the forests and lakes of central Finland. (He might also have traveled via the coast, to Abo, but that route was much longer and the road was notoriously ice choked.) He must have had this part of the journey in mind—cold, lonely, lost, and scared—when he wrote to Jefferson from cosmopolitan St. Petersburg: "I find the little French I have of infinite service to me," he remarked, repeating the point (as was his habit) for full effect: "I could not do without it: it is a most extraordinary language. I believe that wolves rocks woods & snow understand it, for I have addressed them in it & they have all been very complaisant to me." Mankind was less helpful, for Ledyard alludes to some sort of difficulty with the authorities in Finland, complaining of the "villainous laws & bad examples of some Governments I have passed thro." Ledyard may have been thinking of this trip when, near the end of his life, he told a friend: "I am accustomed to hardships. I have known both hunger and nakedness to the utmost extremity of human suffering. I have known what it is to have food given me, as charity to a madman, and I have at times been obliged to shelter myself under the miseries of that character to avoid a heavier calamity."

Otherwise, the Bothnia trip didn't merit much comment from him. In Ledyard's mind, his real journey had barely begun.

The St. Petersburg that greeted John Ledyard in March 1786 was like a shimmering young cousin of the Paris he'd left six months earlier—a freshly painted, newly built boomtown of tremendous wealth. He was instantly enthralled by "this Aurora Borealis of a city."

The city's very existence was the product of one man's outsized ambition. Less than seventy-five years earlier, in 1703, Czar Peter the Great had erected the first log buildings at the swampy mouth of the Neva River. Now St. Petersburg's citizens flaunted the latest foreign fashions in art, thought, and dress. The new Russian capital was determined to become a center of European culture.

Peter was the first Russian ruler who leaned westward, toward Europe; indeed, he was the first Czar in a long while who had even set foot outside Russia. Moscow, the old center of the Russian empire, was too Asiatic for his taste. St. Petersburg, with its Baltic seaport, seemed an ideal spot from which to lead Russia into Europe. When the German-born Catherine the Great assumed the throne in 1762—usurping her own estranged husband, who was Peter's last surviving descendant—she continued Peter's work. She dug a network of canals across the Neva delta so that St. Petersburg rivaled Stockholm as the Venice of the North. Famous architects were imported from Scotland and Italy to build fabulous palaces and government buildings on the marshy land in the latest rococo styles. She stocked her palaces and royal academies with the finest European paintings and professors.

Almost as soon as he'd thawed out from his long trek, Ledyard called on one of those learned gentlemen: Professor Peter Simon Pallas, a German-born naturalist (though Ledyard called him a "Sweed") who had been a disciple of Linnaeus and was an acquaintance of Sir Joseph Banks. A resident of St. Petersburg for more than twenty years, the forty-six-year-old Pallas had traveled extensively in Siberia, and his specimens filled the science museum of the Hermitage palace; some of them are still on display, including a large mammoth skeleton.

Penniless and filthy after three months of overland travel, Ledyard must have presented a pathetic sight to Pallas, although his ability to speak French might have redeemed him somewhat. (Pallas also spoke English, and corresponded voluminously with Banks and other English naturalists.) "I dined in a shirt that I had worn four days," Ledyard confessed sheepishly to Jefferson. "And he has yet more shirts than shillings," Jefferson reported to a friend, John Banister, a Virginian who'd met Ledyard in Paris. "Still, he was determined to obtain the palm of being the first cirumnambulator of the earth. He sais that having no money they kick him from place to place and thus he expects to be kicked round the world."

Yet Pallas did not hesitate to take the American under his wing. The German scientist was an influential man at Catherine's court. She was eager to expand Russia's dominions, but like Peter, her interests lay mainly toward Europe, and southward to the Black Sea. Only after Pallas translated for her the Englishman William Coxe's *Account of the Russian Discoveries Between Asia and America* her interest in Siberia was piqued. Like Ledyard, Jefferson, and Jones, she, too, had heard of the voyage of La Pérouse, and she was concerned about what it meant for her own toehold on North America, which then consisted of scattered fur-trading camps on foggy Alaskan isles. When Pallas proposed that she sponsor her own voyage of discovery to the northeastern Pacific, including Kamchatka and Alaska, she readily agreed.

As the head of the expedition, which was commissioned in 1784, Pallas had helped to install Lieutenant Joseph Billings, who had recently exchanged an undistinguished Royal Navy career for a more lucrative job with the fledgling Russian fleet (as would John Paul Jones, who joined the Russians in 1788 as a rear admiral to fight the Turks on the Black Sea). Billings had also sailed with Cook, as the assistant to astronomer William Bayly on board the *Discovery*, and had later served as master's mate to another Cook alumnus, Lieutenant James King. On the basis of this rather slender experience, the twenty-seven-year-old Billings "was therefore supposed to be well qualified for such a command," sneered Ledyard's old friend James Burney. Billings was also a bit of a spendthrift: In January 1783, he'd landed in London's King's Bench Prison for nonpayment of a 23-pound debt, and appealed to Sir Joseph Banks for rescue.

Billings's Russian patrons spared no expense in equipping his expedition. When he finally departed, in August of 1785, he had at his disposal no fewer than one hundred men, dozens of charts, expensive instruments, and enough supplies to construct and outfit two ships once the expedition reached Okhotsk, a tiny settlement on the Pacific coast of Siberia, more than 6,000 miles distant. Billings also carried enough cash to pay local Cossack and native guides at double the going rate, and to hire as many horses as he would need (they numbered around 2,000, when all was said and done).

Ledyard knew Billings well. As a marine on Cook's voyage, he had often been responsible for guarding the astronomer's tents on shore. Now Pallas proposed that Ledyard join up with Billings's expedition. The plan was essentially the same one that Vitus Bering had attempted fifty years earlier. Billings's expedition would carry its material overland to Irkutsk, more than 5,000 miles, then float another 1,500 miles down the Lena River to Yakutsk, and then overland again for a final 1,000-mile push to Okhotsk, where they would set up a camp and build the ships. The ships would then sail to Kamchatka, exploring up and around the north coast of Siberia, before sailing across to explore the Alaskan coast. Complicated as it was, the expedition perfectly suited Ledyard's needs. He could catch up with Billings in Siberia and tag along with him to North America.

First, however, Ledyard needed to get official permission. Undeterred by Empress Catherine's first rejection, Ledyard had come to St. Petersburg with full confidence that he could somehow obtain a passport for travel to Siberia. He went first to the English consul in St. Petersburg, who explained politely that Anglo-Russian relations did not permit the diplomat to ask such a favor ("Damn his eyes," Ledyard growled in a letter home). Next he applied via the French minister, the Comte de Segur, with Pallas's backing. Two months later, he was still waiting for an answer.

Eighteenth-century Russia was a land of serfs and masters, as brutally unequal as France. Yet in her own way, Catherine was a far more enlightened despot than Louis XVI. She'd stocked the Hermitage with paintings by Rembrandt and Titian, and she purchased the natural-history collection of Professor Pallas, with thousands of specimens of plants, animals, and fossils. A voracious student of the French Enlightenment, she read Rousseau and had corresponded with Voltaire up until his death in 1778; their ideas had rubbed off, a little, and she took some steps to ease the harsh lot of Russian serfdom. Ledyard would have had interesting things to say about Kate of the North. She might even have liked him, too. Well into her sixties by the time Ledyard reached St. Petersburg, the stout, spunky Catherine was still quite fond (to the point of scandal) of vigorous, cultivated younger men. These court favorites, in turn, gave rise to the enduring rumors of her sexual voraciousness. One of her favorites, her longtime lover Gregory Orlov, had helped engineer the removal of her sickly, ineffectual husband from the throne (after which the husband died a suspiciously prompt death). Ledyard's little French would have served him well, since the empress wrote, spoke, and conducted court business primarily in that language.

But they were not to meet. The empress herself had left St. Petersburg on a six-month tour of her domains, marking her twenty-fifth year in power. Her entourage included dozens upon dozens of courtiers, sycophants, ambassadors, and military officers, all carried along on 200 gold-trimmed sledges. Her ultimate destination was the newly annexed Crimea and the port of Stavropol, where she made a great show of reviewing Russia's new Black Sea fleet—which would soon see combat against the Turks, under admiral-for-hire John Paul Jones. Territorial expansion was much on her mind. She had one eye on Istanbul and the other on Alaska.

Back in St. Petersburg, Ledyard sensed the same thing. The quays were packed with ships bound for missions of trade and discovery, he informed Jefferson, with no less than four ships getting ready to sail for the American Northwest. "This & the equipment that went from here 12 months since by land to Kamchatka [i.e. Billings's expedition] are to cooperate in a design of some sort in the northern Pacific Ocean—the Lord knows what," he noted oh-so-innocently (but informatively), adding: "Nor does it matter what with me—nor need it with you, or any other Minister or any Potentate southward of 50 of Latitude." Of course he knew Jefferson would be very interested. Ledyard was talking about the ships captained by G. I. Mulovsky, who was to set sail for Kamchatka and there rendezvous with Billings, whose own expedition was really little more than a supply run. According to Grigory Mulovsky's official orders, his expedition was purely scientific, but following Russian custom these official orders were also completely false: He intended to sail as far down the Alaskan/Californian coast as he could, planting the Russian flag wherever possible. There was a rumor in St. Petersburg that La Pérouse had already reached Kamchatka, so Mulovsky's expedition was seen as urgent and highly secret; and it was this very expedition that Ledyard was supposed to join.

The empress would not return to St. Petersburg until July, which would be too late for Ledyard to set out; he would lose yet another year. He had still not heard from the French ambassador, the Comte de Ségur, to whom he'd applied for help, liberally dropping the names of Jefferson and Lafayette. Ségur was accompanying Catherine on her trip. Ledyard's impatience was appeased by love. He had grown enamored of "a charming little blue-eyed German lass," whom he had met through Pallas. (Madam Parish had evidently been forgotten.) "I wish I could die to night at her feet, or higher up," he would write from the road, six months later. (Still later, he would pant, "I feel inclined to be a slave to my German lass," admitting that he fantasized about cleaning her shoes.)

Yet the attraction was not so strong as to keep him from his journey. In mid-May, still stuck in mosquito-infested St. Petersburg, Ledyard's frustrations boiled over. "You & I had both conceived wrong notions about traveling in this Country," he raged in a letter to William Stephens Smith. "There is no country in Europe & Asia . . . so difficult to pass through as this," he went on. Like many another aggravated traveler in Russia, he blamed his difficulties on "the manners & dispositions of the inhabitants." So, with his typical stubborn naiveté, Ledyard tried a sort of end run, perhaps forgetting that he was in a totalitarian empire. He had befriended a Russian military officer who apparently took pity on him. ("Sir we pay no attention to any thing but *éclat*," the man informed the poor American, who evidently had little in Russian eyes.) The officer arranged to get Ledyard a passport through the Grand Duke Paul, Catherine's son. That was good enough for Ledyard, who probably did not realize that Paul was his own mother's foremost rival, his every move closely watched. Paul believed that he should have ascended to power after his father's death. Catherine never felt terribly secure, in part because she was not even Russian; she had already survived several murky plots in which Paul was a prime suspect. So when Ledyard set out for Siberia on the first of June 1787, he likely did not even realize that he was riding into a political booby trap.

Although it lay some 4,000 dusty, difficult miles from Europe, Irkutsk became known as the "Paris of Siberia," with fabulous parties and (eventually) its own opera house. Ledyard was first repulsed, and later seduced by its rough-hewn glamour. *Courtesy of the Library of Congress*

# Walking to Yakutsk

ON A SWEATY JULY MORNING, I CLIMBED ABOARD A SLEEK but shabby train in Moscow's Yaroslavl Station for a journey into the heart of Siberia. My primary destination was also Ledyard's: Irkutsk, the former frontier outpost near Lake Baikal, a full four days' rail journey and 3,500 miles from Moscow.

There was no Trans-Siberian Railway in 1787, but there was already fairly heavy traffic across Russia, carried by a well-developed post road, the Great Siberian Trakt, which then reached as far as Irkutsk; from there trade routes led into Mongolia and China. There were guest houses every couple dozen miles or so where travelers could stop and eat and change horses. The Trakt was so well used that in some spots the road was wide enough for ten carriages to pass. Traveling across Siberia in the 1880s, the American explorer and writer George F. Kennan (a distant cousin of the Cold War diplomat by the same name) found that the Siberian post service out-hustled our own Pony Express. The vehicle of choice was the kibitka, a kind of covered wagon that jounced over the rough and muddy roads. Some versions of the kibitka actually lacked wheels, since they proved to slow the vehicles' progress in the mud and snow of winter and spring; instead of rolling, the vehicle was simply dragged along. The kibitka drivers had one goal, which was to get the trip over with as quickly as possible, so they drove their horses—and passengers—mercilessly. The pounding was relieved only for short periods, when travelers took boats (or in winter, ice sledges) on great rivers like the Irtysh, the Ob, and the Yenisei, each of which rivals the Mississippi in size. Making the same journey in 1890, en route to Sakhalin Island, the writer Anton Chekhov pronounced himself "a martyr from head to toe." "Kabitka traveling is the remains of the Caravan traveling," Ledyard noted in his journal. "It is your only home—it is like a Ship at Sea."

Our train, called the Sibiryak, was like a modern kibitka caravan, composed of sleek 1950s-style rail carriages painted dark green and mustard yellow. Up front, the Russian plutocrats and foreign tourists were sequestered in their velvet-upholstered "soft class" service; we never saw them. Behind us, the masses wallowed in the squalid *platskartny* (third-class) coaches, which were rather like prison dorms on wheels, except the inmates could bring their own beer and sausages. It was the hottest week of the hottest summer in a century, and as I hurried past the steaming third-class carriages, with men in undershirts hanging out the windows, I thanked my inner snob for not letting me travel among "the people."

Ledyard would have approved of my decision. He was a gentleman, or at least he lived like one whenever he could afford to. But he might have thought me a sucker for shelling out money for a ticket. Ledyard was a master of the art of traveling for free. In relative terms, so was I: A second-class ticket on the Sibiryak cost less than a hundred bucks, or about three cents per mile. Ledyard had done better, traveling at government expense with a load of supplies for Billings's expedition, accompanied by a Scottish physician named Dr. William Brown.

In Ledyard's day, almost nobody made the trans-Siberian trek voluntarily; it was a journey of exile or punishment, for political dissidents and outcasts. When the Trans-Siberian Railway opened in 1906, Western travel writers scrambled aboard, eager to give the world a glimpse of exotic Siberia from a rail-carriage window. The Russian government had stoked expectations at the Paris Exhibition of 1900 by displaying the plushest carriages imaginable, complete with fine restaurants, luxurious compartments, a gymnasium, and even a swinging bathtub that wouldn't spill its contents when the train went around a curve. But the bathtubs quickly vanished (if they were ever actually placed in service), and the restaurant cars fell far short of Gilded Age standards. The trains averaged about sixteen miles per hour, making the trip interminable. Almost immediately, the dominant tone became one of complaint. "The stupidity of the Russian waiter," fumed one American junketeer, "is unsurpassed." (After the Revolution, the railway fulfilled its true purpose, which was to transport political prisoners eastward by the hundreds of thousands.)

I shared a comfortable four-bunk compartment with a fifty-ish couple from Perm, a city on the western slope of the Ural Mountains. Leonid and Svetlana, relatively prosperous engineers, were on their way home from Paris. It had been a once-in-a-lifetime trip; they were still holding hands and smiling a lot. There were no waiters in second class, and the food-service car seemed to be closed. We were watched over, after a fashion, by a tough-looking blond provodnitsa, who dispensed instant coffee and tea in green and gold Sibiryak glasses that matched the curtains. She also prevented foreigners from lingering too long at the train's periodic ten- or fifteen-minute station stops—a valuable service, I soon realized, noting the increasing bleakness of the towns we passed through. I heard one story about an unfortunate tourist who wandered off while his train left without him. His quick-thinking tour guide tossed his suitcase out the window for him. Without it, he'd have been lost: Trans-Siberian trains don't overtake each other, and accommodation along the way has always been sparse.

Ledyard had barely left Moscow when he "began . . . first to feel the want of houses of entertainment." He often slept in his cloak on the floor of the post houses where they stopped. Still, he would have felt grateful that he was getting a free ride in the company of Dr. Brown. They made good time from the beginning. Within a day or two, they overtook the party of the grand duke Paul, en route to Moscow. A few more days and they reached the city of Kazan, some 600 miles east of Moscow, which was where the Russian outback began in those days. The farther east they went, Ledyard noticed, the more hospitable the locals became; Siberians are like the people of the American West, friendlier and more open than their metropolitan cousins.

As we rolled along through an endless pine forest, the sun began to set somewhere in the direction of Moscow. Leonid and Svetlana (named, like many Russian girls of her generation, for Stalin's daughter) grilled me about life in America, about my job, and my car (I drove a Volkswagen Golf and so did they). Before long they'd worked around to every Russian's favorite question: How much money did I make? After two weeks in the country, I'd learned to dodge that one, and they moved on to another biggie: President "Boosh," of whom they were highly skeptical. By contrast, Ledyard found Russians toasting the healths of Benjamin Franklin and George Washington in the farthest-flung Siberian outposts, as he reported to Jefferson (who may have felt left out).

Leonid and Svetlana offered no *na zdorov'ye!* to the American president, but they readily shared some delicious smoked sausages, which we washed down with room-temperature beers purchased on the last station platform. For dessert, I passed around some tart red berries that I had bought from a vendor at the last stop. Svetlana refused any money for the food and beer; Ledyard, for his part, found Siberians "very hospitable," noting, "It is very rare that I can prevail on them to take any thing for what I eat and drink, and when they do it is inconceivably trifling."

Our own train seemed to be traveling through time. As we slipped away from the cities, apartment blocks and factories gave way to thick forests of birch and evergreen, interrupted by small villages of log buildings and wooden churches. Sturdy men strutted around in puffy white shirts, wielding actual wooden pitchforks and driving horse-drawn hay wagons through the muddy streets. Women in long skirts hung homemade clothes on clotheslines and scolded towheaded children. Dogs barked in barren yards. Everyone else ignored the train completely. This was another Russia, one that didn't seem to have changed much since Ledyard had passed through in 1787. We took in the scene of picturesque poverty, until Svetlana broke the silence. "*Rossiya,*" she said, smiling faintly.

Sometime during the course of the night, as the train tickatocked over the Ural Mountains, we crossed into Asia. Leonid and Svetlana had debarked at Perm, often considered to be the last stop before Siberia begins. In Ledyard's day, though, even Moscow was considered vaguely Asiatic by Europeans and Russians alike; the Mongol hordes had thumped up against the city's gates as recently as the 1300s, and their influence was still felt. This was why Peter the Great had created the self-consciously European city of St. Petersburg.

As he bumped east along the Trakt, Ledyard noticed a change in the people he saw. At Kazan, he spotted his first "Tartar," his blanket term for Siberian natives, who indeed look markedly Asian. The man was probably a member of the Tatar tribe, which lives around Kazan and in the western Urals. Ledyard was fascinated by all these "Tartars," for they looked like first cousins to his beloved Ben Uncas, his term to describe the Native Americans he had known in New England and met in Nootka Sound. "They are the same people," he wrote excitedly to Jefferson, "& had not a small sea divided them, they would all still have been known by the same name."

Every middle-school student now knows that Native Americans are thought to have migrated across the Bering Strait from Asia, thousands of years ago. In 1787 this was a radical idea. The different races were thought to have originated more or less separately from one another: Asians in Asia, Africans in Africa. No less an authority than Linnaeus had divided mankind into six distinct subspecies, including *Europaeus, Asiaticus,* and *Americanus.* Jefferson and other like-minded men believed, on the other hand, that all men really were created equal and thus shared a common ancestry (though Jefferson was not quite convinced this was the case for Africans). He and Ledyard had shared many intense conversations on the subject in Paris, though empirical evidence was still in short supply. Before he left, Ledyard had presented his mentor with an enormous handwritten chart detailing the differences and similarities between the Chippewa, Ojibway, and Nootka languages—not a bad piece of work for a self-taught linguist. Ledyard's firsthand observations in Siberia were even more astute, and welcome. Where the conventional wisdom of the time saw differences, Ledyard saw commonality. And as he traveled deeper into Siberia, observing native peoples more closely as they lived among and intermarried with Russians, he became convinced that "the difference of Colour in Man is not the effect of any design in the Creator; but of causes simple in themselves, and will perhaps soon be well ascertained."

Characteristically, Ledyard had reached this conclusion by simple observation. One of his greatest strengths was that he took things at face value, seeing things as they were rather than through the prism of book learning (a virtue, perhaps, of his incomplete education). As he himself put it, "Reasoning from theory downward to facts has exceedingly injured Truth." By British (or even Russian) standards, the Siberian natives had seemed "savage." Ledyard tried to see native peoples on their own terms, just as he had done with Cook. "The Tartar however situated is a voluptuary," he jotted in his journal. "They deviate less from the pursuit and enjoyment of real sensual pleasure, than any other people." He quite approved. "Would a Tartar live on *Vive le Roi*? Would he spend ten years in constructing a watch? In forming a Telescope? In the United States of America as in Russia we have made our efforts to convert our Tartars to think and act like us, but to what effect?"

Fifteen years after leaving Dartmouth, Ledyard was in effect still arguing with Eleazar Wheelock. The Siberian natives' plight was similar to that of the Native Americans he had known in Connecticut and at Dartmouth. By the time Ledyard passed through, Russians had been colonizing Siberia for more than 200 years, since Yermak Timofeyevich and his Cossack soldiers had first pillaged their way east of the Urals. Not long after, the Siberian khans made peace with Moscow, and the Russians began to establish a string of forts and fur-trading towns along key rivers from Tobolsk and all the way to Yakutsk on the Lena River—Ledyard's ultimate destination. The dire climate attracted few voluntary settlers, but priests and missionaries swarmed into the new territories, eager to convert the "savages" (who were, it must be said, not so thrilled to be converted). "The cloak of civilization sits as ill upon them as on our American Tartars," Ledyard noticed immediately, thinking back to his Dartmouth days. "They have been a long time Tartars & it will be a long time before they are any other kind of people."

———

I got off the train at Yekaterinburg, nearly twenty-four hours and more than 1,000 rail miles from Moscow. "Why you go to Yekaterinburg?" Leonid and Svetlana had wanted to know. It was as if I had just arrived in the United States from, say, Perm, and asked to be taken directly to Detroit. Yekaterinburg (or Ekaterinburg) is an industrial city whose best days seem to be well behind it. During World War II, the Soviet government had moved most of its military industries there, beyond the reach of German bombers. During the Cold War, the city (then known as Sverdlovsk, after the first head of the KGB) was closed to foreigners; in 1979 several hundred city residents died of anthrax after a leak from a biological weapons plant. Yet it had been strategically important since its founding in the early eighteenth century, as a center of iron making and as the main jumping-off point for the trans-Siberian road. The only real tourist attraction in town was the massive new onion-domed Church on Spilled Blood, marking the site of the Ipatiev House, where Czar Nicholas and his family were executed by the Bolsheviks in 1918. It opened a week before I arrived, with a huge, politically tinged gala attended by such luminaries as Russian president Vladimir Putin and conductor Mstislav Rostropovich; perhaps they agreed, like Leonid and Svetlana, with the common Russian sentiment that what the chaotic nation needed was a new czar.

I headed in another direction: toward the Sibirsky Trakt. In most of Siberia, the Trakt has all but vanished, like a Russian Route 66—more myth than road. In Yekaterinburg, it turned out to be just another rain-wet four-lane street, with streetcar tracks up the middle. I wandered up the street where the Trakt house was supposed to be: It didn't look promising. Tall concrete apartment blocks loomed on both sides, their grounds overgrown with weeds. The residents had worn footpaths into the mud; there were no walkways. After a few blocks, I came to a neighborhood of rundown wooden houses, with blue shutters. One of these must have been it—a larger, two-story house—but it looked abandoned, like most of the others. The whole area, in fact, was slated for redevelopment, and a number of the old houses were already being demolished to make way for new brick offices and hotels. The post house had long outlived its usefulness. I wandered back toward the center of town and found a faux-Irish pub, a fixture in every Siberian city, and ordered a big steak and a six-dollar Guinness.

Ledyard would have approved. Whenever possible, he liked to travel in style. He loved nothing more than to end a hard day on the road at some country lodging, setting "pell mell upon a joint of Roast" with a bottle of wine and an interesting companion. So after eight dusty and hungry weeks on the road, he was undoubtedly pleased to reach Barnaul, the capital of the Kolyvan province and home to an important salt mine. According to a Russian almanac, which he copied into his diary, he was now some 4,539 "versts," or about 3,000 miles, from Moscow. He had traveled the equivalent of the distance from Boston to Seattle, but he was still less than halfway to Okhotsk. "How I have come this far & how I am still to go further is an enigma that I must disclose to you on some happier occasion," he wrote to Jefferson during his stay there, but his trip had gone easily thus far, compared to what was to come.

In Barnaul ("Barnowl"), he and Dr. Brown were received in fine style. They stayed for three days, met the local governor, and dined with various military men. It was a relief, after grueling weeks on the Trakt, to be drinking wine and indulging in witty conversation once again. One day he and Dr. Brown were invited to dinner, and Ledyard wrote in his journal, "Three hours [later,] I found him in the street bawling out Ivan! Ivan! without a hat & very drunk."

In Barnaul, Ledyard parted ways with Dr. Brown and continued on his own. While he'd traveled anonymously through Scandinavia, this was not possible in Siberia, particularly for an American with tattooed hands. "I am a curiosity myself in this country," he wrote Jefferson. "Unfortunately the marks on my hands procures me & my countrymen the appellation of wild men." The American Revolution was quite the talk, perhaps thanks to a British weekly that had somehow made its way to the provincial outpost.

Ledyard left Barnaul in even better fashion than he'd arrived. The local governor had arranged for him to accompany the mail stage all the way to Irkutsk and assigned a corporal to look after him. First, however, Ledyard had to negotiate a hazard familiar to travelers in Russia: competitive drinking. In the next town, Tomsk, the local commandant (a seventy-three-year-old Frenchman) had him to dinner and kept him drinking "strong Liquors" until well past midnight. "I never was so ill after a debauch," Ledyard groaned in his journal, "as I have been to-day."

He felt better after a swim in the chilly Tomsk River, but worse once he was back on the road. Though it was still only August, the autumn rains had begun, hampering his progress along the Sibirsky Trakt. It rained for days and days, as the kibitka slogged through the endless conifer forests known as the taiga. It was exhausting travel, "driving with wild tartar horses at a most rapid rate of a wild and ragged Country—breaking and upsetting Kabitkas—be swarmed by Musquetoes . . ." By the time he arrived in Irkutsk on August 15, after ten weeks on the road, he wrote, "I was, and had been the last 48 hours wet thro' and thro'—and one complete mass of mud."

When he awoke the next morning and peered through his window—a thin sheet of talc—at the log-cabin metropolis of Irkutsk, he experienced a familiar feeling of dread. "I shrewdly suspect," he scribbled in his journal, "that I shall even here find all

the fashionable follies—the cruel ridiculous extravagance, and ruinous éclat of Petersburg."

Ledyard's first impressions were almost always spot-on. Founded
in 1661 on a bend of the Angara River, as a simple log fort or
*ostrog,* Irkutsk had grown to become the capital of Siberian commerce, flush with new wealth and flaunting the latest fashions
from Europe. The locals had all but replicated metropolitan Russian society, with one crucial difference: These were not the empire's best and brightest, but her outcasts, her rogues, her exiles
and entrepreneurs. Many of the locals seemed to be convicts. "I
find that the worst idea I had formed of the Country, and its
Inhabitants does not require correction," Ledyard wrote in his
journal. "To think of the rascality of this place—10 kopeeks for
shaving me!" Elsewhere in Siberia, he had drunk and dined for a
kopeck or less. He was drastically short of money now, having
been robbed of fifty rubles even before he'd passed Moscow.

Publicly, Ledyard made his own best showing of éclat. Once
he'd dried out and cleaned himself up, he made the social rounds:
He dined with a brigadier, a colonel, and a major one day, and the
next morning went to see Alexander Karamyschev, the director of
the local bank and also a naturalist, to whom he carried a letter of
introduction from Pallas. Karamyschev appeared at first to be
some sort of savior. He was a "man of Science," and a student of
Linnaeus, Ledyard wrote approvingly. Karamyschev was happy to
talk about the local plants and animals and fossils—rhinoceros
bones and pea-sized Siberian apples which he sent to Lafayette. In
the local museum, a room in the town library, he showed Ledyard
some bark cloth from Hawaii, which Ledyard recognized, since
Cook's ships had brought it to Kamchatka eight years before, after
Cook's death. Learning that his guest was interested in the native
Siberians, the obliging Karamyschev summoned three members of
the local Calmuc tribe for Ledyard's inspection. He measured their

heads and ears and jotted down the results in his notebook. Karamyschev even appeared to share Ledyard's opinion of his fellow Siberians. As Ledyard wrote in his journal, "He declared to me that Patriotism and the true solid virtues of a Citizen were hardly known." Within a day, Ledyard was referring to him as "my friend," remarking, "he is very assiduous to oblige me in everything."

More than ever, Ledyard needed friends. If he had been poor at St. Petersburg, now he was practically destitute. Invited to grand dinners, he had to decline because of his tattered clothes; he'd lost most of his baggage on the Elbe, back in Germany, a loss "which I severely feel at this instant." He had sacrificed more items to a pilfering washerwoman. Unlike Major Langborn, he could expect no friendly countryman to come to his rescue. Nevertheless, he was relieved to be back in relative civilization. Already more than 100 years old by the time Ledyard arrived, Irkutsk had transformed itself into the "Paris of Siberia," with a library, a museum, and even an opera house. "I find French and Spanish wines here," Ledyard confided to his journal, "but so mutilated that I was told of it before I knew it to be wine."

The wine had traveled as far as Ledyard had, over the same muddy roads; little wonder it tasted "mutilated." So was Ledyard. His eight-month, 6,000-mile journey had depleted his resources and left him more alone than ever in his life. The oceanic vastness of Siberia only added to his melancholy. He was as far from his home as it was possible to get. Ledyard had set out to cross the North American continent, and in terms of distance, he already had, twice—the trip from London to Irkutsk exceeds the round-trip distance between New York and Nootka Sound. Yet he was still only about two-thirds of the way to North America, he calculated. He had to travel to Yakutsk, the last outpost of Russian civilization, a 1,500-mile journey down the Lena River. There, or in coastal Okhotsk (nearly 1,000 miles farther on), he would meet

Billings and his expedition and, he hoped, for the second time in his life sail back to the continent where he was born.

Though the rail journey from Moscow took only four days, and not ten weeks, the sheer size of Siberia had its own galvanizing effect on the traveler. My railway companions and I sat for hours, mostly in silence, watching the vacant grassy plains slide past, punctuated by the occasional 500-foot-tall smokestack, its plume trailing into the jet stream. Settlements were few and far between, just as they had been in Ledyard's day. In the late afternoon the train pulled to a stop at a small station called Barabinsk, somewhere to the east of Omsk, after traversing a wide, lonely, marshy plain. It was as if this town had appeared out of nowhere. When the train doors opened, we were beset by vendors, the hungriest and most aggressive yet, wielding buckets of berries, plates with a few stale meat-filled rolls, and dozens upon dozens of dried fish. The fish came in all sizes and shapes, from bait-sized things on long stringers, to an impressive two-foot specimen turned yellow from the smoke. They were split open and desiccated, twisted into postures of agony, not unlike their hard-bitten, gold-toothed vendors. When they had finished at our car, the vendors rushed up and down the platform, snarling at one another and shouting at the train passengers. (Near the front of the train, an American tourist group huddled together in terror.) I bought a small container of berries from an old woman, who nodded gratefully. Then another woman appeared in front of me, twisted, wretched, and red faced. I reflexively dropped a few coins into her outstretched hand. *"Nyet!"* the first vendor scolded me. *"Alkash!"* (Drunkard!). Shamed, I scrambled back aboard the train. It seemed like forever before we rolled out of there.

Ledyard had noticed it, too—the Baraba Steppe had been artificially settled by Catherine's regime, which established brand-new villages across the bleak expanse, which could never support human settlement. Ledyard pronounced them "miserable receptacles," and Barabinsk hadn't improved much since then. Now, all across Siberia, the problem was still the same: too many people and not enough resources and jobs to support them. With the collapse of Soviet industry and the gulag system, Siberia simply had more people than it could support.

In the train, people mingled freely from compartment to compartment—if you left the sliding door open, it was considered an invitation to sit down and talk. I found myself sitting on a bunk with two men from Siberia, Georg and Alexsey. Alexsey, the younger, only wanted to give me a hard time about "Boosh," until Georg silenced him and he climbed into the upper bunk for a sullen nap. Then Georg started talking: His name was Georg Aseev, a stocky fifty-three-year-old engineer who was heading home to Novosibirsk, a scientific and technical city that the Soviets had created in the middle of the empty steppe. He had been in Moscow with his wife, who had decided to fly home, because it took four hours as opposed to three days. "I don't fly on Russian airplanes," Georg explained. "My wife is a very brave woman." But I could also tell that that was partly an excuse, and that part of him liked the sense of distance that he felt when he traveled more slowly. When he finally got home, he would feel like he'd really been somewhere. Then it was his turn to interrogate me: where I'd come from, and why, and what I hoped to accomplish by traveling. "You have come a long way," he said, staring out the window. Then he turned to appraise me. "But the real journey is in your mind."

I staggered into the center of Irkutsk a day and a half later. It looked little different from the town Ledyard had described more than 200 years earlier, consisting of "2000 poor log houses and 10 churches." There were the usual Soviet-era cement apartment blocks on the outskirts, stained and shabby, where most of the 400,000

Irkutskians actually live, and a smattering of crummy semimodern buildings downtown, most of which housed various regional bureaucracies; but the heart of the city is composed of weathered wooden houses with brightly painted shutters, in traditional Siberian style. Many of them now were home to Internet cafés and pizzerias and bootleg CD shops. Nonetheless, Irkutsk still felt like a ragged frontier outpost, what Denver might have been a century ago. Surely, I thought, I'd find some trace of Ledyard here.

To help me with translations and research, I hired a local university student, Alexander Nevsorov, a moon-faced twenty-year-old who went by the name of Sasha, and who was supposed to speak the best English in town. At least he was industrious. By the time we met, he had already made himself an expert on Ledyard's life (the details of which mostly, but not entirely, originated in Jared Sparks's biography). My e-mail inbox brimmed with random tidbits about Irkutsk in bygone days. "Hello Bill," a typical message began. "Here's something I've found:

> The popular songs in Irkutsk in 18 century were "Great miles from Irkutsk to Yakutsk"
> and
> "That's enough for you guys to drink someone else's beer"

As far as I could tell, everyone in Irkutsk had their own beer—at bus stops, on park benches, everywhere. It wasn't uncommon to see a stylish young woman on her way from (or to) work, navigating the mud-puddled streets in a skirt and heels, pausing to swig from a warm bottle of Baltika No. 3. I once even saw someone drinking a beer in a museum.

Despite my high hopes, very little of Ledyard's Irkutsk seemed to have survived, apart from a handful of wooden churches whose sturdy, onion-domed towers must have loomed over the muddy town. One institution that did survive was the Irkutsk Museum of Regional Studies, which had grown out of Karamyschev's little collection of curios. In the company of a local historian named Mark Sergeev, who works at the museum, Sasha and I walked the streets in search of the two or three eighteenth-century houses that survived the numerous fires that had roared through Irkutsk in the nineteenth century. We found one old two-story house on a back street, practically disintegrating before our eyes. A visit to the state archives confirmed that most city records had also been destroyed, either by fire or by Bolsheviks. Sergeev knew all about Ledyard, though: He was famous throughout Russia, particularly in Siberia; perhaps "notorious" is a better word, thanks to his later arrest.

Ledyard's rogues and rascals, too, were apparently alive and well in twenty-first-century Irkutsk, now one of Siberia's crime capitals because of its proximity to lucrative and easily plundered natural resources such as timber, oil, and diamonds. Murder, extortion, and carjackings are commonplace. To eat a simple pasta dinner at an ordinary restaurant, I had to pass through a metal detector and endure a pat-down from a serious-faced security guard. On the streets, chaos ruled: Coming out of a church earlier that day, I was confronted by an angry teenager brandishing a plastic cup of what he claimed was HIV-infected blood. I abandoned my dignity and simply fled.

The next day, Sasha and I went to visit one of the most important men in Irkutsk. He was waiting for us in a churchyard a mile or so out of town, and he was stone-cold dead. Although he died in 1795, the tomb of Gregory Shelikov has stood behind the church since 1810, courtesy of his widow, Natalia. His hawkish likeness, in all-black relief, gazes handsomely from the white obelisk, facing in the general direction of the Aleutians. "Here is buried the Russian Columbus," the inscription reads. "He crossed the seas, discovered unknown countries, and seeing that everything on earth is corrupt, he set his sail to the heavenly ocean, to seek treasures celestial, not earthly."

Like Ledyard, Shelikhov was a born explorer who quickly saw the potential value of the American fur trade. He was also a far better businessman. Originally from Rylsk, in southern Russia, he arrived in Siberia in 1773 and went to work at the busy border outpost of Kiakhta, the main crossing point between Russia and Mongolia, only about seventy-five miles from Irkutsk. By 1776 Shelikhov had established himself as an Irkutsk merchant, with investments in more than a dozen ships, all involved in the fur trade. He was also a bit of a dreamer. He envisioned a string of Russian colonies down the American coast, extending from Kodiak Island all the way to California. Never mind that the Spanish already claimed California and were venturing north. In 1783 he had three ships built at Okhotsk, on the Pacific coast, and sailed them to Alaska, where, after overcoming fierce resistance and slaughtering hundreds of native people, he established his own little fur-trading colony, rather like the one that Ledyard had seen on Unalaska (and dreamed of founding at Nootka Sound). The surviving native people were bribed with jobs and gifts, and Shelikhov even brought some of them back to Russia, to be educated at Irkutsk. He had also built churches at his trading outposts, the better to convert native people to Christianity (and the all-powerful Russian Orthodox Church into a Shelikhov ally). His American colonies, he bragged, would someday grow into great cities, populated by prosperous, fur-trading Russians and cooperating Native Americans. (Natalia had accompanied him on that 1783 voyage, and after Shelikhov died of a heart attack in 1795, she took over his company.)

Shelikhov's Kodiak Island outpost made him a wealthy man. He returned to Irkutsk in April 1787, to lay the groundwork for his next venture—a full-fledged Russian-American Company with an imperial monopoly and plenty of capital with which to establish Russian colonies in America. To help his cause, he'd written and published a Ledyardian account of his voyage, replete with self-serving inflations. Shelikhov wasn't the richest or most powerful merchant in Irkutsk, but he was the most visionary—and the only one whom history would remember. So naturally he was quite curious to meet the adventurous American who had popped up in Irkutsk, calling himself a colonel and bragging that he was on his way to that very same coast that Shelikhov regarded as his own. On the morning of August 18, having been in Irkutsk three days, thirty-five-year-old John Ledyard went to meet forty-year-old Gregory Shelikhov.

According to Ledyard's account of their meeting in his journal, he and Shelikhov hit it off. The Russian "shewed some charts rudely descriptive of his voyages," and claimed that there were 2,000 Russians living on the American coast, annually producing some 12,000 furs (like Ledyard, Shelikhov was a great exaggerator). Shelikhov added that he had a vessel waiting at Okhotsk, for a voyage to North America the following summer, and he offered Ledyard passage aboard her. The Russian was so friendly that one later historian mused, "Perhaps Shelikhov had been drinking when Ledyard met him."

Perhaps, though Shelikhov was also apparently keeping careful notes. In an urgent dispatch to St. Petersburg, he gave a sobering account of his meeting with the American. "He asked me with ardent curiosity which places I had visited," Shelikhov wrote, and how far Russian commerce had progressed down the North American coast. "He also tried to find out from me how many Russian vessels were engaged at the present time in the trade." The two men seem to have gotten into a bragging contest. According to Shelikhov, Ledyard had asserted that there were 10,000 Europeans already living on the American coast, north of California.

"And he uttered these words as a threat," Shelikhov wrote, "which I countered by saying that people from other states had no right to exercise power over these areas without permission from the Russian Monarch." Shelikhov also pooh-poohed Ledyard's claim to have sailed with Cook to Kamchatka. And when Ledyard told him of his plan to walk across North America, Shelikhov howled with laughter. He had seen firsthand how native people treated lone white men, at least in Alaska (it usually involved a sharp spear and loss of blood). He'd lost more than one shore party to native arrows, and others were simply never seen again. A solo European traveler would never survive, he insisted. But Ledyard was not dissuaded.

Despite his alarmist tone, Shelikhov knew that Ledyard was a godsend for him. He was trying to drum up royal support for his planned colonies and had asked for generous backing from the empress, including a private army of one hundred men and a huge, interest-free loan. Catherine had already turned him down once. The specter of a British-American spy in Irkutsk, headed for Russia's claimed (but unsettled) American territories, he hoped, might inspire the court to give him what he wanted.

On my first Saturday in Irkutsk, Sasha and I piled into the backseat of a Toyota driven by his Uncle Yuri, a balding fiftyish man with a bushy black beard. In the passenger seat next to Yuri sat Sasha's mother, Anna, a blowsy blond in her midforties. A former radio and TV journalist, she now handled PR for a pulp and paper company, one of many that were busy leveling Siberia's vast forests.

It soon became clear that our lives depended on Anna. Yuri had bought the car cheap, from Australia. It was quite a nice car by Siberian standards, a twelve-year-old Camry with less than 200,000 miles on it. It had one potentially fatal flaw, however: Australians drive on the left, like the English, so the steering wheel is on the right side of the car. This works fine in Australia or England, but in Russia, where they drive on the right, it can be a problem, especially if one is driving on a busy, potholed, rain-slick two-lane road with lots of oncoming traffic, and one still insists on trying to pass slower cars at every opportunity. This is where Anna came in. When Uncle Yuri sensed a break in traffic, he would gun the engine and veer into the oncoming lane, which of course he couldn't see. If there was a car coming—or, worse, a truck—Anna would bark "Nyet!" and Yuri would back off. Otherwise, she sat petrified in the passenger seat. After a couple of rounds of this, I started feeling around between the seats. "What are you looking for?" Sasha wanted to know.

"Nothing," I lied.

"There are no seatbelts," he said. Up front, his mother was now yelling, "Nyet. NYET!"

This was likely the same "miserable road" that Ledyard had ridden, after dinner on the same day he met Shelikhov. While the crafty merchant was composing his missive to Moscow, the American was being escorted to see the magnificent Lake Baikal, the largest freshwater lake in the world (by volume), more than 200 miles long and unbelievably deep. It took Ledyard seven hours of riding, an overnight stop, and a few more hours the next morning to travel the same distance that Uncle Yuri covered in two terrifying hours. At last we crested a rise and saw the whole southern end of the lake shimmering in the afternoon sunlight. Yuri yanked the car off the road at a turnout, and we gratefully got out. It was a crowded dirt parking lot, full of Russians sitting on the hoods of their cars, drinking beer (of course) and eating smoked fish with their fingers. The fish was called omul, a kind of herring that thrives in Baikal's waters and almost nowhere else. Despite the best efforts of the Soviets, who built a paper-processing plant on her shores in the 1950s, Baikal remains amazingly pristine, chemically more pure than Evian water. I'd bought a bottle of Baikal drinking water in an Irkutsk grocery and it was the best I'd ever tasted.

We chose the best-looking fish, and Anna haggled expertly with the vendors, who were tough, henna-haired women. For a couple of dollars, we came away with a sack full of fish and another bag of lukewarm beers. Yuri drove us to a seaside fishing village, where we ate on the dock while watching hefty drunk guys doing cannonballs into the fifty-seven-degree water. The fish was delicious, smoky and tender, the best thing I had tasted in weeks.

Ledyard also sampled the smoked omul, but he spent most of his day at Baikal aboard a boat, taking soundings in a drenching rain. (He was, after all, a man of "some science.") The lake gets very deep very quickly, ultimately reaching more than a mile at its deepest point; just a few yards offshore, Ledyard found that he was unable to touch bottom with a fifty-fathom line. On the way home, he and Karamyschev dined with Erik Laxmann, a transplanted Swede who operated a glass factory near Baikal. Laxmann's son Adam, a twenty-one-year-old army lieutenant, agreed to accompany Ledyard on his next stage, to Yakutsk. They would leave in a few days.

First, however, Ledyard had to pay his respects to the governor-general. In terms of raw square mileage, tall and handsome sixty-one-year-old Ivan Varfolomeyevich Iakobi was the most powerful man in all of Russia, governing more territory than all of Europe's kings and queens put together. He ruled over an immense swath of Siberia, including Irkutsk and Kolyvan provinces (Barnaul was in Kolyvan), stretching from the Yenisei River all the way to Kamchatka. By 1787, he was a year away from retiring, living in a grand style that would not have been out of place in St. Petersburg, keeping forty musicians on retainer for his parties while some

6,000 serfs tended his personal landholdings. Iakobi gladly supplied Ledyard with a letter of introduction, which Jared Sparks was somehow able to obtain in 1821. "He is a pretty good man," Iakobi wrote, "and his intention inclines toward joining up with a certain secret naval expedition." The recipient, Alexander Marklovsky, the governor of Yakutsk, was instructed to "uniformly render him assistance in every possible way and to deliver him to the above-mentioned Expedition without the slightest delay."

The letter is dated August 25, 1787, and that same afternoon Ledyard found himself in a kibitka once more, bound for the great Lena River, which would carry him to Yakutsk; that is, if he survived the two-day ride in the kibitka, with its "cursed unbroke Tartar horses," who kept galloping out of control. He had to keep alert so he could leap from the wagon before it overturned, which it often did. "90 versts more will probably put an end to my Kabitka Journeying for ever," Ledyard scribbled in his journal that night. Once again, he was quite wrong.

It was nearly midnight when the vodka bottle came out. We had to be at the airport by six the next morning, but Anna Nevsorova insisted, thrusting a tiny glass of chilly liquid in my face. Uncle Yuri nodded encouragingly, while Sasha, a confirmed teetotaler, shook his head. "It's a violation of human rights," he scolded his mother. But I had no choice, and down it went, as cold and crisp as the deepest Baikal waters. They were giving me the good stuff. I banged the glass down for more.

Very early the next morning Sasha and I boarded a sturdy-looking propeller plane of a certain age, owned by Angara Airlines, and took off for the interior. Like Ledyard in his kibitka, we were headed for the Lena, which would take us more than 1,500 miles to Yakutsk, deep in the heart of Siberia. The plane was our kibitka, a sort of flying covered wagon, and it pitched and plunged wildly as we passed through the clouds. A little more than ninety minutes later, we touched down at a tiny airfield on an island in the middle of a wide, bending river. This was Kirensk, one of the oldest towns on the river. It felt like the end of the world.

Except for the rusty freighters anchored in midriver, Kirensk looks as it must have when Ledyard had passed through in 1787: a collection of tumbledown log buildings on an island. Some of the houses were occupied, some were in ruins, and still others were both occupied and ruined. There was also a memorial to Allied aviators who had crashed in the surrounding wilderness while ferrying planes from Alaska to Murmansk during World War II. (Kirensk had been a key stop on the Murmansk run, with the largest airfield between Yakutsk and Krasnoyarsk.) Only a few of the wreck sites have ever been found. Across the river, huge piles of wet, freshly cut logs waited to be loaded onto barges. Tied up at a wharf was our destination, the river steamer *Blagovechensk*.

Named for a gritty, depressing city in the Russian Far East, she was a thing of beauty, 168 feet long and rounded at both ends, with a spacious catwalk that completely encircled the upper deck. A steam-powered side-wheeler, with enormous paddle wheels on either side of her, the *Blagovechensk* had been built in Hungary in 1959, but she looked like something that might have traveled the Mississippi River with Mark Twain at the helm. Inside, she was paneled in glorious hardwood, with skylights and an inlaid Bolshevik hammer and sickle in the foyer. Our first-class tickets for the five-day voyage came to about $120. We would leave the next morning.

By the time Ledyard reached Kirensk, on the morning of September 4, 1787, he was already sick of the journey. It had taken almost a week to travel the 200 miles downriver from Kachuga, the highest navigable point on the Lena, where he had traded his kibitka for an open boat. That was already much farther than his youthful trip down the Connecticut, and in the cramped confines of their boat Lieutenant Laxmann's company was wearing thin. "My rascal of a soldier stole our brandy got drunk and impertinent," he fumed in his journal. "I was obliged to handle him roughly to preserve order." To speed the journey, Ledyard noted, he had "fixed a little sail to our boat." Thus equipped, and with the help of a swift current, they covered as much as eighty miles per day. At Kirensk, a town of about 700, they were able to stock up on food, and Ledyard met the local commandant, who wisely chose to keep his wife hidden from the dashing American. "The reason was because he was jealous of her," Ledyard wrote, no doubt starving for female companionship by that point. "I have observed this to be a prevailing passion here."

Although the Lena ranks among the world's ten longest rivers, flowing more than 2,700 miles from its source in the mountains near Lake Baikal to the Arctic Ocean, its upper reaches much resemble the Connecticut that Ledyard knew so well. In spots, it is only about a hundred yards across, with a fast current flowing between high, forested hills. Every few hours we'd pass a clearing or a lonely cluster of log houses, and sometimes the ship would glide to a stop, at which point rugged-looking men would buzz out in their motorboats to collect supplies for the coming winter: crates of food, ammunition, salt (for curing meat, I supposed), and, of course, vodka. Then we'd be on our way, through unbroken wilderness. No wonder Stalin established five gulag camps along the Lena's banks.

Rivers are the highways of Siberia, both in summer and winter. The *Blagovechensk* and its sole surviving sister ship, the *Krasnoyarsk*, were the Lena's summer lifeline (a third steamer had sunk after a collision with a cargo ship, and a fourth was being cannibalized for spare parts). They plied the river between May and September, connecting the little river towns and bigger cities like Vitim and Olekminsk, isolated mining centers that were otherwise almost impossible to reach. Our ship carried a handful of foreign and Russian tourists (including one well-dressed bearded gentleman who operated some sort of Amway-like cosmetics-sales company), but most of the passengers were traveling on business or to visit family. For them, the *Blagovechensk* was the cheapest way to go.

There was one group of about a dozen men from Uzbekistan who occupied the very cheapest berths in steerage, below the waterline. They spent most of their time on the upper deck, smoking and chatting with the first-class passengers. Their leader, whose cropped, thinning hair and long face made him resemble Kevin Spacey in *The Usual Suspects*, told me they were on vacation. Siberia seemed an odd choice for a vacation, I observed. He shrugged and offered me a cigarette. When they disembarked, late one night, at the brightly floodlit mining and logging outpost of Olekminsk, the Kevin Spacey look-alike organized them into an efficient human chain that unloaded staggering quantities of heavy cargo bales. When I waved goodbye, from the deck, he stared right through me.

It had been raining for two days straight, and I was glad to be in a cozy river steamer rather than an open wooden boat. Then as now, settlements on the Lena were few and far between, so Ledyard undoubtedly camped out many nights. On shore, he uncovered some intriguing rocks and some fossils, including one that he believed to be an elephant bone (probably mammoth), which he sent to Irkutsk for his friend Pallas. He also stopped at the Lensky Stolby, a series of towering stone pillars along the right-hand shore, some reaching more than 250 feet high. By that point, he was just a day or two from Yakutsk and glad to be done with the "very fatiguing passage."

Fatiguing, but beautiful. On the *Blagovechensk*, the passengers spent most of their days at the rail, slowly circling the metal catwalk around the upper deck as pine-cloaked Siberia floated gently past: the little log-cabin homesteads, a shaggy horse in a field, soaring fish hawks, and drifting rain clouds. Where the river was shallow, we could see the current running across the stony bottom, pulling us toward Yakutsk and the Arctic Ocean. "I cannot say that my voyage on the Lena has furnished me with anything new," Ledyard wrote to William Stephens Smith from Yakutsk, still enchanted, "& yet no traveller ever passed by scenes that more constantly engage the heart & the imagination."

I was standing at the rail one day when someone addressed me in English, a rare thing in Siberia. It was a young Polish backpacker whom I'd seen belowdecks with his three friends. They were two couples in their midtwenties, beautiful in a tanned, shaggy, sandal-wearing kind of way, and they'd staked out a place for themselves by the lower-deck gangway. They were traveling deck class, lacking even the money for the poorest cabin, and I had always felt a tad guilty walking past them to the ship's one poor restaurant, or to buy beer and snacks from the ship's kiosk. We struck up a conversation as I offered him some of my beer. They were headed for Yakutsk, he said, and then the Arctic. He and his friends, all just out of university, hoped to hitch a ride from Yakutsk on a cargo barge bound for the river's mouth, where there is a desperate little town called Tiksi, surrounded by the vast, labyrinthine Lena Delta and hundreds of miles of barren tundra.

He wasn't quite sure what they would do there. The tanned young Pole seemed oblivious to the idea that the locals might not actually want them in Tiksi—and that, in fact, there might not be any jobs there, or even food; and that they had no money; and that winter was only weeks away. He didn't know much about Tiksi, but the idea of Tiksi, the ultimate Arctic outpost, had obviously seduced him; the others gladly followed. They'd made it this far, camping in strangers' yards and enjoying Siberian hospitality. They would be fine, he was sure of it. And I couldn't help but think of Ledyard, as he traveled this same river, not doubting for a moment that he would be able to continue onward, as far as his will desired. His clothes were shabby, his money nearly gone, while behind him, in Irkutsk and Moscow, eyebrows were being raised over the American's presence in the Russian east. To Ledyard's mind, though, he was almost home. All he had to do was reach Okhotsk and board the ship Shelikhov had promised him. "Two frozen stages more," he wrote hopefully from Yakutsk, "and I shall be beyond the want or aid of money, until emerging from her deep deserts, I gain the back of the Atlantic States."

As late as the 1940s, John Ledyard was still sufficiently famous that the Travelers Insurance Company used him in advertisements; this scene illustrates a passage from his Siberian journal, about Yakut natives storing water in the form of ice blocks.

# The Icebox

I N THE LATE 1940S, READERS OF *NATIONAL GEOGRAPHIC* MAGAZINE
might have happened on an odd advertisement, featuring an
illustration of what looked like an Eskimo couple hauling
blocks of ice on a sled. Designed to resemble an actual *Geographic*
article, the ad was headlined, "What John Ledyard Discovered in
Siberia's 'Icebox'"—namely, that the native Yakuts, who could
not dig wells into the frozen earth, stored their winter's water in
their front yards, in the form of ice blocks. In the same way,
warned the Travelers Insurance Company (based in Ledyard's un-
beloved Hartford, Connecticut), a modern man needed to protect
his own family against future hardship: "He does this through
insurance."

Ledyard would have found the whole concept of insurance
absurd. "He did not burden himself with baggage, and he never
thought about the future," observed his friend Peter Simon Pallas,
in St. Petersburg. "No man was less anxious about his life and his
fate." He lived in a world of best-case scenarios. He hadn't
planned on spending the winter of 1787–88 in the "icebox," but
he had arrived in the north at exactly the wrong time. When he
left Irkutsk in late August, the wheat fields were brimming with
grain; by the time he landed at Yakutsk, three weeks later, winter
had swept down from the Arctic, and the local boys were spinning

their tops on the ice. He rode into town on an ox-drawn sledge, through six inches of snow. It was the 18th of September.

He was in a real hurry now, a desperate hurry. On the river, he had spent whole nights awake at the helm rather than stopping. He still hoped to reach Okhotsk, where he might possibly catch a late-season trading vessel straggling over to Alaska, or at least Kamchatka—perhaps the ship that Shelikhov had promised him. He went to see Alexei Marklovsky, the local commandant, with his letter from General Iakobi in Irkutsk. The commandant received him with the utmost courtesy. It was a great honor to have a guest from so far away. He would be happy to be of service to his visitor. "Sir continued he," Ledyard recounted, "the first service I am bound to render you is to beseech you not to attempt to reach Okhotzk this winter: he spoke to me in French. I almost rudely insisted on being permited to depart immediately & was surprized that a Yakutee Indian & a tartar horse should be thot incapable to follow a man educated in the Latitude of 40."

The standoff lasted for more than two days—but then, Ledyard wouldn't even have reached Yakutsk if he hadn't been stubborn as a Yakut horse. The exasperated commandant finally summoned a local trader who often made the journey, to attest to the dangers of traveling to Okhotsk in the horror of Siberian winter. The commandant then pitched in with a generous offer of hospitality, which Ledyard had no choice but to accept. He would stay at Yakutsk for the winter, at the commandant's expense. Already he had a sneaking suspicion that he was being manipulated, and he regretted revealing so much about his plans. "I should . . . have said less to them about the matter," he lamented in his journal, "if I had not been naked for want of cloaths & with only a guinea & ¼ in my purse—& in a place where every necessary of life is dearer than in Europe & clothing of any kind still dearer by the same comparison."

Once again, winter had overtaken him and spoiled his plans. So had poverty, his constant since his father had died twenty-five years earlier: "that meager devil POVERTY who hand in hand has traveled with me o'r half the globe," he wrote in his journal. How differently his fate might have evolved if only he'd been able to tap the idle wealth he'd seen all around him, in Connecticut and Philadelphia, Paris and London, even St. Petersburg. "Ye sons of ener[v]ating Luxury," he moaned, "ye Children of wealth and idleness! What profitable Commerce might be made between us, had you the will, and I the power to enter on the trade."

Like the Polish backpackers I'd met on the *Blagovechensk,* Ledyard had made it down the Lena thanks only to the generosity of Siberian villagers he had met along the way. They had given him food and provisions and often refused to take any payment in return. "They fill their table with <u>every thing</u> they have to eat and drink," he wrote. He was also well provided with clothes, for Marklovsky had taken pity on him in his shabbiness. Ledyard now strutted about Yakutsk clad in a reindeer coat that was trimmed with moose, with an ermine cap and fox-fur gloves, not to mention his reindeer boots, even as he began to realize that he might never see Nootka Sound, much less the Mississippi River or New York. He closed the journal passage on a rare note of resignation. "I submit," he sighed. Writing at the dawn of the Cold War, biographer Helen Augur saw Ledyard as a victim of a sort of proto-Bolshevik conspiracy, perpetrated by "the enemy." But Ledyard saw the Russians as indifferent allies, at worst.

Although Ledyard's well-being was not the commandant's first concern, as we'll see, it soon became clear that he had done Ledyard a kind of favor by keeping him in Yakutsk. The frontier outpost sits well above 60 degrees north latitude, and winter in the permafrost zone makes January in Hanover seem like June in Tahiti. The temperature dropped lower by the day, and gales blew down from the north. "The Atmosphere," Ledyard observed, "is constantly charged with Snow." He began keeping a "Thermo-metrical Diary," which lasted until November 19th, when it got so cold that the mercury in his thermometer froze (which it does at minus thirty-eight degrees Fahrenheit) and it broke. The Lena River froze solid as well, and the ice cracked, and sang, and sighed all day and night. As Ledyard put it later, "The Houses & Rivers keep a contual Cracking & all Nature groans beneath its Rigour."

Not much happened in Yakutsk in winter. Founded in 1632 as a Cossack fort and fur-trading station, the simple log village was even older than Irkutsk, with a population in Ledyard's day of several hundred souls and many more dogs. A great lover of animals, Ledyard observed that the canines were used not only for pulling sleds but also for hunting game, and were thus "esteemed there nearly in the same degree that horses are in England." He soon learned that the Russians were as jealous of their dogs as of their wives. One day he went for a walk with commandant Marklovsky's dog, which led to a contretemps. "An ordinary Russian will be displeased," Ledyard remarked, "if one endeavours to gain the good will of his Dog." There was friction with young Lieutenant Laxmann as well: "A pretty little puppy has come to me one day & jumped upon my knee," Ledyard wrote in his journal. (His own dogs, by this point, were long gone.) "I patted his head & gave him some bread; [Laxmann] flew at the dog in the utmost rage & gave him a blow that broke his Leg." Ledyard says he gave Laxmann a thrashing in return: "The Lesson I gave him on the occasion has almost cured him—but I have told him to beware how he disturbs my peace a third time by his rascally passion, & he has done it."

Ledyard was near the end of his rope, at least as far as the Russians were concerned. "I have observed . . . that the Russians in general have very few moral Virtues," he scrawled in his journal. "The body of the people are almost totally without." Under imperial military policy, Russian officers who served in Siberia were awarded two promotions automatically upon their departure, with a third to come on returning to Moscow, regardless of merit. This may be why Ledyard had given himself a promotion, from ex-British sergeant to American colonel. "I have before my eyes the most consummate Scoundrels in the Universe," he wrote scornfully, "of a Rank that in any other civilized Country would insure the best virtues of the heart & head, or at least common honesty & common decency."

With six to eight months of winter ahead of him, Ledyard took stock of his surroundings. The "savage" Siberian native people interested him more than the allegedly civilized Russians, and he began studying them closely. The customs and manners of the Yakuts, he found, compared favorably to the drunken behavior of the Russian military goons and greedy fur men. "The Tartar is a Man of Nature—not of Art," he wrote in his journal, clearly under the influence of Rousseau. "His Philosophy is very simple—but sometimes very sublime—let us enumerate some of its virtues—He is a lover of Peace—no Helen, & no System of Religion has ever yet disturbed it. He is contented to be what he is. Never did a Tartar I believe speak ill of the Deity, or envy his Fellow Creatures. He is hospitable & humane—He is constantly tranquil & cheerful—He is Laconic in Thoughts Word & action—they do not prostitute even a Smile or a Frown any more than an European Monarch."

Where Shelikhov and other Russians in Siberia saw a Greater Russia, extending even to North America, Ledyard saw the Russians as invaders and occupiers of another, equally legitimate realm: a vast "Tartar" nation stretching almost from Kazan to the

Pacific, including Tatars in the Urals, Buryats near Irkutsk, Tungus (or Evenk) and Yakuts (or Sakha) around Yakutsk. He had read extensively about Siberia in Banks's library, but nothing of what he read resembled what he saw. "I find nothing material said about this great people by any Writer whatever," he fumed; "Steller ought to have been hung and Le Bruyn burned," he added, meaning Georg Steller (naturalist on Bering's 1741 expedition, whose journals Captain Cook had carried) and the Dutch painter Cornelius le Bruyn, who had traveled from Archangel to Astrakhan in 1701–1703. Their notes on Siberian peoples, if any, tended to be secondary to observations on plants, animals, fossils, and rivers, as though the natives were just another species of deer. "When the history of Asia & I will subjoin America . . . is as well known as that of Europe," Ledyard predicted, "it will be found that those who have written the History of man have begun at the wrong End."

The Sakha only seemed to have been conquered by the Russians, he realized. In many ways, the Russians had become more like Sakha. While the Russians had built European-style houses for the native people, the Sakhas actually preferred their own yurts, round huts lined with canvas and furs, with a fire in the center and (usually) two rooms, one for the livestock and one for the people. Built half underground, the yurts were actually warmer than the Russians' drafty log houses. The Russians had altered their own dress, as well, draping themselves in cozy furs and skins so that they almost resembled Sakha themselves. Russians who had spent a long time in Yakutsk even adopted native pronunciation. The shortage of women in the Far East led many Russian men to marry native women and have children with them. Ledyard seems to have entertained the idea himself. As he learned to speak Sakha (or so he thought: He was really speaking Russian), one of his first phrases was a question, for a girl: "Will you come and live with me at Kamchatka?"

Even if someone had agreed to go to Kamchatka with him, or anywhere else, Ledyard could not have left. It was as impossible for him to escape Yakutsk as it was to live there anonymously. Almost since its founding, Yakutsk has been the end of the line for exiles and dissidents and criminals of all stripes. Surrounded by miles and miles of uninhabited tundra, and subject to bitter cold and freezing fogs, Yakutsk more than lived up to its billing as a "prison without walls." Little wonder that Stalin built several gulags in the wilderness between Irkutsk and Yakutsk. Anyone who tried to leave on foot would surely die.

The Yakutsk summer is almost as severe as the winter. When Sasha and I staggered off the *Blagovechensk,* at ten o'clock on a mid-August morning, the temperature already topped ninety degrees Fahrenheit, en route to a hundred. The streets were dusty and dry. Yet just a few yards below our feet, the ground remained frozen year-round. Now home to 200,000 people, Yakutsk is the world's largest city built entirely on permafrost. The climate makes it difficult to grow food and impossible to dig wells—hence the blocks of ice that Ledyard observed the locals storing in their yards. (Milk, too, was delivered in frozen hunks.)

Because of the permafrost, the modern city is built almost entirely on pilings. Water mains and sewer pipes also must be carried above ground, so the city looks like some sort of huge oil refinery. Strolling through an old part of town, I soon saw why. During the brief subarctic summer, the ground thaws into a boggy mess, and even buildings sink down into it. Some of the older homes in Yakutsk have subsided right down to their first-floor windows. I, too, wanted to sink into the earth: Since leaving the boat, I'd been in the full grip of "traveler's sickness," an ailment from which Ledyard almost certainly suffered but which he scarcely ever mentions, in hundreds of pages of diaries and letters. His health, surely, was far more robust than that of the average man. "I believe it is curious that I am so often exposed to the Small Pox without taking it," he wrote elsewhere in his journal. He never even mentions the "flux," the eighteenth-century term for diarrhea.

Ledyard would be stunned though perhaps not surprised by Yakutsk today. The former fur-trading outpost and quasi-penal colony, which remained so throughout the Soviet era, is now one of Russia's wealthiest cities, a worldwide center for the production of industrial diamonds. Even more startling, the Sakha are now firmly in charge. With tremendous reserves of diamonds and oil, the Sakha Autonomous Republic thrives in a state of semi-independence from Moscow, with its very own strongman in charge. When I arrived, a new opera house had just opened, and a new museum was under construction. The main street, Prospekt Lenina, was filled with Sakha men and women wearing business suits and expensive wristwatches.

Sedentary and domesticated, the Sakha had always adapted well to Russian domination. Ledyard was more intrigued by their rivals, the wild Tungus, a tribe of nomadic reindeer herders and huntsmen who ranged from the Yenisei River (into which Lake Baikal drains west of the Lena) all the way to Okhotsk, on the Pacific coast. Like the Iroquois, they lived in bark wigwams. Like the Tahitians, they were often tattooed. The Tungus were warlike and quarrelsome, fighting duels with knives and bows; the early Russian settlers learned to stay away, though the Tungus did make excellent guides. Ledyard admired their fearlessness: "They are often found dead," he wrote approvingly, "having pursued the Chace down some precipice." More recently, the Tungus were decimated by disease and by Soviet oppression; many were slaughtered or shipped off to labor camps. A small remnant of Tungus clung to their old ways—including, I'd heard, their traditional shamanic religion.

After two days in bed, I felt well enough to venture forth in search of the last remaining "Tartars." They weren't difficult to find. All it took was a well-placed inquiry, and I was off with two friends on a high-speed taxi ride into the bush country surrounding Yakutsk. After a tooth-rattling trip over a washboard gravel road, our once-luxurious Volga turned down a narrow lane that wound between stands of evergreens. The road ended at a cluster of frame houses, in the middle of which stood a familiar-looking structure: A Native American–style tepee, where a slim fellow in western clothes and funky sunglasses was waiting for us. I assumed he was some sort of tour guide who would take us to see the "real natives," in their authentic costumes, performing a hokey tribal dance for us. His name was Sasha. "I am an Evenk," he said, using the Tungus name for their own tribe. About thirty years old, he was born during Soviet times, so his native names were given a proper Russian disguise. His Russian name, Alexander, derived from his Evenk nickname, Oleksu, which means "squirrel." His grandfather had been a reindeer herder, while his parents were both university-educated engineers. "I am half city, and half traditional," Sasha told us.

He was one of 30,000 Evenk who had managed to survive Soviet purges, the corrosive force of modernity, and an orchestrated Russian campaign against shamanism. Despite the best efforts of Russian Orthodox missionaries and Soviet secret police, the Evenk believe in shamanism. Sasha estimated that 90 percent of Evenk shamans were killed by the Russians after World War II. The very word "shaman" comes from the Evenk language, meaning "one who knows." The Evenk revere all of nature, believing that animals and even plants are spirits. (Sasha's unspellable Evenk last name meant "he who knows animals inside and out.") They didn't understand why the Russians were so greedy for furs. "The greatest sin," Sasha said, "was to kill more than you need."

Some shamanic rituals served a practical purpose. For starters, Sasha put us through a purification ceremony, which consisted of waving a smoking bundle of green herbs around our bodies. The smoke smelled really good, and it drove the fierce mosquitoes away. Soon they were back, crawling up my nose and on the inside of my glasses, and I reached for the insect repellent. "The Evenk solution to the problem of mosquito," Sasha said, watching me, "is patience."

The Siberian natives' solution to the problem of Russians, as it turned out, was also patience. Unlike the Sakha, however, the Evenk have no shining capital city, no prosperous diamond mines or Mercedes limousines. Their God is still the reindeer, useful for food and for pulling their sleds across the taiga in search of elk. (Although, Sasha admitted, snowmobiles and 4x4s were handier for hunting.) His family kept a couple dozen scrawny reindeer in a paddock, including a puzzled-looking albino specimen who nuzzled up to me, with velvet antlers and soft, round eyes. I tried to forget about her two hours later, as we ate a tasty reindeer stew, washed down with vodka.

The next day, I rode a bus with a friend to the outskirts of Yakutsk, where a group of Russians and Yakuts had gathered for a very different purpose: a Christian baptism at a small church set beside a clear lake. The ceremony had just finished, and the priest came to greet us, clad head to toe in a sopping wet white linen suit. His cheeks were rosy and he was still gasping from the cold water. I remembered a line in Ledyard's journal, written after he'd watched a group of Yakuts attending a Christian service. "There are but very few of the Yakutee who have embraced the Christian religion," he observed, "& those who have perform its duties with a species of sarcastic Indifference that is very curious." At this ceremony, anyway, he was wrong: Far from indifferent, just-baptized young men and women stood and talked to their families and friends, giddy and excited in their soaked clothes.

My friend was an American missionary in her forties named Sue, who had come to Yakutsk via Dallas Christian College and a painful divorce. In a few weeks she was headed for the wilds of Yakutia, where she planned to spend the next year or two living in a small village, helping nurture a tiny group of Christian converts there. On her first visit to the village, she'd bought the store's only two Cokes. As we made our way into the crowd, a young Yakut woman ran up to her. "Katia!" Sue shouted, but her excitement gave way to a questioning look. Katia was supposed to have been baptized today, but her clothing was completely dry. "I couldn't do it," she explained sheepishly. "I was all ready to do it, but then something wouldn't let me." Sue gave her a hug. "That's okay," she said comfortingly. "That's okay."

Situated far down the Lena River, Yakutsk ("Jakutsk" in this map) was part fur-trading station and part open-air prison; the surrounding wilderness was so unforgiving that anyone who tried to escape would certainly die. Local authorities prevented Ledyard from continuing on to the seaside outpost of Okhotsk, and kept him there into the winter of 1787–88. *Courtesy of the Library of Congress*

# Prisoner without a Crime

THE OUTSIDE WORLD HAD NOT FORGOTTEN ABOUT LEDYARD while he was marooned at Yakutsk. From Paris, Thomas Jefferson had apprised Charles Thomson, secretary of the Continental Congress, of Ledyard's plans: "He is a person of ingenuity and information," he wrote candidly. "Unfortunately he has too much imagination. However, if he escapes safely, he will give us new, various, and useful information."

Jefferson had a boundless thirst for information. He was extremely eager to find out what Ledyard might learn, in Russia as well as North America. In Paris, he had instructed Ledyard in methods for determining the height of mountains and the width of rivers, using a long, pointed stick. To help him take measurements, Jefferson suggested that Ledyard make two marks on his forearm, exactly one English foot apart; he could use the marks, and the position of the sun, to calculate his latitude. If Ledyard ran out of paper deep in the deserts of North America, he might make notes on his own skin, via a coded system of tattoos. His body would thus have been more than a "substitute for cash," as he'd written Isaac so long ago; it would become a substitute for paper as well. (Whether Ledyard actually adopted these suggestions is not known.)

Closer to hand, some of the Russians who Ledyard had met were beginning to wonder just what sort of information this

American really sought, and for whom it might prove useful. After their August interview, Gregory Shelikhov had worked himself into a froth over the American's plans. He got the ear of Governor-General Iakobi, who also dispatched his own alarmed letter to St. Petersburg. In the letter, dated November 7, 1787, Iakobi informed Prince Alexander Bezborodko, Catherine's minister of foreign affairs, that Ledyard, "an American squire," had appeared in Irkutsk with sketchy-looking travel documents and a dubious story. He had a passport issued at St. Petersburg and a travel order from the local post office there (since he was traveling with the mail coaches). But the travel order authorized him only to go as far as Moscow, where he was supposed to have asked permission to continue through Irkutsk to Okhotsk. (He hadn't bothered, needless to say.) What's more, his stated purpose—"to obtain information relating to natural history"—seemed fishy. After all, that was what every Russian explorer/spy since Bering had been told to say about their own secret missions. Iakobi had largely echoed Shelikhov's concerns (his letter appears to have been written from the merchant's notes) but as governor of most of eastern Siberia, he carried a lot more official weight than a mere merchant did.

Everything Ledyard did or said provided grounds for suspicion: The American was supposedly even curious about the Kuril Islands, a forlorn string of fog-shrouded rocks that Russia has guarded jealously, for some reason, to this very day—very nearly going to war with Japan over them during the last century. "He failed to obtain information about these," the apparatchik smugly declared (despite his "ingenious questions"), "and finally stated that those whose forces are the stronger would naturally have the first right to occupy these islands." (If anybody wanted them, that is; even today, the Kuriles are barely inhabited.)

He was probably not even an American, Iakobi opined. "It could very easily be the case that he was sent here to reconnoiter the area for the English," the most distrusted people of all, he theorized. (Captain Billings, who actually was English, was somehow exempt from such suspicion.) As further proof of Ledyard's trickery, Iakobi forwarded along two intercepted letters that Ledyard had intended for Pallas and Banks. He couldn't read them, he admitted, but the Count might still find them interesting. (Indeed: "I might as well look for figgs and grapes here as information," Ledyard had written to Pallas, going on to criticize the overall moral character of Russians for several more pages.) Lastly, Iakobi had written secretly to Marklovsky, the commandant at Yakutsk, instructing him to "try to convince [Ledyard] to stay in Yakutsk because of the difficulty of the winter passage from there to Okhotsk, so that he can be detained there inconspicuously until I have obtained more detailed information about his situation, while giving him assurances that he will be sent to Okhotsk at the first convenient time for travel." In the meantime, Marklovsky was instructed to "not let the least of his shifty undertakings escape . . . observation."

Marklovsky had done his job well (and Helen Augur was not wrong that Ledyard was conspired against, although definitive proof did not surface until the 1980s). Ledyard knew nothing of the intrigues swirling around him, so he reckoned it a lucky break when Joseph Billings and his party appeared unexpectedly in Yakutsk, in late November of 1787. Billings now planned to winter in Yakutsk returning to Okhotsk the following spring. "At Yakutsk we found, to our great surprise, Mr. Ledyard, an old companion of Captain Billings's, in Cook's voyage around the world," wrote Billings's official historian, an Englishman named Martin Sauer. "He then served in the capacity of corporal, but now called himself an American colonel, and wished to cross over to the American Continent with our Expedition, for the purpose of exploring it on foot." "Colonel" Ledyard was delighted to see his old shipmate, and they renewed their acquaintance. "I went to live with him a few days after at his Lodgings as one of his Family & his Friend," Ledyard wrote happily in his journal. Billings agreed to let Ledyard ride over to North America aboard one of his ships, which was supposed to sail the following summer. "I was happy," Ledyard wrote later. "Every difficulty was done away. In the language of my dear Sauvages I had a clear sky & smooth waters."

Both Billings and Ledyard were headed for the same place—the northwest coast of North America—the only difference being that Ledyard was traveling alone and unequipped, while Billings had hundreds of men and the treasury of the Russian Empire at his disposal. Just by reaching Yakutsk, Ledyard had Billings one-upped. "If the Empress had understood the characters of the two men," wrote James Burney, who'd known both on Cook's voyage, "the commander of the expedition would probably have been ordered to Moscow, and Ledyard . . . would have been appointed to supply his place."

But Billings remained firmly in charge. Ledyard actually found Billings "so much improved since I last saw him before now," he confided. Although his friend remained "as rough in his address as a Russian bear," Ledyard did not hesitate to compare his leadership abilities to those of Cook himself—at least that was what he wrote to Pallas, who had chosen Billings for the job. Superficially at least, they had some common interests. Like Ledyard, Billings was fascinated by the "Tartars," their customs and appearance. He showed Ledyard his own journals, which were full of observations about shamanic religion, as well as native birth and marriage rituals. (Ledyard had more than a passing interest in the latter, given his efforts to learn Yakut pickup lines. He undoubtedly envied Billings's native mistress, who had accompanied him on his travels.) They had read many of the same writers, such as Thomas Pennant, the English naturalist who had traveled in Siberia, and

Jonathan Carver, the American explorer who had traveled to the Great Lakes and upper Mississippi River Valley in the 1760s. But Ledyard sensed some caginess on the part of his English friend. Billings had just completed the first phase of his expedition, exploring the area around the mouth of the Kolyma River, which empties into the Arctic Ocean around the northeasternmost point of Siberia—looking, in effect, for a Northeast Passage by which Russian ships could more easily reach Alaska. Ledyard knew he was wasting his time. "It has ever appeared to me ridiculous to attempt it after the voyage of Captain Cook," he wrote to Banks. As a result of this red-herring hunt, however, it now seemed unlikely that Billings and Ledyard would reach North America for two more years. In the meantime, Ledyard offered to help his friend explore the Korean peninsula, which the Russians (by the way) seemed interested in colonizing. Ledyard pumped him for more information, which was slow in coming. "Perhaps some accounts will be kept secret from me," he confided to his journal, "but as others will naturally transpire in the course of my acquaintance with him I shall write them as they occur."

Like Ledyard, Billings was fascinated by the Siberian native peoples. He was relying on them to help complete his mission, and Ledyard praises his relatively humane treatment of them compared with the brutal Russians. Billings was a keen observer of their customs and showed Ledyard his journals, which described (among other things) their strange-seeming method of giving birth while standing. (Billings's own Sakha mistress was pregnant at the time.) He even gave Ledyard a gift of a "Tartar froc," made of spotted reindeer calfskin by the Chukotski natives of far northeastern Siberia. Ledyard was more worried about the native practice of taking enemies' scalps, which he'd heard about in Alaska and witnessed in Hawaii; would the Native Americans engage in similar barbarities? Billings had not been to Alaska yet, so he could not say. "Pray there is not an analogy," Ledyard fretted, "between the custom of scalping & that of taking the Foreskins of the Enemy."

He would have realized by then how lucky he had been to have stayed in Yakutsk in September. The trip to Okhotsk was not merely arduous; it was deadly, requiring many frigid river crossings and the traverse of the forbidding Verkhoyansk Mountains. The road, such as it was, was strewn with the bodies of horses that had simply fallen over and died of cold and starvation. Billings had left the Kolyma River on October 8 and had not reached Yakutsk until November 13th, "having suffered inconceivable hardships from the severity of the cold, and traveling on horseback," Martin Sauer wrote.

As December deepened, the sun all but disappeared from Yakutsk. Ledyard and Billings compared notes on the cold: Billings had recorded temperatures of minus sixty-four degrees Fahrenheit at Yakutsk. This was so cold that it would make a glass of strong French brandy thicken like coagulated blood, Ledyard observed. Ice coated the insides of the windows of his house. Yet fire was a constant danger, and one night a church in Yakutsk burned completely to the ground. In the right wind conditions, it would have taken the whole neighborhood with it. In late December, Billings decided he urgently needed to go to Irkutsk, ostensibly to check on his next batch of supplies, which had been sitting there for months. He invited Ledyard to come along, and on the 29th of December, together with Sauer, they set off on the long trek up the frozen Lena.

Irkutsk was much more agreeable than Yakutsk; even in winter its social life buzzed like that of Paris, thanks to General Iakobi and his lavish parties. If Ledyard was still annoyed by its "ruinous éclat," he doesn't say; his journal entries during these weeks in Irkutsk are remarkably terse. He also doesn't mention Shelikhov, though he must have seen him. Shelikhov had just returned from St. Petersburg, where he'd had a private audience with the empress to discuss his fur-trading plans. Ledyard still suspected nothing. Then one evening in late February, about six weeks after Ledyard, Sauer and Billings had returned to Irkutsk, Sauer's card game was interrupted by a messenger from General Iakobi. The empress had ordered that one of the Billings party, "an Englishman," was to be arrested and sent to Moscow for questioning. Sauer went with the guards to find John Ledyard already under arrest—as a French spy, Ledyard told him incredulously. He had already sent for Billings, whom he hoped could vouch that he was no spy. Billings was at dinner with Governor-General Iakobi, and refused to come to the aid of his former shipmate. "It was an absolute order from the Empress," Sauer reported that Billings told him, "and he could not help him. He, however, sent him a few rubles, and gave him a pelisse [fur-lined coat]; and I procured him his linen quite wet from the wash-tub. Ledyard took a friendly leave of me, desired his remembrance to his friends, and with astonishing composure leapt into the kibitka, and drove off, with two guards, one on each side."

Though it spelled the end of his attempt to cross North America, Ledyard's arrest made him more famous than did any other single event in his life. He was downright infamous in Russia itself, where history texts made sure to mention the first American "spy" to be captured in Siberia. In the Russian version of his story, Ledyard is not a hero but a villain—and a boorish one at that. According to Gavriil Sarychev, a Russian lieutenant with Billings's expedition, Ledyard was an ungrateful grifter who treated his hosts with haughty contempt—the very first Ugly American, if you will. "[At Yakutsk] he met with still greater kindness, being admitted to the house and table of the commander [Marklovsky], and receiving as a present from him a warm dress, more fitted for the cold season, which had commenced: and yet, the only return which Mr. Ledyard made for this extraordinary hospitality was to calumniate and abuse everyone; and finally challenge his benefactor for remonstrating with him on the impropriety of his behaviour." Ledyard had gotten so angry that he had apparently challenged Marklovsky to a duel. Even his friend Martin Sauer had to agree: "Ledyard's behavior, however, had been haughty," he conceded, "and not at all condescending, which certainly made him enemies." Chief among these, it seems, was his old friend Karamyschev, to whom Ledyard now referred as "that scoundrel."

Ledyard himself could not fault Billings, the one man who might have saved him. "We were like brothers," he wrote a few months later, the memory of his ordeal still fresh. Perhaps he sensed that Billings was in over his head, and that he would spend the next two years accomplishing absolutely nothing in his attempt to explore the Bering Strait and Alaska. Sauer would carefully record Billings's failure for posterity.

The real reason for Ledyard's arrest remains vague and a matter of dispute. His own early biographers agreed, however, that he was the victim of a great injustice, to have had his great dream shattered, as one nineteenth-century observer put it, by "the Caprice of a Woman." Even Jefferson, in his foreword to the official account of the Lewis and Clark expedition, accused the empress of having first given permission to Ledyard, and then, when he'd gotten to within 200 miles of Kamchatka, changing her mind. He corrected himself in his autobiography a few years later, for his own letters showed that Catherine had denied Ledyard's petition from the outset, calling his plan "chimerical." (Also, Ledyard had gotten nowhere near Kamchatka, which is another 1,500 insurmountable miles from Yakutsk.)

Most puzzled about the reasons for his arrest was Ledyard himself, but he barely had time to think. The soldiers hustled him westward at breakneck speed, through all the dreariness of late winter in Siberia. The kibitka journey was so miserable and bumpy that Ledyard barely wrote in his journal at all until he neared Moscow. ("Thank heaven a petticoat appears!") He slept in the kibitka, or sometimes on the floor of a guesthouse, as at Nizhni Novgorod, about 400 miles east of Moscow: "In a vile, dark, dirty, gloomy, damp Room; it is called quarters; but it is a miserable Prison." He reached Moscow sometime before March 10, having covered 3,000 miles in less than thirty days. "It is more than 20 days since I have eat," he wrote in his journal, at a rare stop for rest. He was emaciated and very ill. "Thus I am treated in all respects (except that I am obliged to support myself with my own Money) like a vile Convict." This was no accident. "I did not neglect to give instructions to the police officers assigned to him as to what sort of treatment he should be given on the journey," General Iakobi bragged secretly to Catherine.

Ledyard had not even been told of his exact offense, and still believed he had done nothing wrong. Anticipating Dostoyevsky, he called himself "a Prisoner without a Crime." There was no more mention of his being a French spy. (If anything, Ledyard had been working for the English.) Justifiably or not, Shelikhov and his fellow merchants saw Ledyard as a threat to their own interests in North America. Ledyard understood this, on some level: "[H]im who travels for information must be supposed to want it," he'd mused in a letter to William Smith from Yakutsk, "& tho' a little enigmatical it is I think equally true that to be traveling is to be in error."

His primary error had been to leave St. Petersburg without the empress's permission. When she finally learned (probably from Shelikhov) that the American had disobeyed her, she ordered him arrested at once. She had been having a difficult winter. Her health was poor, and as the year 1788 dawned, war with Turkey seemed inevitable. The French and English were perpetually annoying her with their plots and intrigues, and she knew the Swedish navy would zip in and attack St. Petersburg at the slightest opportunity. Now this American—a "colonel," no less—had defied her orders and was snooping about on the backside of her empire. It was therefore very easy for Ekaterina to sign her name to the December 21, 1787 order for Ledyard to be removed from Irkutsk, brought back for interrogation, and then expelled from the empire, with strict instructions never to return. In another note, she chided Baron von Grimm, whom she perhaps saw as "Le Dijar's"—Ledyard's—enabler, that "what is discovery for others is not always discovery for us."

In Moscow, Ledyard was interrogated by General Peter Eropkin, the empress's commander-in-chief there. Ledyard's notes of their conversation are now lost, but his answers evidently satisfied the general, and he was allowed to continue on. He was not done with the imperial bureaucracy, however, and as he neared the Polish border—and freedom—he was subjected to a maddening interview with General Peter Passek, commandant of the Belarusian provinces, at the town of Moghilev (in what is now Belarus). Brimming with indignation, Ledyard told the general that he felt grossly insulted by the empress—in particular, by her refusal to specify the exact offense for which he had been transported 4,000 miles under guard. Passek tried to defuse him with "a most endearing politeness," which only annoyed him more. After subsisting for weeks on minimal food, Ledyard was now served tea and addressed in French, which eased his pain somewhat. "He said I thought too rigidly of the affair," Ledyard wrote,

> & went on to tell me by complimenting his Mistress, as the most wise, amiable, prudent, & humane Sovereign in Europe & concluded for the moment with this most condoling & sensible Remark; that whatever Reasons her

Majesty had for her proceedings she had only politely told me that my Visit to her Dominions was disagreeable & desired me to discontinue it. "Had I not been waited on to the place of my destination by a Guard?" You have not been prisoner, [he said,] you have not lost your Liberty &c &c, and then begun in Proverbs to tell me "that Sovereigns had long Arms."

That finally set Ledyard off. "Yes by God M. le General yours are very long Eastward," he shot back, according to his own account. "If your Sovereign should stretch the other Westward she would never bring it back again entire, & I myself would contend to lop it off." Of course, he well knew why he was arrested: He was traveling without permission; only Ledyard believed that normal rules did not apply to him and his grand quest.

Later, after a hot Russian bath, his first in weeks, and four bottles of wine from the border-town commandant, Ledyard mellowed a bit. General Passek had been quite kind to him, in the end, and he lingered in Moghilev for four days, regaining his strength. When he left, Passek provided him with one of his own servants as an escort, a young man who spoke passable French. Another Russian officer gave him a present of six precious lemons and some delicious white bread—and made certain that a coachman who had snatched five rubles from Ledyard's purse was well and truly flogged. When his guards left him on the border of Poland, Ledyard told a friend a few months later, "They told him, that if he returned to Russia, he would certainly be hanged; but that if he chose to go back to England, they wished him a pleasant journey."

When he crossed the bridge from Russia into the Polish town of Tolochin (now Talashin, in Belarus), on the evening of March 18,

1787, Ledyard almost swooned for happiness. "O Liberty! O Liberty!" he wrote. "How sweet are thy embraces!" He was back in Europe at last. "After being absent 9 years from my Mother whom I almost adore," he gushed in his private journal, "I did not meet her with greater Raptures than I do thee."

He was understandably happy not to have to worry about being robbed again, or betrayed à la Karamyschev (or Shelikhov), or inexplicably arrested. He was, in short, free again. Released at last from grip of the Russian Empire, he had time to think, and rest, and write again in his journal. As he surrendered the hard-won miles across Siberia, he had come to realize what it meant to be an American abroad. He now saw himself as a citizen of the world, a missionary for the ideals of his newborn nation, which he'd not seen in four years. An attack on him was an attack on Liberty itself, so he had to remain strong: "Resignation would be a crime against the noble Genius of my dear native country." In a passage that perhaps ought to be inscribed over the front door of the White House, he added, "Methinks every Man who is called to preside officially over the Liberty of a free People should once— it will be enough—actually be deprived unjustly of his Liberty that he might be avaricious of it more than of any earthly possessions."

Yet however badly he had been used, Ledyard knew he was far better off than the peasants he saw by the roadside, in Russia and in Poland. They seemed little more than slaves, and certainly worse off than the Siberian native peoples (who in their own way were more free than their Russian conquerors). He had always hated slavery, though his grandfather's household included at least two slaves; now the mere sight of one made him uncomfortable. "I become concerned to think and act for him," he wrote, "and have not time to do either."

As he traveled across the plains of Poland with a Russian trader to whom he'd paid forty rubles, Ledyard's own grand expedition had devolved into something more resembling Sterne's *Sentimental Journey*, a farcical account of a carriage ride across a strange land with a motley array of characters. Poland proved much more difficult going than Russia had been. As appalling as Ledyard had found the tyranny of Catherine the Great, he had to admit that it had produced a good infrastructure. The roads in Poland, on the other hand, were almost impassable, choked by rain and mud. Some days they made barely fifteen miles, or about one mile per hour; in Russia, his imperial kibitka had averaged as much as ten to fifteen miles per hour. It took another six weeks to travel the few hundred miles across Poland to Vilna, then to Danzig, where matters improved quite a bit when he acquired a lovely Jewish girl as a traveling companion—"The distressed girl of Dantzic"— overriding the complaints of his drivers, who feared she would bring bad luck and sickness to the horses. Reaching Königsberg (now Kaliningrad), in late April, he was able to cash a note for five guineas on Joseph Banks, just enough to get him back to London. But he was not the same man who'd left England just eighteen months before.

"No state's, no Monarch's minister am I, but travel under the common flag of humanity," he wrote, in a soliloquy that leaps off the page of his journal. "Commissioned by myself to serve the world at large, and so the poor, the unprotected wanderer must go where sovereign will ordains. If to death why then my Journey is over sooner and rather differently from what I had contemplated. If otherwise, why then the Royal Dame has taken me rather much out of my way, but I may take another route. The rest of the world lies uninterdicted."

# PART FIVE
# Passage to Glory

# The Saturday's Club

B
Y MAY 24TH, LEDYARD WAS BACK IN LONDON, WHERE HE
paid a call on Sir Joseph Banks at his mansion on Soho
Square. Banks had eagerly followed Ledyard's progress
across Siberia, via such letters as had escaped confiscation by the
authorities. Now Banks had an intriguing new proposal for Ledyard, whose character he'd accurately assessed when they had met
two years earlier. Banks promised him "an adventure almost as
perilous as the one from which he had returned," in the words of
a mutual friend. He now wanted the American to explore Africa.

Banks had become president of the Royal Society in 1778,
and he now managed a broad portfolio of adventurers and expeditions. In May of 1787, at his urging, the first ships full of
settler-convicts had set off for New Holland, now known as Australia, which he had helped to explore with Cook's first voyage. In
1789, he would send an expedition to the South Seas to obtain
samples of the miraculous breadfruit tree, for possible cultivation
in the Caribbean. (His only mistake was his choice of captain,
William Bligh.) A 1788 portrait of Banks by John Russell reveals
a solid, jowly man, with intense dark eyebrows and a round drinker's
nose. He is holding an illustration of the surface of the moon, as
seen through his friend William Herschel's telescope, suggesting
that Sir Joseph's interest in exploration extended even beyond

Earth's atmosphere. For the moment, his fancies had turned toward Africa, where he'd spent three weeks during his return voyage with Cook, sampling the flora and fauna of the Cape of Good Hope. (He also admired the women of the Cape: "Had I been inclined for a wife," he wrote in his journal, "I think this is the place of all others I have seen where I could best have suited myself.")

Like Banks, Ledyard had first touched African soil on the voyage with Cook. While freezing in Yakutsk, he dreamed of retiring to sunnier climes—after he'd finished up with Asia and North America, that is. "Africa explored," Ledyard had written self-confidently from his open-air prison, "I lay me down and claim a little portion of the Globe I've viewed—may it not be before." So of course he was interested in the rich man's scheme.

Banks sent Ledyard to see his lieutenant, Henry Beaufoy, for the details. The son of a wealthy vinegar merchant, Beaufoy was immediately taken by Ledyard's bold presence. "Before I had learnt from the note the name and business of my Visitor," he recalled later, "I was struck with the manliness of his person, the breadth of his chest, the openness of his countenance, and the inquietude of his eye." Beaufoy spread the map of Africa on a table and traced the proposed route: Ledyard would travel by ship to Alexandria, and then to Cairo. From Cairo he would continue south, following the Nile Valley to a kingdom called Sennar, located in present-day Sudan; and from there he would go westward to the Niger River, whose exact location and direction of flow was still only guessed-at. Much of the map of the "Dark Continent," in fact, consisted of empty white space, truly terra incognita. Even on paper, it seemed an absurdly long journey; it would almost certainly prove to be a one-way trip. To Ledyard, giddy after his return from Siberia, and with thousands of miles already behind him, it seemed like nothing. "He said, he should think himself singularly fortunate to be entrusted with the Adventure," reported Beaufoy, who became one of Ledyard's most ardent admirers. "I asked him when he would set out? 'Tomorrow morning' was his answer."

Beaufoy was stunned. He was about Ledyard's age, a Quaker member of Parliament who took a leading role in the antislavery movement of the day. Like Ledyard, he was a nonconformist thinker who was curious about the world. His brother, Mark Beaufoy, had recently become the first Englishman to scale Mont Blanc, in France. But the slightly built Henry had never met anybody like Ledyard:

> His person, though scarcely exceeding the middle size, was remarkably expressive of activity and strength; . . . his manners, though unpolished, were neither uncivil nor unpleasing. Little attentive to differences of rank, he seemed to consider all men his equals, and as such he respected them. His genius though uncultivated and irregular, was original and comprehensive. Ardent in his wishes, yet calm in his deliberations; daring in his purpose, but guarded in his measures; impatient of control, yet capable of strong endurance; adventurous beyond the conception or ordinary men, yet wary and considerate; and attentive to all precautions, he appeared to be formed by nature for achievements of hardihood and peril.

Beaufoy would become the next in a string of young and wealthy men to fall under Ledyard's spell. Ledyard told the Englishman that he had spent years living among Native Americans, learning their manners and customs so that he could travel among them with ease. He said he had arrived in St. Petersburg without stockings or shoes (which may be true, though at the time he complained only about his lack of clean shirts and funds). Before leaving for Africa, Ledyard entrusted Beaufoy with his papers, and after he died Beaufoy's eloquent account of Ledyard's character and exploits did much to enhance his friend's fame.

By taking on this hastily conceived mission, Ledyard was in fact making a terrible mistake, one reminiscent of Cook, who had hurried on to his third and fatal voyage without allowing himself sufficient rest. Ledyard was deeply exhausted, even if he didn't realize this amid all the excitement of his triumphal return. His Siberian adventures had already made him famous, and his weeks in London were a social whirl. He was, at last, a "celebrated Traveller"—a respected vocation in the eighteenth century. He carried himself with new confidence, buying fine new clothes with Banks's money and living at the Green Man and Still, a tavern and inn on Oxford Street in central London. (His bill there amounted to four pounds twelve shillings and sixpence, or almost $800.) He found time to sit for a portrait by Carl Fredrik von Breda, a Swedish pupil of Sir Joshua Reynolds, paid for by Banks, who had the painting hung at Somerset House, the home of the Royal Society.

Yet despite the impression of vigor that he made on Beaufoy and Banks, Ledyard was anything but healthy. The past two years had aged him badly, as his old family friend James Jarvis had noticed. "An American face," the glib Ledyard told him, "does not wear well like an American heart." He had suffered frostbite of his nose and ears at Yakutsk, and he had actually collapsed from hunger and exhaustion on the rough journey home from Irkutsk. "I was so weak & ill with fatigue (for the first time in my life) that I fell asleep as I lay," he had written, still weary several days later. Even as the kibitka thundered onward, over very bad roads, Ledyard could not be roused. "I was never before sensible of a weakness of body," he admitted. But he nevertheless insisted to Isaac that "a few days rest among the beautifull daughters of Israel in

Poland re established [my health] & I am now in as full bloom & vigour as 37 years will afford any Man."

Of course, it was impossible for Ledyard to leave "tomorrow morning," chiefly because the organization that was to fund his expedition had not yet been formed. On June 9, 1788, Banks and Beaufoy went across town to St. Alban's Tavern in Pall Mall for a special meeting of the Saturday's Club, a group of influential London gentlemen with an interest in agriculture, exploration, and social drinking. Besides Beaufoy and Banks, the nine members in attendance on that Monday included William Pulteney, one of the richest men in England; the antislavery Earl of Galloway; Sir William Fordyce, a noted doctor; and thirty-three-year-old Lord Francis Rawdon, who had been a notoriously brutal British officer in the American Revolution. (While stationed on Staten Island in 1776, Rawdon commended his men for their habit of raping local women: "The fair nymphs of this isle are in wonderful tribulation," he wrote gleefully.)

Their common interests included abolition, a hot political topic, and from there Banks steered the discussion toward Africa in general. By the end of the meeting, the members had agreed to form an "Association for Promoting the Discovery of the Interior Parts of Africa," whose goals included geographical exploration and also (as the idealistic Beaufoy put it) to ensure that "the conveniences of civil life, the benefits of the mechanic and manufacturing arts, the attainments of science, the energies of the cultivated mind, and the elevation of the human character, may in some degree be imparted to nations hitherto consigned to hopeless barbarism, and uniform contempt."

Each of the twelve founding members agreed to contribute five guineas (about $1,000) for three years; the five committee members also produced an additional fifty guineas each to fund the first two expeditions. The association had a clever marketing strategy: Membership was strictly limited, and its proceedings were kept confidential, which of course meant that everybody talked about it and wanted to join. Thanks to the slavery issue, interest in Africa was intense. Although the continent lay just across the Strait of Gibraltar, very few Europeans had actually penetrated beyond the coast. Its Mediterranean shores were guarded by the hostile Barbary States, and the rest of the coastline belonged to slave traders and pirates. The most contemporary travelers' accounts of the interior were those of Leo Africanus, a sixteenth-century Moroccan convert to Christianity who had traveled through the Sahara; and Sharif Idrissi, a Muslim geographer of the twelfth century. They had managed only slight improvements on the work of the ancient historian Herodotus. More recently, in the 1770s, a mad Scotsman named James Bruce had reportedly managed to reach the source of the Blue Nile, in Ethiopia; his account had still not been published, and there were those who doubted that he'd really made it as far as he had claimed. That was why the map of Africa, circa 1788, was as sketchy and inaccurate as the charts of the Northwest Passage carried by Captain Cook. The coastline was documented, but the interior consisted of but "a few names of unexplored rivers and of uncertain nations," as Beaufoy wrote. In between, as the great Irish satirist Jonathan Swift put it, mapmakers had "placed elephants for want of towns."

One of those few towns exerted a shimmering allure: Timbuktu, also known as Tambuctoo, Timkitoo, and a dozen other farcical variations that were as inaccurate as the myth of Timbuktu itself. It was said, via various vague travelers' tales—including those of Leo Africanus—to be surrounded by gold mines, if not actually made of gold itself. (In actuality, its most precious commodity was salt.) Real or mythical, Timbuktu was the ultimate goal of the first explorer hired by the Association. His name was Simon Lucas, a thirty-year-old Englishman who had been kidnapped by Barbary pirates and held as a slave in Morocco for three years. He had taken advantage of the opportunity to learn Arabic, and when he returned he secured a job as an interpreter at the Court of St. James. Lucas would start at Tripoli and proceed south, across the Sahara, to Fezzan and beyond.

The other explorer-for-hire was John Ledyard, bound for Cairo. His route would take him south along the Nile, then west (after a quick jaunt over to Mecca) to the Niger River. The association allocated seventy guineas ($12,500) for Ledyard to equip himself, in addition to the thirty guineas that Beaufoy had already advanced him for his living expenses in London. Once in Cairo, he could draw another fifty pounds from the English consul there, George Baldwin, followed by thirty pounds sterling at the holy Muslim city of Mecca (which seems highly unlikely, to say the least). This was a bit less than the 250 pounds allotted to Lucas, but Ledyard had traveled across Siberia and back on next to no money at all, so he was thrilled.

He wrote a long letter to Isaac immediately, his first in two years. The association already had 200 members, all of whom were important gentlemen, he said; until he, Ledyard, had come along, they had been unable to find anybody bold enough to travel to Africa. Most impressively, he claimed that his patrons had appropriated some 1,500 guineas for his journey. "The King has told them no expence is to be spared," he informed his cousin. However, he assured Isaac, "My heart is on your side of the Atlantic. . . . Do not think that because I have seen much & must see more of the World I have forgot America." As if to underscore the point, he had his friend Jarvis take Isaac his most valuable belongings, including the furs he had worn through two Arctic winters. He would not be needing them any longer.

Ledyard had been living well on the generosity of Banks. According to scraps of receipts that somehow found their way to San

Francisco's Sutro Library, he purchased six fine shirts and a "suit of cloaths," and also provided himself with new shaving supplies, which he undoubtedly needed. He bought an umbrella, as if he were preparing to explore London and not Africa; though he did purchase "leathern pantaloons" and a pair of pistols, as well as four hatchets for his trip to the nearly treeless Sahara. (Perhaps he was remembering their value to Cook, as currency more than as tools.)

He was well aware that he might not return. Indeed, he seems to have been preparing for that possibility. When the Breda portrait was finished and hanging in the Royal Society's Somerset House, Ledyard hired a young apprentice painter to dash off a quick copy on paper, which he sent to his mother. He also wrote a wistful letter to his friend Sir James Hall, who was in Edinburgh at the time. "I want to talk a month with you without interruption," he wrote. Were he not to return, he suggested an appropriate epitaph for himself: *Sic Transito.* In late June, on the day he was to leave for Cairo, he appeared at Beaufoy's office to say goodbye. "If I live," he declared solemnly, "I will faithfully perform, in its utmost extent, my engagement to the Society; and if I perish in the attempt, my honour will still be safe, for death cancels all bonds."

# Almost Universal Blindness

L EDYARD'S FIRST GLIMPSE OF AFRICA BORE LITTLE RESEM-
blance to the crisp and largely blank map that Henry
Beaufoy had laid out before him in London. The
Egyptian port of Alexandria was noisy, dirty, and hot: "a scene
wretched & interesting beyond any other that I have seen," he
wrote to Jefferson, shortly after his ship arrived there in early August. The first sight that greeted him was a vast burial ground,
a sea of white tombstones on white chalky soil, under the blind-
ing desert sun. The strange land's impressions assaulted him:
"poverty, rapine, murder, tumult blind bigotry, cruel persecution,
pestilence."

Contemporary Alexandria showed no signs of ever having
been one of the ancient world's great centers of learning and culture. The only evidence of the city of antiquity was Pompey's
Pillar and Cleopatra's Needle, a sixty-eight-foot tall obelisk that
now resides on the banks of the Thames, having been stolen by
wealthy Egyptophiles in 1878. "No man of whatever turn of
mind can see the whole without retiring from the scene with a sic
transit Gloria mundi," he wrote Jefferson, the phrase apparently
much on his mind since he had left London five weeks earlier. He
felt ill-prepared for his great journey. "I have read but little of
Egypt and have heard less," he confessed.

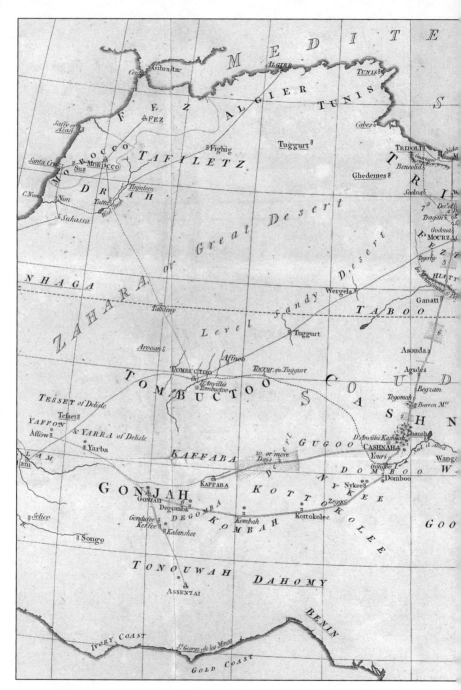

Eighteenth-century maps of Africa, like this 1790 sketch by James Rennell
for Sir Joseph Banks, tended to have a lot of blank spaces. Ledyard planned
to travel south from Cairo, following the Nile River to Sennar, in the region

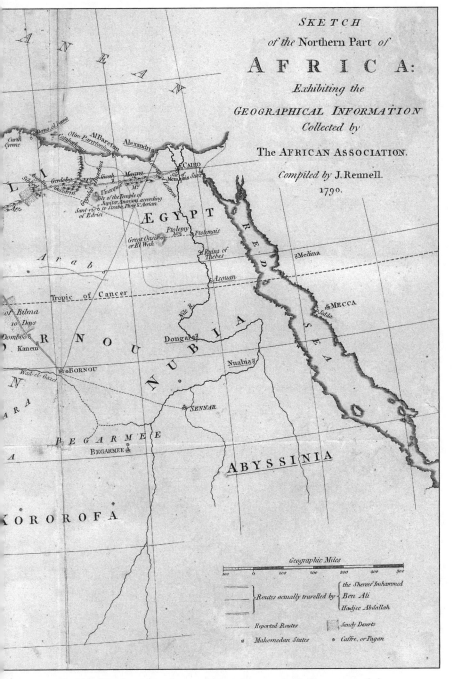

SKETCH
of the Northern Part of
A F R I C A :
Exhibiting the
GEOGRAPHICAL INFORMATION
Collected by
The AFRICAN ASSOCIATION.
Compiled by J. Rennell.
1790.

marked Nubia; from there he would travel west to seek the source of the
Niger River. *Courtesy of the British Library*

Ledyard had barely made it to Alexandria at all. In Paris he fell sick with a cold, which kept him there for a week; he somehow managed to avoid Jefferson, who was still angry with him for working for the British. At Marseilles, he had gotten into some kind of fracas with Stephen Cathalan Jr., Jefferson's wine and produce merchant, who was supposed to help Ledyard on his way to Egypt. Apparently Ledyard lacked the proper papers for traveling to the Holy Land, and the French official in charge of the port refused to make an exception. Ledyard had enlisted Cathalan to help him. "I shall ever think tho he was extremely polite that he rather strove to prevent my embarking at Marseilles than to facilitate it," he huffed to Jefferson, no doubt restraining himself because he had sent the letter via Cathalan (who, naturally, opened it and read it before appending his own indignant version of events). In the end, Ledyard simply sneaked aboard a ship as it was about to depart, leaving the poor bureaucrat to gnash his teeth in vain. "Mr. Lediard is a different kind of person," Jefferson later apologized to Cathalan. "He is American, justement timbre pour aller chercher les sources du Nil et assez sage pour en rendre bon compte"— meaning "crazy (cracked) enough to go and search for the sources of the Nile, and yet clever enough to give a good account of his journey." He was the perfect adventurer, in other words.

One of Ledyard's first acts, on arriving in Egypt, was to try and mend fences with Jefferson as best he could from afar. "You thought hard of me for being employed by an English association, which hurt me very much," Ledyard wrote. He sought to make amends by giving Jefferson more of the "information" that he so coveted—notwithstanding Ledyard's strict pledge of secrecy to his employers.

When Napoleon led his army into Cairo in 1798, a decade after Ledyard, he brought with him a smaller army of "savants"—

artists, scholars, botanists, and writers—who compiled a magisterial twenty-two-volume *Description de l'Egypte* that documents the entire Nile Valley, from Alexandria to Aswan, and which served as the definitive work on Egyptology for more than a century. Full of gorgeous drawings—crisp views of pyramids and mosques, musicians playing in almost empty streets, turbaned men lounging beneath spreading water cypresses—the *Description* made Cairo seem nothing like the dusty, noisy, smelly city into which Ledyard arrived in late August 1788, after a five-day voyage up the Nile in the company of an English merchant named Hunter. Indeed, the scenes before his eyes little resembled the Cairo described by other travel writers, from the Frenchman Claude Étienne Savary to Leo Africanus, and going all the way back to Homer and Thucydides. "Sweet are the songs of Egypt on paper," Ledyard complained, anticipating the debunkery of Mark Twain nearly a century later. "Who is not ravished with gums, balms, dates, figs, pomegranates, with the circassia & sycamores," he continued, "without knowing amidst these one's eyes ears mouth nose is filled with dust eternal hot fainting winds, lice bugs mosquitoes spiders flies—pox itch leprosy, fevers, & almost universal blindness."

In his letters and journals, Ledyard barely mentions such wonders as the Sphinx, which he would have seen with its nose intact. The pyramids impressed him, but only negatively, as a testament to Africa's lack of liberty. "He who has seen an Egyptian pyramid has seen a monument of human weakness as well as power," he had remarked in his Siberian journal, before he ever saw one himself. Cairo itself was "a wretched hole and a nest of vagabonds," with no hint that it had ever been the seat of a great civilization. Even the fabled Nile failed to impress him. "It is a mere mud puddle compared with the accounts we have of it," he wrote to Jefferson. The mighty sovereign of rivers was scarcely wider than the Connecticut or the Thames. "What eyes do travelers see with," he wondered. "Are they fools, or rogues?" Cairo didn't even seem as hot as he expected, perhaps thanks to his shade-giving London umbrella: "I think I have felt it hotter in Philadelphia in the same month."

Cairo in the late eighteenth century was a semiautonomous backwater of the Ottoman Empire, ruled over by the oppressive Mamelukes, a soldier caste descended from Georgian slaves. The city itself was a medieval maze of crowded, narrow passageways, thronged by a population of about 250,000 people, not counting slaves. The city was divided into quarters, each closed off from the other by gates, and surrounded by huge trash dumps, which loomed like miniature pyramids. European visitors were extremely rare, and Ledyard could find nowhere to sleep but a miserable Augustinian convent that catered to Christian travelers.

Ledyard sought out the Venetian consul in Cairo, a merchant named Carlo Rosetti who was pioneering the overland trade across the Isthmus of Suez. Rosetti impressed Ledyard with his array of Venetian beads. To Ledyard's great disappointment, Rosetti failed to invite him to lodge at his home, but he did introduce him to Aga Mohammed, a top minister to Ismail Bey, the de facto ruler of Egypt. Mohammed told Ledyard that as he went south he would meet people who could change themselves into the form of animals. And what did Ledyard think of this, he wondered? "I did not like to render the ignorance, simplicity, and credulity of the Turk apparent," he wrote in his journal. "I told him, that it formed a part of the character of all savages to be great necromancers . . . [and] that it rendered me more anxious to be on my voyage."

Aga Mohammed had another, more practical issue to discuss with Ledyard. "He asked me how I could travel without the language of the people where I should pass," Ledyard wrote. This was certainly a valid concern, since Ledyard's French would be of no service to him outside Cairo, and unlike his colleague Simon

Lucas he had neglected to learn Arabic. "I told him, with vocabularies," Ledyard snorted. "I might as well have read to him a page of Newton's Principia." Unfazed by the ill-mannered American, Mohammed agreed to provide letters of recommendation and introduction through "Turkish Nubia" (southern Egypt) and to the mysterious kingdoms beyond. The annual caravans would soon be arriving from Darfur and Sennar, he said, and Ledyard could travel with them when they returned to the south.

Still stuck in Cairo in mid-October, Ledyard ventured into the slave markets, seeking more information about the caravans. Though he traveled with one of Rosetti's aides, he didn't get far, for the Muslim slave traders (whom he calls "Jelabs") did not like Europeans, or "Franks," snooping around, and Ledyard complained that he was "rudely treated." The 20,000 slaves brought to market annually, he learned, were not bound for Europe or America, but for households in Cairo and across the Middle East. Europeans were not even permitted to purchase slaves. He returned to the market two days later, alone this time and better disguised as a Turk—an outfit that would have rendered him instantly recognizable to his Dartmouth classmates, who remembered his "enormously large loose Turkish breeches" for as long as they lived.

Here again was Ledyard the great transiter, the crosser of divides between East and West, "civilized" and "savage." As a boy in Connecticut, he had played with the sons of "Ben Uncas," and as a young man at Dartmouth he had lived and studied with Iroquois and Caghnawaga and Huron. He'd bedded down with Polynesian kings, reveled with Russian fur traders and camped with Siberian nomads. He saw himself, always and above all, as "a friend to Mankind." In Cairo, however, he felt the full brunt of racism and religious intolerance—directed, for the first time, at him. He had finally reached a cultural divide that he could not bridge, an Other he could not know, not least because he didn't understand Arabic.

And for the first time in his experience, the Other had the power. "The humiliating situation of a Frank would be insupportable to me—but for my Voyage," he wrote Jefferson, lamenting his treatment at the hands of "a banditti of ignorant fanatics." He thought he knew the cause of the trouble: "Religion does more mischief than all other things," he declared, perhaps thinking back to the bitterly divisive Great Awakening of his childhood. "In Egypt it does more than in most other places."

In the slave markets of Cairo, he saw his first black Africans, brought up from Sennar and Darfur, both now part of Sudan (and where slavery reportedly exists to this day). He was amazed by the height of the Sudanese, and by the great brass rings in their noses and their colorful beads, and by their hair, which was so plaited and plastered that it called to mind "one of Uncle Toby's wigs," from *Tristram Shandy*. He was bold and curious enough to ask the slaves—who were mostly women—how he would be treated if he visited their country. They replied "that they should make a King of me, and treat me with all the delicacies of their country," he wrote, quite eager to be on his way.

He returned several times to the slave market, increasingly impatient, and by October 25th had found a merchant who would guide him to Sennar. This man, he wrote to Beaufoy, was a "Procurer at Cairo to the King of Sennar," which meant he was in good hands. Ledyard would travel with the caravan, the aga's letters in hand. A few more weeks, he wrote, and he should be on his way; he reckoned the trip to be about 600 miles. The association would hear from him next, he promised, at Sennar.

Meanwhile, Ledyard's colleague and competitor Simon Lucas was making progress in Tripoli. He was as unlike Ledyard as it was possible to be: He was a lifelong civil servant, not an adventurer, and had made sure the king would continue his eighty-pound annual salary while he was absent. Also, he had actually prepared for the journey he was to undertake. Staying in London until August, Lucas had equipped himself with a compass, a watch, and the obligatory pair of pistols, but he also had a more important skill: his Arabic. Dressed in Arab clothing, including a skullcap, robe, and yellow slippers, with his long, dark hair, he joked that he resembled "a London Jew in deep mourning."

Tripoli was the most dangerous of the North African ports. It had thrived on the success of the Barbary pirates and the Saharan caravan trade; luckless European sailors were still sold in its slave market. Lucas hoped to negotiate his safe passage with the local pasha, Ali Karamanli, but was rejected. Patient and undeterred, he would finally leave Tripoli in February 1789, with a camel caravan led by slaves returning to the south. But shortly after he left, fighting broke out between the bedouins and the pasha's army, and his guides abandoned him. Lucas had the means, and the language, but not the courage (or foolhardiness) to continue, and he cautiously decided to turn back. By late July 1789, he was back in London, safe and sound, ready to go back to work. History promptly forgot him.

Ledyard, on the other hand, was preparing for immortality. It took at least two months for his letters to reach Europe, sometimes more; with each dispatch, Banks and Beaufoy grew more excited. They found Ledyard's writing to be intelligent and perceptive, especially for someone whom they had first considered merely "a bold but illiterate adventurer," as Banks later confessed to Thomas Paine.

Early in 1789, the letters from Ledyard stopped—because, it was assumed, he was already deep in the desert. In his last note to Jefferson, he'd described his plan: to leave with the Sennar caravan for the 600-mile trip into the deserts of Nubia. "There my present conductors leave me to my fate," he wrote. But fate caught up with him first, and that spring the "melancholy tidings" reached London: Ledyard was dead.

The caravan had apparently not left in November after all. Nor did it leave in December. Ledyard had been in Egypt for more than four months, marked by delays and mistreatment of various kinds, and his patience was at an end. He was conscious, too, of what he considered to be his obligations to the African Association. "I have the eyes of some of the first men of the first kingdom on earth turned upon me," he'd written Beaufoy, sounding grandiose even by his own standards. "I am engaged by those very men, in the most important object that any private individual can be engaged in: I have their approbation to acquire, or to lose; and their esteem also, which I prize beyond every thing, except the independent idea of serving mankind."

He dared not disappoint. He was a celebrated explorer now, though also a failed one so far. After all the rigors of his Siberian trip, which had taken him nearly halfway around the world by land, he still had not made it to North America. Now he was stymied by the caravan leaders, who would not leave until they had a fair wind, or so he was told. (A reasonable notion, given the dangers of Saharan sandstorms.) Some years, the caravans did not go at all. Adding to the uncertainty, there was an uprising in the south that might have made travel impossible anyway. Ledyard was stuck in Cairo, his great mission collapsing on his shoulders. Then one day, probably in early January, as he lay in his filthy room at the convent, he felt rumblings in his stomach and sweat on his brow: telltale signs that something was wrong.

The reports to London were contradictory and incomplete (and, by the time they reached Jefferson in Paris, second- and thirdhand). According to Rosetti, who had written to Ledyard's merchant friend Hunter on January 27, 1789, Ledyard had been "transported to anger against the persons who had engaged to conduct him to [Sennar] because they delayed setting out on their voyage for want (as they said) of a fair wind. He was seized with a pain in his stomach occasioned by bile and undertook to cure himself. Excessive vomiting ensued, in consequence of which he broke a blood vessel." Beaufoy also had a March 4, 1789, letter from George Baldwin, the British consul in Cairo, essentially confirming the story: "Mr. Ledyard took offence at the delay and threw himself into a violent rage with his conductors which deranged something in his system that he thought to curb by an emetic, but he took the dose so strong as at the first or second effect of its operations to break a blood vessel."

Before he left London, Ledyard had been instructed in basic medicine by none other than John Hunter, a renowned London doctor who had also helped to support his Siberian journey. An expert on venereal diseases, Hunter had intentionally infected himself with syphilis for research, and a type of chancre had been named after him. His training had apparently not helped Ledyard, however. At the first sign of sickness, according to Beaufoy, Ledyard had swallowed a dose of "acid of vitriol"—sulfuric acid, which was sometimes used to treat digestive disorders. When that only worsened the pain, he followed the "incautious draught" with an even more violent cure, tartar emetic (potassium antimony tartrate), a poison which was often used as a medicine in the eighteenth century, but which thankfully went out of general medical use in about 1800. The emetic proved too powerful, and Ledyard began vomiting violently, breaking a blood vessel in the process.

Baldwin reported that it took three agonizing days for Ledyard to die; Rosetti put it at six, with his final breath passing on January 10, 1789. Either way, it was a miserable and lonely way to die—as a stranger in a hostile land, in his tiny convent room, and with the unavoidable realization that he was dying by his own hand. Ledyard's illness was clearly caused by his own temper, and his attempts to cure it were extreme, even rash. Both Baldwin and Rosetti's accounts stop just short of saying that he intentionally poisoned himself. He had survived Cook's fatal voyage, a wintertime trek across Siberia (not to mention around the Gulf of Bothnia), and a solo trip down the wild Connecticut River in a handmade canoe. He could not survive his own temper. To the end, Ledyard was his own worst enemy.

John Ledyard was buried in an unmarked grave in a small cemetery reserved for the few Englishmen (and women) who happened to meet their fate in Cairo; his tomb has never been found. All we have is that last letter to his mother, written from London in June, in which he'd composed his own farewell.

"Born in obscure little Groton, formed by nature and education to move in the small circle of domestic life, behold me the greatest traveller in history," he'd written, "excentric, irregular, rapid, unaccountable, curious, &, without vanity, majestic as a comet. I afford a new character to the world, and a new subject to biography."

# Afterlife

Death was far kinder to John Ledyard than his brief, arduous life had been. In the spring of 1821, a curious notice appeared in newspapers up and down the East Coast. A "gentleman in New Hampshire" was undertaking a biography of Ledyard, "the celebrated traveller," and wished to hear from anybody with remembrances or letters, "particularly respecting the early part of his life." The notice gave the address of a Mr. J.S. in Concord, New Hampshire.

One of the first to reply was one Daniel Ledyard, of the Manhattan Bank in New York. He identified himself as a cousin of the celebrated Traveller—he was the son of Isaac Ledyard, in fact—and he expressed his displeasure. In no uncertain terms he demanded that J.S. "proceed no further in this business." Besides, Daniel Ledyard went on, the Reverend Jared Sparks of Baltimore was already engaged in the very same project, and the family, "although very averse to this gentleman's intentions," had agreed to cooperate as far as possible. The fellow in New Hampshire would be well advised to drop his biography altogether. "J.S." was, of course, the one and only Jared Sparks; the Concord address belonged to his friend Richard Bartlett, who was helping him with his research. Bartlett forwarded the letter with a note: "Mr. Daniel Ledyard of New York seems to be in great agony lest 'the gentleman in New Hampshire' do some violence to his deceased kinsman's reputation," he chuckled, "but I have humanely put his heart at ease by assuring him that J.S. are the initials of your names, and that I act only as your friend & agent."

Long after he died, John Ledyard's family remained torn between pride in their kinsman and fear that he would bring scandal to their name. Within a year of John's death, Isaac had begun to put together his own biography of his cousin and confidant, using the letters and diaries that he'd lovingly preserved. He wrote to Sir Joseph Banks, politely requesting his cousin's journals from his trips to Siberia and Egypt. Five months later, he got a snooty reply from Richard Price, a noted clergyman, economist, and associate of Banks and Beaufoy, who had kept Ledyard's journals. "[Mr. Beaufoy] has no reason for doubting that you are the person you say you are," Price informed Isaac, "but having never before heard of you, he expects I believe to receive some further information about you."

Beaufoy may have seen Isaac as a competitor: He was already at work on his own sketch of Ledyard, which he published as the centerpiece of the first *Proceedings of the Association for the Discovery of the Interior Parts of Africa*, printed in 1790. Beaufoy thus became Ledyard's first biographer, and his account of Ledyard's life and character helped define the Traveller as a hero for the ages. Ledyard, he wrote, "seemed from his youth to have felt an invincible desire to make himself acquainted with the unknown, or imperfectly discovered regions of the globe." He had sailed the South Seas with Cook and had tramped across the snows of Siberia and the sands of Africa, clad in rags, sometimes without shoes. It almost didn't matter, as Beaufoy noted in passing, that Cairo was already well-trod ground, and that Ledyard had added little to the body of observation of that place.

Not everybody was so taken by Ledyard's performance. "Ledyard...was a very unfit person," wrote a later traveler named William George Browne, who visited Egypt in 1792, " & tho' he had lived, would not have advanced many leagues on the way, if the judgment of people in Egypt [i.e. George Baldwin] concerning him be credited." The explorer James Bruce finally surfaced with the information that Ledyard had chosen the wrong route. "He is either too low or too high," he wrote. He might try Abyssinia, he suggested, but "very lucky he will be if he ever arrives there; & still more so if he ever comes back; but I confidently say he shall not, nor do any thing worthy of repeating, even tho' he had language."

Yet the *idea* of Ledyard, the solitary wanderer who endured Christlike sufferings and died alone, was tremendously potent. The very impossibility of his planned journey—to ascend the Nile and then to traverse Africa from east to west—only enhanced the allure of the doomed romantic explorer. Ledyard's death also drew attention to the group that had employed him; by 1791, the African Association would have 109 paying members, including the historian Edward Gibbon, the brewer Samuel Whitbread, and the potter Josiah Wedgwood.

Ledyard's heroic fame also attracted other would-be explorers, whom Banks and Beaufoy sent one after another to their deaths. Major Daniel Houghton set out for Africa in October 1790. The fifty-year-old Houghton possessed some of Ledyard's "intrepidity of character," according to Beaufoy, but he also had "an easy flow of constitutional good humour," that might get him through the inevitable bad patches. Perhaps learning from Ledyard and Lucas's difficulties in the Sahara, Banks and Beaufoy sent him to the Gambia River, in west Africa; he would ascend the river for several hundred miles, then travel overland to the east, ultimately reaching the Niger and, of course, Timbuktu. But he was captured and tortured by African chiefs who regarded him as a spy, and he ultimately starved to death in captivity. News of his death took more than a year to reach Banks in London.

In 1794, Banks heard from a restless young medical student named Mungo Park, who was averse to entering what he considered to be a dull profession. Banks arranged for him to sail to Java aboard an East Indiaman as an assistant ship's surgeon. He performed well enough on this test voyage that the following year, the association dispatched him to Africa, to complete the journey Ledyard (and now Houghton) had attempted. Park also chose to enter the continent via the Gambia River. He made it several hundred miles inland before things started to go wrong. Like Houghton, he was held captive, beaten, robbed, and nearly died from fever, but he finally reached the Niger River, in present-day Mali, in 1796. He returned triumphant to England, married, and settled into life as a doctor in Edinburgh. A decade later, feeling restless, he returned to Africa and led a party up the Gambia River once again. This time, the rainy season caught up with him, and by the time he reached the Niger his forty-man party had been reduced to nine, all in various stages of disease and dementia. Not long after they passed the fabled city of Timbuktu, Park and his remaining men disappeared on the river; they are thought to have drowned. And yet, when Melville's Ishmael contemplates his place among the great travelers of history, two names come to mind: the intrepid Park and the hapless Ledyard, who had failed to get past Cairo.

It was Beaufoy who had ensured Ledyard's fame by reaching back into his Siberian journal to extract (and edit) the most famous passage Ledyard ever wrote: his celebrated "commendation of women."

> I have always remarked that women, in all countries, are civil, obliging, tender, and humane; that they are ever in-

clined to be gay and cheerful, timorous and modest; and that they do not hesitate, like men, to perform a generous action.—Not haughty, not arrogant, not supercilious, they are full of courtesy, and fond of society: more liable, in general, to err than man; but in general, also, more virtuous, and performing more good actions than he. To a woman, whether civilized or savage, I never addressed myself in the language of decency and friendship, without receiving a decent and friendly answer—even in English billingsgate. With man it has often been otherwise . . .

Though likely written in an idle moment at Yakutsk, it became Ledyard's most enduring piece of prose, his posthumous calling card; quoted, misquoted and pirated for decades after his death. Beaufoy himself had edited Ledyard's text, snipping out a key sentence: "Those who have been used to contemplate the female character only in societies highly civilized and polished may think differently from me," he'd written; he was talking only about women from places "where nature only dictates." No matter. While the rest of his Siberian journals did not see print until the 1960s (except for Sparks's copious excerpts), this passage was reprinted immediately and often, often so highly edited as to be unrecognizable: Sometimes it appeared in verse. ("Thro' many a land and clime a ranger / With toilsome steps I've held my way / A lonely unprotected stranger . . .")

Ledyard's paean appealed to women as well as men; one young lady, who gave her name only as Anna, was moved to respond in verse, in a poem published in the *Columbian Gazetteer* in 1797. The last two stanzas read:

> *Undaunted amidst unnumbered woes,*
> *He brav'd black Bothnia's wintry blasts;*

*Travers'd, Siberia's drifting snows,*
*And chill Kamschatka's frozen wastes . . .*

*For Ledyard's hand, o grateful deed,*
*Around our injured sex's brow,*
*Twin'd a fair garland, formed with heed,*
*Whose buds shall ne'er forget to glow.*

Had he survived, gallant Ledyard would have gladly twined a garland or two around fair Anna's brow. But by the time she wrote, this Ledyard—the hearty swain, the man's man who embraced life wherever he found it, who drank wine by the bottle and romanced Parisian prostitutes—was rapidly disappearing. In his place, his biographers would erect a sort of wax figure: a man of pure, impossible desires.

Isaac Ledyard was the first to attempt to tell the story, as he wrote to Henry Seymour, "of all that is remarkable in the life, character & adventures of our Dec'd relative." Isaac eventually did manage to dislodge a copy of John's journal from Banks and Beaufoy, and he enlisted the help of his brother-in-law Philip Freneau, a noted Revolutionary-era poet and political commentator. Freneau was a passionate Jeffersonian, and his politics may have hampered his poetry, but it certainly didn't dampen his output: He penned dozens of ballads and satires, often quite pointed, while serving as editor of the Jefferson-friendly *National Gazette.* One of his most famous works was a poem entitled "On a Honey Bee." In 1797, he printed a small advertisement in his own magazine, *The Time-Piece,* promising a full and complete biography of John Ledyard for the price of twelve shillings. The response was promising. Subscriptions poured in from every state, including Virginia; Isaac had sent order forms to Thomas Jefferson, to distribute to his friends. A year later, Freneau informed readers that the manuscript was in the hands of a printer. It was to be called *The Interesting Travels of John Ledyard, with a Summary of His Life.*

But the book never appeared. The manuscript had indeed been sent to a printer in Philadelphia, along with the family's copy of John's portrait by von Breda, which went to an engraver. At the last moment, however, Isaac apparently had second thoughts and stopped the publication. According to his son Daniel, Isaac had "concluded, with the advice of his friends, to abandon this intention, the account of his travels being too incomplete to answer the public expectation." The engraver later died in a yellow fever epidemic that swept through Philadelphia, and the painting was lost in the chaos. (The original stayed in London, and eventually made its way to Sweden when von Breda returned there, according to one of Sparks's correspondents, but it disappeared after his death. Some of Ledyard's friends had copies made, but they, too, are lost.)

After Isaac's own death in 1803, also from yellow fever, the Ledyard family apparently decided that it could do without a biography of their famous relative. Jared Sparks was not one to give up easily, but it took years to persuade them. Born in 1789, three months after Ledyard had died, he developed an adolescent fascination with the legend of the Traveller; he had scribbled Ledyard's "Commendation of Women," as rendered by Beaufoy, into one of his student notebooks. A carpenter's apprentice who had somehow managed to win a scholarship to Phillips Exeter Academy, Sparks earned money by teaching school at Havre de Grace, Maryland, before entering Harvard in 1811 as a twenty-three-year-old freshman. After graduation he went back to teaching, but felt so stifled that he applied to the African Association in 1816, volunteering for a journey even more ambitious than Ledyard's. He intended, as he wrote to a Harvard friend, to "go into Africa at Tetuan, or Mogadore, to spend some little time in

Morocco, and to start with a caravan at Tafilet, or some other place, to cross the Great Desert to Tomboctoo . . . to learn as much as possible of its manners, customs, political institutions, etc., and also of the trade which is carried on with it from various parts, and such other information as can be obtained from the respective countries." As if that weren't ambitious enough: "After leaving the Niger, [I will] proceed if possible to the Cape of Good Hope, otherwise to Abyssinia, or through Darfur to Egypt, or through Fezzan to the Mediterranean, or to Benin, or Loango or Congo, or to the southeastern coast of Africa, or to any place, in fact, which may be thought expedient or practicable."

The African Association turned down this open-ended proposal, and Sparks went on to lead an altogether more sedate life. He had taken up arms against the British when they attacked Havre de Grace in 1813, but that was the extent of his physical adventures. He became a prominent Unitarian minister and was appointed chaplain of the U.S. House of Representatives in 1821, while he was working on the Ledyard book. In his spare time, he also served as the editor of the famed *North American Review*, one of the earliest American literary magazines. In 1849 he became president of Harvard, from which he retired in 1853. His one great journey was a trip through the South, during which he kept a rather stuffy, not-very-Ledyardian journal. His true métier was biography, and he became an important (and controversial) historian of the revolutionary period and later served as editor of the first *Library of American Biography*—in which his own life of John Ledyard took a prominent place.

Ledyard had been his first work and his labor of love, although he also proved Sparks's most elusive quarry—as he would for generations of biographers to come. Through lengthy negotiations with the Ledyard family, he had managed to shake loose some letters and reminiscences from various cousins, including

Isaac's compilation of John's journals and papers. It actually proved easier to write the lives of men like Jefferson and Washington, whose movements and temperaments were less erratic, and who left thousands of pages of letters and documents rather than a few dozen scattered scraps. Ledyard never kept any of the letters he received, and only a few of his correspondents bothered to save his missives to them. After Dartmouth, he almost never stayed in one place more than a few months, with the exception of his eighteen-month stint in Paris during 1785 and 1786.

Reconstructing Ledyard's peripatetic life sent Sparks on one wild goose chase after another, chasing down stray letters and tidbits of recollection. He had a half-dozen friends and correspondents supplying him with newspaper clippings and possible sources. He visited Jefferson at Monticello; he corresponded with Lafayette; he interviewed one of Ledyard's half-sisters, as well as his Seymour cousins and his old Uncle Tom, who was well into his eighties and bragged that he still did not need eyeglasses. Sparks even visited the house where Ledyard was born, in Groton, and actually touched a lock of Ledyard's hair. "[It] resembles flax on a distaff," he reported. That was as close as he would get to the man.

"I hope it will be finished next year," he wrote to a friend in 1822, optimistically. He was off by six years. Sparks's *Life of John Ledyard, the American Traveller: Comprising Selections from His Journals and Correspondence* was not published until 1828. The book evidently sold well, for a second edition appeared the following year, and it was soon published in Britain and in Germany. Public interest in Ledyard remained so strong that Sparks revised and reissued the book in 1847 and again in 1864.

But Sparks was not quite Ledyard's Boswell; he was more like Parson Weems, the Washington biographer who invented the famous (and apocryphal) story about the cherry tree. Sparks's

Ledyard was a Victorian minister's hero, full of noble ideals and free from earthy passions. In many places, Sparks edited Ledyard's words to smooth out his prose—and to suit his own worldview. For example, in Cairo Ledyard had observed, "Religion does more mischief than all other things. In Egypt it does more than in most other places." Sparks changed this passage to read, "Religion does more mischief in Egypt than all other things," which is not quite the same thing. Later, Sparks would come under fire for selectively editing Washington's letters, removing the general's uncharitable comments about the patriotism and virtue of New Englanders. As the English historian Lord Mahon noted, "Mr. Sparks has printed no part of the correspondence precisely as Washington wrote it; but has greatly altered, and, as he thinks, corrected and embellished it." The biographer Willard Sterne Randall accuses Sparks of pruning and adjusting facts to create a "Washington myth." (Later historians also complained about Sparks's habit of selling Washington's papers, including important journals from the French and Indian War, to autograph collectors.)

Sparks was not entirely to blame for the sanitizing of John Ledyard: By the time he saw Ledyard's papers, they had already been copied and smoothed over by his relatives, while many of the originals had long since disappeared. In the end, frustrated in his quest for new information, Sparks simply resorted to quoting Ledyard's much-edited journals and letters at length. One reviewer complained that the resulting 325-page biography was a bit skimpy for the price, but the Ledyard family was quite pleased with his work.

Other writers took Sparks's tidying-up even further. One anonymous Victorian scribe actually dragooned John Ledyard into serving as a role model for young boys, in a slim volume entitled *The Adventures of a Yankee, or the singular life of John Ledyard*, published in 1831. Young Ledyard loved his mother, the author insisted (correctly), skipping quickly over his frothy adolescence to his later life of virtuous suffering on behalf of God and man, "wading amidst the frozen snow of Siberia, or panting amidst the burning sands of Africa." In closing, the author finds Ledyard's character "well worthy of... imitation. In his disposition he was amiable; to his benefactors always grateful; and in the exhibition of disinterestedness he had few equals. With his decision, energy, perseverance, fortitude, and enterprise, living as they do in better times, what may we not expect under the auspices of a smiling Providence from our American youth?"

Squire Ledyard and Reverend Wheelock must have convulsed in their graves. They might not have recognized the John Ledyard portrayed by Jared Sparks, but Sparks's Ledyard was the one who would live into posterity. His *Life of John Ledyard* was so imposing that it deterred other biographers for well over a century. Still, there was no shortage of biographical sketches of Ledyard, beginning even before Sparks. Herman Melville owned a copy of William Mavor's *An Historical account of the most celebrated voyages, travels, and discoveries, from the time of Columbus to the present period*, published in 1796; nearly every library in the land contains Samuel Smucker's popular 1858 compendium *The Life of Dr. Elisha Kent Kane and Other Distinguished American Explorers*. Writing in the 1920s, author Henry Beston included Ledyard in his *Book of Gallant Vagabonds*. "He was a son of the new, native-born and native-minded culture which was springing up in the hearts of Americans during the last half of the 18th century," he declared in his essay on Ledyard. "His place is with Daniel Boone and the lords of the frontier."

In 1855, an American industrialist named W. C. Prime traveled to Cairo in search of his hero's tomb. He was a descendant of the Reverend Prime, in whose library young Ledyard had "feasted twelve days" while trying to get a job as a minister or school-teacher. He visited the Christian monasteries and churches of Cairo, interviewing monks and priests, and he interrogated the "custodians of pretended records, which proved to be no records, and after all I was left to the longest interviews with my own imaginations, in the wonderful glamour of Egyptian evening lights, when the sun was going or had gone down into the Libyan desert." He found no grave site.

Earlier, Jared Sparks himself had proposed erecting a monument to Ledyard in Cairo, inspired by the grand tombstones he'd seen in Père-Lachaise cemetery in Paris. Shaped like an obelisk, the marker would be inscribed simply (and mistakenly):

JOHN LEDYARD
THE AMERICAN TRAVELLER
BORN IN CONNECTICUT, 1751
DIED AT CAIRO, 1788
ON HIS WAY
TO THE INTERIOR OF AFRICA

But no monument was ever built, which is perfectly fitting. With no earthly remains, no marble tombstone or bronze statue, Ledyard lives on as he should: only in spirit.

# EPILOGUE

# The River

ONE MAY MORNING A COUPLE OF YEARS AGO, I STEPPED carefully into the stern of a red Old Town canoe and pushed gently away from the dock, drifting out into the Connecticut River. My craft was weighed down by my backpack, wrapped in plastic garbage bags to keep my clothes and sleeping bag dry, as well as a canister of propane fuel, a huge plastic water jug, and my paddling partner, a twenty-four-year-old recent graduate named Jamie Salmon. On the river, we joined six other canoes, each similarly laden with gear and sleepy paddlers, and as the morning fog began to lift, we nosed our boats slowly downstream.

In my wallet was a hundred dollars that I'd withdrawn from an ATM at the Ledyard National Bank, in Hanover. Looking back, we could see a small knot of friends, still waving from the dock of the white clapboard Ledyard Canoe Club. Just to the left of it, a bronze plaque marked the spot where Ledyard had launched his famous dugout canoe in 1773. More than half a century later, blinded and crippled by age, his classmate Ebenezer Mattoon—one of the boys who helped Ledyard craft his escape vehicle—had pointed out what he thought was the stump of the very tree Ledyard had felled. The monument itself had inspired a poem by Richard Eberhart titled "John Ledyard," which I'd just read in the Dartmouth library. It begins:

*The stone entablature*
*By the river*

*Tells us*
*Of a youth who made a canoe*
*From a cedar,*

*Descended the Connecticut,*
*Discovered far places,*
*Died the great voyager*

*Far from home,*
*Lost in Africa,*
*Youthful, valiant, destroyed.*

*That was in another century.*
*The incised bronze fades,*
*His name only remembered*

*By insignificant lovers in the Spring*
*Who read his story*
*And clasp each other . . .*

Another Dartmouth poet, Robert Frost, called Ledyard "the patron saint of freshmen who run away." (Frost himself had dropped out after one term.)

The current swirled faintly around the support pillars of the Ledyard Bridge, which joins the towns of Hanover, New Hampshire and Norwich, Vermont. When it opened in 1859 it was the only toll-free bridge across the Connecticut, which is only fitting. More than most people, Ledyard appreciated a free ride. (There was also a river steamer named the *John Ledyard*, which made the difficult passage from Hartford to Bellows Falls, Vermont, starting in the late 1820s.) The river itself was not free, however. A mile or so downstream, the current stalled against a concrete dam, one of a half-dozen such barriers that we would encounter on the trip downriver. Most had been erected in the early twentieth century, transforming the river into a string of slender lakes (one of them buried Bellows Falls, which Ledyard had narrowly avoided). We would have to paddle, and portage, and paddle some more; there would be no time for reading the classics. It was a very different river from Ledyard's free-running Connecticut, and a very different world.

My companions included a dozen soon-to-graduate Dartmouth seniors, who were adventurous enough to take a weeklong canoe trip, energetic enough to paddle all day long, and sufficiently irresponsible to skip five days of classes at the frantic end of the term. Jamie Salmon had graduated two years earlier and was finally getting ready to start a teaching job at a private school. This was his second Trip to the Sea, an annual tradition since the 1920s, when a group of students had impulsively paddled the 206 miles to Long Island Sound. Every year since then, a small Dartmouth flotilla has taken to the river in Ledyard's wake. Recently, in Ledyard's honor, the students had begun a "Strip to the Sea," paddling through Hartford in the nude—or, as Ledyard might have put it, "in an unconstrained situation."

Long after he died, Ledyard was still inspiring adventure. Actually, he was still alive when the first Boston ships, the *Columbia* and the *Washington*, set out for the Northwest coast in September 1787, their owners practically drooling over Ledyard's tales of the luxurious pelts that awaited them at Nootka Sound. Since Ledyard was not available, his old *Resolution* shipmate Simeon Woodruff had shipped aboard the *Columbia* as a guide, for a cash advance that was eight times greater than the salary of the ship's captain (who put him off the ship at the Cape Verde Islands). The ships would return with only modest profits, but the Northwest fur trade would create some of the greatest American fortunes.

Ledyard had paved the way for other explorers as well, start-ing with Mungo Park, who completed the African journey Led-yard had vainly attempted—and then, like Ledyard, disappeared into the beyond. The Canadian fur trapper Peter Pond read Led-yard's journal and wondered if an explorer might cross from Alaska over to Siberia, the very opposite of the trip Ledyard had attempted. Ledyard had also, in the end, provided indispensable information to Thomas Jefferson. The third president had re-fused to give up the idea of exploring North America from coast to coast, and finally, more than fifteen years after meeting Ledyard, he found the right men in Meriwether Lewis and William Clark. Thanks to Ledyard, Jefferson knew that any such expedition had to start in the East and head West. In November of 1805, Lewis and Clark would stand on the Oregon coast, looking out at the Pacific—twenty-seven years after Ledyard had first spotted the far shore of his native continent from the deck of the *Resolution*.

Ledyard inspired other, lesser explorers, from young Jared Sparks to James Cochrane, an American military officer who tramped across Siberia in his footsteps, in the 1830s. There was Ishmael, of course, Melville's fictional world traveler, who surren-dered himself to the sea and his fate—to be, in his words, "thumped" around the world. And as Henry David Thoreau paddled down the Merrimack River, he imagined that a traveler he saw on the shore was Ledyard, crossing the fog-cloaked river to the farther shore: "It may be Ledyard or the Wandering Jew. Whence, pray, did he come out of the foggy night? And wither through the sunny day will he go? We observe only his transit; im-portant to us, forgotten by him, transiting all day."

On the river, we talked of another would-be Ledyard: the legendary Dartmouth freshman who had taken to the river in the spring of 2002, fed up with school and everything it represented. He bought a well-used canoe out of a local man's garage and stocked it with food, water, and a tarp. On April 21, almost the very day Ledyard had left in 1773, he and a friend had paddled under the Ledyard Bridge and down the river. The friend came home after two days, but the freshman continued: descending out of the New England hills past Hartford, and then on to Old Saybrook, where the river empties into Long Island Sound in a broad tidal sweep.

He didn't stop there, but kept going, along the shore and through the Cape Cod Canal, around Boston and up the coast of Maine to the Kennebec River, where he turned inland, as if seeking his own Northwest Passage. He traveled upstream now, sometimes paddling and sometimes hauling his canoe against the current, like the modern-day reincarnation of some intrepid frontier fur trapper. A true explorer, after all, sees the whole world as new again. A short pickup-truck ride took him into the St. Lawrence River watershed, which in turn delivered him to the Great Lakes by June. He spent the next three months descending the Mississippi River all the way to New Orleans. There he judged he had gone far enough, and he took a job on a tugboat— like Ledyard, a laborer.

Ledyard himself had been in no hurry to get downriver, and neither were we. While my fellow paddlers had earned admission to the Ivy League, and had done well enough to stay there, most of them looked forward to graduation with a mixture of relief and dread: relief to be finished with school, dread of what would come next—a job, obligations, the swift and inevitable curtailment of freedom. The creative writing majors seemed especially doubtful about the future. Ledyard would have sympathized with them. His whole life was a quest for freedom, from institutions, obligations, and especially money ("It is a vile Slave!" he ranted in a letter from Siberia). An eternal adolescent in some ways, he abhorred anything that would "clip the plume of haughty Genius."

As the current carried us along, past the broad-shouldered bulk of Mount Ascutney, the woods closed in behind us, and it became possible to imagine the river as Ledyard had seen it, balancing in his hand-hewn canoe, with only a bearskin for warmth and some dried venison to eat, and two great books for company, riding the spring flood toward his gloriously imagined destiny.

# ACKNOWLEDGMENTS

THIS BOOK WOULD HAVE BEEN IMPOSSIBLE TO WRITE WITH-out the work of four previous scholars, beginning with Jared Sparks, whose research notes proved invaluable. In the 1960s, Sinclair Hitchings and Kenneth Munford produced a brilliant edition of Ledyard's journal of his voyage with Captain Cook, which by then had been out of print for about 180 years. Stephen Watrous then completed the picture with his 1966 collection of Ledyard's Siberian journals and letters, most of which had never before been published.

I was also given aid and comfort by the library staffs of the New York Historical Society; the Rauner Special Collections Library at Dartmouth (especially Sarah Hartwell); the Library of Congress, Manuscripts Division; the Connecticut Historical Society; the Connecticut State Archives; the New London County Historical Society; the Massachusetts Historical Society; and the Sutro Library in San Francisco. In England, the British National Archives; the British Library; and the Natural History Museum all provided helpful guidance and essential documents.

Numerous magazine editors supported this endeavor, whether they know it or not, including June Thomas, Alex Heard, John Brodie, and Lee Michaelides. Alexander Nevsorov helped with research in Irkutsk, and Emily Copeland did at Dartmouth. I am also indebted to Alan Ledyard, Cass Ledyard Shaw, and John

Ledyard Teague, for their research and insights into their famous relation. John and Julia Hamilton gladly lent their guest room, as did Sarah Gifford, and Andrew Zimmerman; Bill Gifford and Adda Gogoris; and Monique Burns. Larzer Ziff, Wey Lundquist, and William Spengemann provided insight and helpful conversation.

A crack team of readers spotted errors, omissions, and plain clumsiness in the manuscript: Bill Spengemann, Wes Kosova, Jay Heinrichs, Beverly Baker, Stephen Rodrick, and the lovely and talented Elizabeth Hummer. My official editor, the brilliant Tim Bent, "got" Ledyard immediately, and believed in him enough to take the project with him to Harcourt. My tireless agent, John Ware, provided guidance (and the much-needed nudge) at every step of the way. I drew further inspiration, in different ways, from the memories of Leonard Welles, my grandfather, and Katharine Jones Baker. Finally, much of this book was written in the company of "two great dogs," Theo and Elizabeth.

MOUNT GRETNA, PENNSYLVANIA, MAY 2006

# NOTES

## Abbreviations:

| | |
|---|---|
| DCA | Dartmouth College Archives |
| JLP | John Ledyard's Papers, three-volume transcript (copy in Dartmouth College Library). |
| Sib | Ledyard and Watrous, 1966, *Journey Through Russia and Siberia, 1787–1788:* the journal and selected letters. |
| JLJ | Ledyard, 1963, *A Journal of Captain Cook's Last Voyage to the Pacific Ocean.* |
| JCC | Cook et al., 1955, *The Journals of Captain James Cook on his Voyages of Discovery.* Volume III, Parts One and Two. |
| NYHS | New York Historical Society, Ledyard Collection. |
| PTJ | Jefferson and Boyd, 1950, *The Papers of Thomas Jefferson.* |
| Sparks/MS | Papers of Jared Sparks, Houghton Library, Harvard. |

## INTRODUCTION · Damned to Fame

**"I this moment receive a letter from Ledyard"** See Thomas Jefferson to Thomas Paine, May 19, 1789 (revised May 21) in *The Papers of Thomas Jefferson* (Julian P. Boyd, ed. Princeton: Princeton University Press, 1950–2003), p. 136; also Paine to Jefferson, June 17, 1789, in PTJ, pp. 197–99.

**"a man of genius"** Jefferson wrote two accounts of Ledyard, this one from his 1821 autobiography, and a somewhat longer and slightly different sketch of Meriwether Lewis, written in 1813. See Jefferson, *Autobiography* (with an introduction by Dumas Malone, New York: Capricorn Books, 1959); and Lewis, *History of the Expedition Under the Command of Captains Lewis and Clark* (1814).

**starting in Kentucky** In April 1789, Jefferson wrote to James Madison: "[Ledyard] promises me, if he escapes through this journey, he will go to

Kentuckey and endeavour to penetrate Westwardly from thence to the South Sea." July 19, 1788, in PTJ, pp. 381–2.

**"good & extraordinary man"** See Lafayette to Thomas Storrow, April 16, 1823, in Sparks MS at Harvard, Houghton Library. The Ledyard name was not unfamiliar to Lafayette, who had met John's cousin Benjamin Ledyard during the American Revolution.

**"damned to fame"** See Ledyard to Isaac Ledyard, April 9, 1786 (original in NYHS); Beaufoy, *Proceedings of the Association for the Discovery of Interior Parts of Africa,* which also contains an account of Ledyard's travels and death in Cairo.

**"the great New England traveller"** See Melville, *Moby-Dick,* p. 36. In *Return Passages* (New Haven: Yale University Press, 2000), Larzer Ziff gives probably the best and most insightful literary-critical look at Ledyard's life and work to date, including an excellent comparison between Ledyard and Ishmael. See Ziff, pp. 17–57.

**portrait of Ledyard** After Sparks's biography appeared in 1828, he got a letter from an American traveler who had seen Ledyard's portrait in Stockholm. In his preface to the 1847 edition, Sparks notes that the portrait was then "in the possession of the artist, who was then far advanced in life. It is doubtless the same that is mentioned by Ledyard as his 'Swedish portrait.' " Sparks tried to obtain the painting, but found that it had disappeared after Breda's death, when the artist's possessions were sold and dispersed. Sparks, *Life of John Ledyard,* p. 5.

**"locomotive machine"** We owe this unforgettable image to Ledyard's Dartmouth classmate and future Massachusetts judge, Colonel Ebenezer Mattoon, in a letter to Sparks. A contemporary Ledyardian, Weyman Lundquist (chairman of the Ledyard National Bank in Hanover) has described him just as memorably, as a "man of a thousand footnotes."

**"Little attentive to differences of rank"** In James Burney, 1819, *A chronological history of north-eastern voyages of discovery,* p. 280.

**Breathless valentine to Ledyard** See Augur, 1946, *Passage to Glory,* p. 3. While entertainingly written and reasonably well researched, particularly regarding Ledyard's family and milieu, Augur's work suffers from leaps of the imagination and invented thoughts and dialogue.

## PART ONE · Landlocked

## The Squire's Revenge

Key sources on the early history of Groton and New London include Frances Manwaring Caulkins's *History of New London, Connecticut: From the First Survey of the*

*Coast in 1612 to 1860*; Caulkins, *Stone Records of Groton* (Norwich, CT, Free Academy Press, 1903); and most importantly, *The Diary of Joshua Hempstead* (New London, CT: The New London County Historical Society, 1999). See also: Charles R. Stark, *Groton, Conn. 1705–1905* (Stonington: The Palmer Press, 1922).

On the Ledyard family, Cass Ledyard Shaw's comprehensive genealogy, *The Ledyard Family in America* (West Kennebunk, ME: Phoenix Publishing, 1993); and Charles B. Moore, "John Ledyard, the Traveller," New York Genealogical and Biographical Record, 7:2–8, January 1876. Ledyard family wills and church records may be found at the Connecticut State Archives in Hartford.

**the first recorded descent of the river** According to the account of the canoe trip in John Ledyard's Papers, he traveled down the Connecticut "with an Indian whom he had persuaded to accompany him." No other source or witness, including Ledyard, mentions a Native American copilot, but that does not mean that he didn't have one. This tidbit must have originated with Isaac Ledyard, who helped compile the papers—and who likely witnessed John's homecoming first hand. Also, some anonymous French fur trapper might have descended the river before Ledyard.

**not a single barrel of molasses** See, e.g., Willard Sterne Randall, *Benedict Arnold: Patriot and Traitor* (New York: William Morrow, 1990), p. 42.

**fruitlessly searching** See Hempstead, *The Diary of Joshua Hempstead*, whose entry for Saturday May 5, 1750, reads: "my Son Robert is Come fro So-Hold in Quest of his Daughter Abigail who is come away privetly with John Ledyard of Groton (her mothers Sisters Son) because her parents Refused to give her to him to wife." On Wednesday, "Son Robert went away for home Early in the morn & met Danll youngs Brown with Jno Ledgyard Junr and his Daughter Abigail in the Boat a Coming home. Maryed last Sunday night att Seatauket. Got a Lycence of Doctor Mawason [Muirson] who had Blanks (to Dispose of) from the Govr."

**this uneasy union of cousins** One Ledyard genealogist, Alan Ledyard, believes that Abigail was actually pregnant with John at the time of her and Captain John's elopement; this seems unlikely, for infants were typically baptized within a few months of birth. Oddly, however, Joshua Hempstead does not mention the birth or baptism of his granddaughter's child.

**Pequots and Mohegans** The two reservations from Ledyard's time still exist, in southeast Connecticut, and each is now home to massive casinos: the Pequots' Foxwoods Casino Resort and the neighboring Mohegan Sun have made their communities (on either side, interestingly, of the town now called Ledyard, Connecticut) two of the wealthiest towns in America. For the history of the contemporary Pequot tribe, see Kim Isaac Eisler, *Revenge of the*

*Pequots* (New York: Simon & Schuster, 2001); and Brett Fromson, *Hitting the Jackpot: The Inside Story of the Richest Indian Tribe in History* (New York: Atlantic Monthly Press, 2003).

**not all of the loot was recovered** Caulkins, 1895, *History of New London, Connecticut*, pp. 462–467.

**"no life Lost of any humane Creature"** Hempstead, p. 602.

**Captain John's ship *Greyhound*** reported in the Boston *News-Letter*, December 1757.

**Arnold was in London** See, e.g., Willard Sterne Randall, *Benedict Arnold: Patriot and Traitor* (New York: William Morrow, 1990), p. 38.

**"Strange scene of bankruptcy and ruins"** The Squire is quoted in Oscar Zeichner, *Connecticut's Years of Controversy* (Chapel Hill: University of North Carolina Press, 1949), p. 47.

**The Reall Christian** was a somewhat obscure religious treatise, published in England in 1742 and advocating a proto-Unitarian view of God. In the context of Captain John's will, where no other books were named except the Bible, its inclusion seems pointed. The will, along with those of Youngs Ledyard and Squire Ledyard, resides in the Connecticut State Archives at Hartford. How the widow Ledyard managed to lose her property—which had apparently been purchased with an inheritance from her side of the family—remains somewhat murky. Sparks skims over the episode, though Ledyard relatives insisted to him that some sort of skullduggery took place—notably, Abigail Ledyard's niece's letter to Sparks, in Sparks MS. Property records of the time are also somewhat inexact but they do clearly indicate a transfer of a sizable piece of property by Groton Ferry, from the Squire to William and Ebenezer Ledyard, in 1771.

**to replace the sons he mourned** See Cass Ledyard Shaw, *The Ledyard Family in America*, p. 42. Reverend Whitman's eulogy for Squire Ledyard was published in pamphlet form in 1771, no doubt at the estate's expense. See Elnathan Whitman's sermon, "The death of good men compared to a sweet, refreshing sleep," 1771.

**"a broken and distressed family"** John Ledyard to Abigail Ledyard Moore, September 1783 (original in Dartmouth College Archives).

**unexplained and tragic disaster** As described in the *Connecticut Courant*, May 26, 1766. The story of John selling the Squire's horses was told to Jared Sparks by Ledyard's cousin Henry Seymour.

**"Lord and Lady Mayoress"** John Ledyard to Isaac Ledyard, July 1785, original in NYHS. For a more balanced sketch of Tom Seymour, see Sparks's notes, and also Seymour's own account of Ledyard in Sparks's research notes. (At eighty-eight years of age, Seymour still swam every day and bragged of not needing glasses.) Two of teenage John's letters to his mother, dated 1766 and 1767, are in the files of the Southold Historical Society.

## Shut Out and Set Free

Eleazar Wheelock's letters and papers, including Dartmouth day books and expense ledgers, are in the Dartmouth College Archives and are catalogued in *A Guide to the Microfilm Edition of the Papers of Eleazar Wheelock* (Hanover, NH: Dartmouth College Library, 1971). Also useful, in a way, were Wheelock's annual reports to his English board of trustees. Sparks's research notes proved especially helpful here, especially his interview with James Wheelock, youngest son of college founder Eleazar, and letters from various Ledyard classmates, in Sparks MS 112, at Houghton Library, Harvard. For more on Dartmouth's early history, see: Frederick Chase, *History of Dartmouth College and the Town of Hanover, New Hampshire* (Cambridge, MA: J. Wilson & Sons, 1891); James Dow McCallum, *Eleazar Wheelock* (Hanover, NH: Dartmouth College Publications, 1939; reissued by Arno Press, New York, 1969); and McCallum, ed., *The Letters of Eleazar Wheelock's Indians* (Hanover, NH: Dartmouth College Publications, 1932).

"the first carriage of this kind ever on Dartmouth plain" Jared Sparks's exchange with James Wheelock, son of Eleazar, dated November 12, 1821; and January 29, 1822; in Sparks MS 112.

"the bad conduct and behaviour of such as have been educated here" Quoted in McCallum, *Eleazar Wheelock*, p. 132.

A bright Mohegan named Samson Occom See William Deloss Love, *Samson Occom and the Christian Indians of New England;* and Harold William Blodgett, *Samson Occom* (Hanover, NH: Dartmouth College Publications, 1935); and *Samson Occom: Collected Writings from a Founder of Native American Literature*, ed. Joanna Brooks (New York: Oxford University Press, 2006).

the Deerfield Massacre of 1704 The survivors' story is told in John Williams et al., *The Redeemed Captive Returning to Zion* (Boston: S. Kneeland, 1758); see also Evan Haefali and Kevin Sweeney, *Captors and Captives: The 1704 French and Indian Raid on Deerfield* (Amherst: University of Massachusetts Press, 2003).

"All things converged on Wheelock" For Wheelock's health and general harassed-ness, see McCallum, *Eleazar Wheelock*, pp. 180–83; Wheelock's 1741 diary quoted in Joseph Tracy, *The Great Awakening.*

to Walpole ... to get provisions Chase, in *A History of Dartmouth College and the Town of Hanover*, p. 259, says they went to get water, but this seems strange given that Hanover sits on a river. On Governor Wentworth and the condition of New Hampshire roads, see Paul W. Wilderson, *Governor John Wentworth and the American Revolution* (Hanover, NH: University of New England Press, 1994).

**"make a lordly fire"** Nathaniel Kendrick, quoted by his grandson Ariel Kendrick, in Chase, p. 184.

**"to blow stinky horns"** One of the few students to hit back against Wheelock, Francis Quarles Jr. believed he was being punished for allegedly mistreating one of Wheelock's sons. Letters of Quarles and his father, Francis Sr., who really did sue Wheelock, are in the Dartmouth College Archives; also quoted in McCallum, *Eleazar Wheelock*, p. 188.

**"all manner of nise"** In January 1773, Daniel Simon, Daniel Babbitt, Benjamin Buet, and Peter Pohqunnopput wrote to Wheelock, complaining of their Native American neighbors and "the injur that is done to our studies by the Indians that lives in the room against us they interrupt our studies so that many times we cannot get so much of our recitations as we should do" (original in DCA). That same month, Wheelock wrote to Governor Wentworth, lamenting that because of drink, "several of my Indians appear rather to be paganized than civilized & Christianized by their coming." This information, needless to say, was omitted from his reports to the British lords.

**"disappeared without notice to his comrades"** According to Sparks's research notes, from an interview with John's cousin Henry Seymour: "While Ledyard was at Dartmouth he absented himself without permission of the college government and made a tour among the six nations of Indians on the borders of Canada. During this period he made some progress in learning their languages, & becoming acquainted with their manners, and enured himself also to hardship and fatigue." Tom Seymour agreed, noting that while at Dartmouth, Ledyard "acquired a tincture of the languages and manners of the natives of the forrest." Ledyard did seem to know a great deal about native languages and customs; he might, indeed, have taken a trip or two to Native American country, but he might also have learned those things from his fellow students, or even from the Pequots and Mohegans ("Ben Uncas," as he called Native Americans) he had known around Groton. There is no evidence of any missionary trip by Ledyard in Wheelock's papers: He would have eagerly expected Ledyard to bring back recruits; and while he enumerates every one of Ledyard's sins, going AWOL is not among them; in Sparks, *Life of John Ledyard*, pp. 23 ff; notes are in Sparks MS 112, Houghton Library, Harvard.

**"well satisfied not to take another such jaunt"** James Wheelock to Jared Sparks, January 29, 1822, in Sparks MS; also, petition to spare Caesar, dated February 8, 1773, original in DCA.

**"bids fair to make a good scholar"** Wheelock by this point was feeling misled, if not betrayed. He had apparently visited Seymour (and probably Ledyard) personally, in Hartford, to entice Ledyard to come to Dartmouth. He believed that the young man had some kind of inheritance, as he explained in a January 7, 1773, letter to Tom Seymour: "I am in great strait for the money, and would pray you if you can to transmit it to me as soon as may be . . . ," original in DCA.

**"Christ crucified is no news surely in N York"** John Ledyard to Elizabeth Ledyard, New York, March 13, 1772. Original in NYHS.

**the river poured over Bellows Falls** Sparks sent a messenger, George Ticknor, to Walpole, the town nearest Bellows, but nobody there remembered Ledyard's passage. There was, however, a portage around the falls for logs. While it's almost certain that Ledyard's handmade canoe would have capsized one or more times on the trip downriver, he may have exaggerated the Bellows Falls story for effect.

**"our minister laughed most heartily"** John Ledyard to Isaac Ledyard, July 1785, original in NYHS.

**"When I sit down to write"** Both Wheelock's letter of May 1, 1773, and Ledyard's May 23 reply are in DCA.

**The Squire's coat was too large** Story of the Squire's coat from Sparks's interview notes with Ebenezer Avery, who also made Ledyard's linen breeches, in Sparks.

**"I bestrided my Rosinante"** John Ledyard to Isaac Ledyard, describing his trip through Connecticut, Long Island, and New Jersey, quoted (in full) in Sparks, *Life of John Ledyard*, pp. 35–39.

**"I was shut out"** John Ledyard to Eleazar Wheelock, May 23, 1773, in DCA.

## PART TWO · Voyages

Sinclair Hitchings's and Kenneth Munford's superb 1963 edition of *John Ledyard's Journal of Captain Cook's Last Voyage* (Corvallis: Oregon State University Press, 1963), with its extended biographical introduction, remains the best piece of Ledyard scholarship anywhere. Hitchings's research notes (at Dartmouth's Rauner Special Collections Library) were also helpful. For the voyage as a whole, all roads lead to, or from, J.C. Beaglehole, editor of *The Journals of Captain James Cook on his voyages of Discovery* (1955); and his huge biography, *The Life of Captain James Cook.* Also useful were Richard Hough, *Captain James Cook;* Anne Salmond, *The Trial of the Cannibal Dog: The Remarkable Story of Captain Cook's Encounters in the South Seas,* 2003; Glyndwr Williams, *Voyages of Delusion: The Quest for the Northwest Passage,* 2003; and miscellaneous officers' journals in the Public Record Office especially that of James Burney (in the British National

Archives, at Kew, outside London). Those seeking an entertaining, easy-to-digest introduction to the compelling story of Captain Cook should start with Tony Horwitz's *Blue Latitudes: Boldly Going Where Captain Cook Has Gone Before* (New York: Henry Holt, 2002).

## Seven Years' Ramble

**"carrying himself with a martial air"** Sparks, *Life of Ledyard*, p. 43; Sparks interview with John Deshon, Sparks MS.

**"a rough passage of forty days"** This letter, dated January 15, 1774, is the first document in John Ledyard's Papers; even at age twenty, Isaac Ledyard had the foresight to save his cousin's letters.

**mock duel with the mainmast** Henry Channing to Jared Sparks, May 24, 1822, in Sparks MS 153. Sparks chose to omit this anecdote, as well as the even more disturbing one about the dead man's skull.

**"over to Stonington to visit the Ladies"** Channing to Sparks, March 1822, reporting his interview with Ebenezer Avery, Sparks MS; See also Zug, *American Traveler*, p. 28.

**"seven years' ramble"** Ledyard to Isaac Ledyard, January 15, 1774, in JLP.

**"weeping upon his mother's neck"** Sparks, *Life of Ledyard*, p. 168; also Sparks interview notes with Mrs. Anne Ledyard Hodge, in Sparks MS.

**"I know not what to write"** John Ledyard to Isaac Ledyard, January 15, 1782, in NYHS.

**smoky scars of September 6** For more on Arnold's New London raid, see Willard Sterne Randall, *Benedict Arnold: Patriot and Traitor* (New York: William Morrow, 1990).

**not clear whether or not he saw any combat** Ledyard always insisted that he sought to avoid combat against his own people, but records of his whereabouts are scarce. The New York Historical Society has an odd letter, purportedly from Ledyard, dated October 1782, from "Hospital, Italy," that might indicate his deployment to the Mediterranean rather than the American theater, but the handwriting is too loose to be convincingly his. When John took the time to write, he usually had so much to say that he covered every square inch of every page. It's also unclear how such a letter would have made its way from Italy to America, across an ocean and a war zone.

**"the least of two evils"** Ledyard's "memorial" is reprinted in full in Helmut Lehmann-Haupt, *The Book in America*, pp. 88–90.

**"they are not Ledyards"** Sparks interview with Anne Ledyard Hodge, Sparks MS.

**"He knew how to command"** Beaglehole, *Exploration of the Pacific*, p. 312; see also Hough, *Captain James Cook.*

**"no inconsiderable sum"** John Niles to Jared Sparks, in Sparks MS. The *Jour-*

*nal* is still available in many libraries and for purchase from used-book dealers, for around $15,000.

**"a few episodes discreditable to the British"** Beaglehole, in JCC, p. ccviii. Beaglehole takes a dim view of Ledyard, finding him "most untrustworthy" and accuses him—falsely—of bestowing barren Christmas Island with "deserts, forests, mountains, and ferocious animals." (Actually, Rickman did that.) JCC, p. 261 note.

**"the very essence of the lands he visited"** See Ziff, *Return Passages,* pp. 17–57.

**"faithfully narrated from the original MS."** Rickman was finally credited thanks to F.W. Howay in 1921: "Authorship of the Anonymous Account of Captain Cook's Last Voyage," *Washington Historical Quarterly,* vol. 12 no. 1, January 1921. See also letters from "R.W.," in Sparks MS 112.

**With what education I know not** Burney, pp. 280–81.

## Resolution *and* Discovery

**This modern *Endeavour*** After sailing round the world for the last several years, the *Endeavour* replica is now moored—permanently, alas—at the Australian National Maritime Museum in Sydney (http://www.anmm.gov.au/). For a somewhat different account of sailing aboard *Endeavour,* see Tony Horwitz, *Blue Latitudes,* pp. 9–41.

**"Thus did we resemble the ark"** JLJ p. 8; Cook says that if they had only had some women, the ship would have made "a compleat Ark."

**"the dregs of piracy, prison, and dockyard inn"** Beaglehole, *Exploration of the Pacific,* p. 11.

**three ritual dunkings** "This is one of those absurd customs which craft and inconsiderate levity has imposed on mankind," huffed William Anderson, the ship's surgeon.

**"a Ship Built of Ginger Bread"** Beaglehole, JCC, p. xciii.

**"our Watch"** The Harrison chronometer is, of course, the subject of Dava Sobel's *Longitude* (New York: Walker, 1995).

**"deserves the severest reprehension"** Anderson's journal, in JCC 735–37; "Our situation for a few Minutes was very alarming," Cook admitted in his journal, in JCC, p. 12.

**to seek the fabled Northwest Passage** Cook's sailing instructions are in JCC, pp. ccxx–ccxxiv.

**he even applied for the job of expedition historian** See Burney, pp. 280–81. Ledyard's writing sample, or something resembling it, in handwriting very much like his, can be found thrust into Captain Clerke's voyage logs, at the Admiralty Archives at Kew.

**The marines were sea soldiers** For more on the marines, and British naval life in general, see (among others) Nicholas A.M. Rodger, *The Wooden World*, and Julian Thompson, *The Royal Marines: From Sea Soldiers to a Special Force* (London: Sidgwick & Johnson, 2000).

## Noble Savage

**a raging case of the "French pox,"** Salmond, p. 370.

**"amongst many other useless items"** For notes on Omai's equipment, see JCC, p. lxxxviii; Cook's comments are in JCC, p. 522 (for example).

**Cook failed to meet the locals' expectations** Anne Salmond calls this a turning point in Cook's relations with native peoples, citing numerous other examples when Cook would fail to behave in ways they would understand (curiously, for a Cook revisionist, she seems to be condemning him for not using violence when the islanders expected him to). Salmond, *Trial of the Cannibal Dog*, p. 317.

**"my heart suggested other matters"** JLJ, p. 32. Although Ledyard portrays himself as the sole witness to this encounter with Paulaho, Samwell reports an almost identical scene in his journal, and Cook also remarks on the practice of "patting" massage, which he experienced firsthand. It is likely that Ledyard, in his capacity as a marine guard, accompanied some of the officers to Paulaho's tent.

**"never slept better"** Melville, *Moby-Dick*, p. 32.

**"the full exertion of extreme power"** Ledyard's version of the Finau-Paulaho saga is at JLJ, pp. 37–42.

**"At this Omai was highly offended"** Samwell's account of the incident is at JCC p. 1032; also see James Burney's Journal.

**"like St. George going to kill the dragon"** John Rickman, p. 180 ff.

**Cook had the carpenters reinscribe the cross** JLJ, p. 46. Apparently Ledyard was the only chronicler to note that Cook erased the Spanish inscription, which renders his account "most untrustworthy," in Beaglehole's view. JCC, p. cix(fn).

**enormous "poo-poos"** Omai's speech in Rickman, p. 139.

**"[but] Omai rejected my advice"** JCC, p. 193.

**"in short his ignorance and vanity were insupportable"** JLJ, p. 59.

**"mere conjugal fidelity"** JLJ, p. 20.

**"could scarcely be repaired in a century"** Heinrich Zimmermann, *Zimmermann's Captain Cook*, p. 67.

**"without ever a woman among them"** JCC, p. 239.

**"Nor did Omai seem disposed to take a wife"** JCC, p. 239.

**"so ambitious of being the only great traveler"** JCC, p. 241.

"the more unhappy" JLJ, p. 60.

tattoos depicting a man on horseback JCC, p. 242 fn.

## Northwest Passage

"It soothed a home-sick heart" JLJ, p. 71.

"that glorious creature man" JLJ, p. 69.

"I had no sooner beheld these Americans" JLJ, p. 71ff.

"fricassee of rats" Rickman, p. 232.

the very hull of the *Resolution* After the next storm, the *Resolution* sprung a serious leak and it was discovered (according to Ledyard) that rats had eaten through the hull to its copper sheathing. JLJ, p. 78.

"human flesh is most delicious" JLJ, p. 73. Samwell and Cook and Clerke said the natives offered human "hands," which can perhaps include a bit of arm, or perhaps Ledyard's arm came with a hand attached; they differ as to whether it was cooked (Ledyard), dried (Clerke/Samwell) or relatively fresh (Cook). The natives' cannibalism was very real, however, and later they would try to sell the English a little girl, indicating she was good to eat; the asking price was a small hatchet. Clerke, in JCC, p. 1329.

"pointing towards Hudsons or Baffins Bays" JCC, p. ccxxii.

evidence that no such thing existed For a more thorough account of attempts to find, or to pretend to have found, the Northwest Passage, see Williams, *Voyages of Delusion*, especially pp. 239–280.

"Map of The New Northern Archipelago" See Williams, pp. 290–95; and JCC, pp. lxi–lxiv.

"and not for want of looking" Quoted in Williams, p. 286. (Also see pp. 287–334.)

"This is an American indeed" JLJ p. 72.

"harpoon made from a mushel shell" See JLJ, pp. 76–77; and Ziff, p. 30. Ben Uncas was chief of the Pequots, but had rebelled to form the Mohegan tribe in the 1630s, and proceeded to ally himself with the English to make war on his former tribe.

"in such a frightful situation" JLJ, p. 84. See also Cook's version of the same story, in JCC, p. 388: "Providence had conducted us . . . where I should not have ventured in a clear day."

"pale languid and poor" JLJ, p. 89.

after reaching seventy-one degrees north latitude The ships turned around not far from what is today named Ledyard Bay, Alaska.

"one in particular seemed very busy to please me" For Ledyard's account of his exploration of Unalaska, see JLJ, pp. 91–100; for Cook's version, see

JCC, p. 449: "On the 8th I received by the hand of an Indian named Derra-moushk a very singular present considering the place, it was a rye loaf or rather a pie made in the form of a loaf, for some salmon highly seasoned with peper &ca was in it. He had the like present for Captain Clerke and a Note to each of us written in a language none of us could read. We however had no doubt but that this was from some Russians in our Neighbourhood and sent to these our unknown friends by the same hand a few bottles of Rum, Wine and Porter which we thought would be as acceptable as any thing we had besides, and the event proved we were not misstaken. I also sent along with Derramoushk and his party Corpl Ledyard of the Marines, an in-teligent man in order to gain some further information, with orders, if he met with any Russians, or others, to endeavour to make them understand that we were English, Friends and Allies."

"so we pigged very lovingly together" Samwell's journal, in JCC, p. 1,144; Samwell, unlike Ledyard, was not writing for his friends, neighbors, and family.

"Nor had they the least idea . . ." Cook, in JCC, p. 449. The Yakutsk merchant Gregory Ismailoff, who came to the *Resolution* later, also knew little of the American continent.

## Fatal Paradise

the men's enormously swollen penises Many of the Hawaiian men had come to the ship to seek treatment, reports surgeon Samwell, in JCC, p. 1,152; Cook was horrified and ashamed at what his men had wrought, which strengthened his desire to prevent a renewed outbreak.

"my mutinous turbulent crew" JCC, p. 479.

"the laurel that was hereafter to adorn his brows" JLJ, p. 102.

"the multitude on the beach fell prostrate" Ledyard's account of Cook's land-ing on Hawaii, JLJ, p. 105.

"Lono" . . . "Orono" Ledyard, like most of the English, did not fully under-stand who or what was Lono ("Orono," as he had it), in JLJ, p. 104. For more on the much-debated Lono, see also Salmond, p. 390; Robson, 2004; and Samwell, in JCC, pp. 1161–2.

sneaking out to meet their mistresses on neutral ground Ledyard's account of this difficult guard duty is at JLJ, pp. 107–8.

snowy cone of Mauna Loa An active volcano, Mauna Loa is not normally snow-covered. Ledyard, Clerke, and King all report that both Mauna Loa and nearby Mauna Vila were snowy in January 1779.

"an uncommon attachment to each other" JLJ, p. 112; for the significance of the name-exchanging ceremony, see Salmond, pp. 402–3.

"make their pastime of the people" JLJ, p. 135; since James King recalled a similar disturbance on the ships' return to Kealakekua Bay, Hitchings suggests that "there is a possibility that Ledyard, writing four years afterward, may have mingled recollections of the two events"; in JLJ, p. 224.

"Our return to this bay" For Ledyard's version of the events around Cook's death, see JLJ, pp. 141ff. He more or less parallels the official version, no doubt much rehashed on the ships and given by Clerke, based on reports of Lieutenant Molesworth Phillips, who commanded the marine guard with Cook that day. See JCC, pp. 531ff.

tipped with an English bayonet The spear that killed Cook was also said to be a dagger, a Hawaiian knife, etc., but the metal itself was certainly English. The shaft of the spear, made into a cane, sold at auction in 2003 for $250,000. Salmond and others say that Cook could not swim to save himself.

"The above is a mistake" Letter from R.W., in Sparks MS 112; it seems at least possible that R.W., who wrote from New York but seems to have come from Connecticut, may have been related to Ledyard's friend and shipmate Simeon Woodruff, of Litchfield. See also Kenneth Munford, "Did John Ledyard Witness Captain Cook's Death?" in *Pacific Northwest Quarterly*, April 1963.

"unreasoning, irrational, and violent" See Obeyesekere, pp. 3–22; also Sahlins, pp. 64, 80, 266–73. More recently, the historian Anne Salmond intervened in this vitriolic dispute, pronouncing both sides in error (but especially Obeyesekere, who she says misinterpreted the rituals of the Makahiki). See Salmond, pp. 403–404.

## PART THREE · The Enterprize

Key sources for this section include, besides Ledyard's own writings: *The Papers of Robert Morris, 1781–1784*; the *Papers of Thomas Jefferson*; Dumas Malone, *Jefferson and His Time*; and William Howard Adams, *The Paris Years of Thomas Jefferson*. See also Walter Isaacson, *Benjamin Franklin*; Edmund Morgan, *Benjamin Franklin*; Evan Thomas, *John Paul Jones*; papers of John Holker, Blair McClenachan, Tench Tilghman, and others at the Library of Congress; Mary Malloy, "Boston Men" on the Northwest Coast.

## A Simple Plan

"How can a Man or a Woman marry" John Ledyard to Isaac Ledyard, January 15, 1783, in JLP; unedited original in NYHS.

"I am a violent Whig, and a violent Tory" John Ledyard to Isaac Ledyard, January 1783, in NYHS.

**"I am a native of North America"** Ledyard's letter to Lord Sandwich, with Gore's cover, dated June 21, 1781, is at ADM 1/1839; reprinted in JCC, 1565.

**"an obscure unassisted genius"** The Russians were pulling his leg, but for Ledyard's moist-eyed description of what he thought was Bering's ship, see JLJ, p. 99.

**"There is no knowing who will be principle merchants"** Ebenezer Ledyard was replying to Tom Seymour, who had asked him to provide a position for his son Henry. "There is no knowing who will be principle merchants Six Weeks hence or in the Spring. The final evacuation of this place & change of government here, threatens a material revolution in the Merchantile Line. Those who are now in much business and expect to continue have daily applications from Gent'n for their sons, who offer a handsome Fee, besides boarding & Lodging them out at their own expense" (original in NYHS).

**the Crooked Billet** For Franklin's early days in Philadelphia, see for example, Isaacson, *Benjamin Franklin.*

**"sixteen sail of seven different maritime powers"** This, and passages below, from John Ledyard to Isaac Ledyard, May 1783, in JLP.

**"What a noble hold he instantaneously took of the Enterprize!"** John Ledyard to Isaac Ledyard, June 1783, in JLP.

**Morris urged his business partners to adopt Ledyard's plan** The documents pertaining to Morris's venture with Ledyard are sketchy at best; there is no record, for example, of his meetings with Ledyard, except for Ledyard's own letters. The editors of *The Papers of Robert Morris* have pieced together an excellent account of Morris's involvement in the China trade, from 1780 to 1785, including his dealings with Ledyard. (Nuxoll and Gallagher, eds., *The Papers of Robert Morris, 1781–1784,* vol. 8, appendix I, pp. 857 ff.), from which most of the details in this chapter are drawn.

**"Ledyard's account, in its minutest details, was verified"** Sparks, *Life of John Ledyard,* p. 180.

**"with whom he had a Short Acquaintance"** Duer to John Holker, October 1783, in *The Papers of Robert Morris,* p. 867.

**"the hardest flight is highest crowned"** Copy of John Ledyard's letter to his mother from New York, November 1783, in Sparks MS 112.

**"without money or friends"** Comfort Sands to Jared Sparks, March 14, 1822, in Sparks MS 112.

**"The flame of Enterprize, that I excited in America"** John Ledyard to Isaac Ledyard, November 15, 1784, in JLP.

## The Sport of Fortune

**"that I John Ledyard shall hop, skip, and jump about"** John Ledyard to Isaac Ledyard, October 12, 1784, in JLP.

**Isaac Ledyard led his own full and accomplished life** For more on Isaac, see Cass Ledyard Shaw, *Ledyard Family in America*, pp. 41–44. The "Mentor" and "Phocion" exchange was published and widely circulated, as was Isaac's "Essay on Matter." In 1782 Isaac wrote to General George Washington, inquiring about his pending court-martial, but seems to have resigned before it took place. See Washington to Isaac Ledyard, January 11, June 23, and August 28, 1782.

**"as clumsy and Gothic as the devil"** John Ledyard to Isaac Ledyard, August 14, 1784, in JLP.

**"The Devil is in it, said I"** John Ledyard to Isaac Ledyard, July 1785. In this long, extraordinary letter, Ledyard details his failed negotiations in L'Orient, followed by his move to Paris; spanning several pages, with five supplements describing Paris, this letter is also interesting for the contrast between the original, at NYHS, and the edited version, in JLP.

**Pirate Jones** See Evan Thomas's superb biography, *John Paul Jones* (New York: Simon and Schuster, 2003), pp. 4ff. Unfortunately none of Ledyard's letters to Jones have been found.

**"bought for a bagatelle"** Jones and Ledyard's proposal is reprinted in *The Life and Correspondence of John Paul Jones*, published in 1830 from manuscripts in the possession of his niece, Janette Taylor.

**La Pérouse was fitting out in L'Orient** See Jefferson to Jones, August 3, 1785, in PTJ. Also Jones's reply, October 5, 1785, copy in Library of Congress, MS Division.

## Man of Genius

**"Such a set of moniless rascals"** Ledyard to "Monecca," in JLP.

**"My friend, my brother, my Father"** Letter from Ledyard to Thomas Jefferson, dated London, November 25, 1786; original in NYHS, and copy in PTJ.

**"Your worthy Virginian"** Ledyard to Isaac Ledyard, July 1785.

**"crucify the thirteen stripes"** John Ledyard to Isaac Ledyard, August 28 (?), 1784; copy in JLP.

**"the sole and professed purpose of mutual prostitution"** This and the passage below from John Ledyard to Isaac Ledyard, July 1785; original in NYHS, redacted copy in JLP.

"nothing on but my shirt" Letter to Isaac, July 1785, in NYHS.

"a journey, which would astonish his countrymen" Notes of Sparks interview with Thomas Seymour, Sparks MS.

"he has the lounging swaggering salt water gait" Ledyard to Isaac Ledyard, July 1785.

"after I have seen Kate, of the North" John Ledyard to Isaac Ledyard, February 1786. For more on "Kate," see Henri Troyat, *Catherine the Great*; Carolly Erickson, *Great Catherine*; and Miriam Kochan, *Life in Russia Under Catherine the Great.*

"Mr. Ledyard's proposals to Her Imperial Majesty" Ledyard's petition is reprinted in Nina Bashkina et al., *The United States and Russia*, pp. 222–23.

"I am like one of Swift's Hughhainums" Ledyard to Isaac Ledyard, April 8, 1786; original in NYHS. The Houyhnhnms were a race of intelligent horses encountered by Gulliver (who much preferred them to the "Yahoos").

"The villainous unprofitable life I have led" Ledyard to Isaac Ledyard, August 8, 1786; original in NYHS.

"She thinks it chimaerical" Jefferson to Ledyard, August 16, 1786, in PTJ; reprinted in Watrous, p. 108. Ledyard was already in London, pursuing alternate routes.

Ledyard had devoured Jonathan Carver's account An American-born army officer who traveled to the Mississippi Valley, Carver, like Pond, seems to have done nothing to persuade Ledyard to make the journey from the East Coast. The "chimera" of a Siberian route was preferable to the known difficulties of the Ohio Valley and beyond. See Jonathan Carver, *Travels through the interior parts of North America*, 1798; and Norman Gelb, *Jonathan Carver's Travels through America.*

"She made me a voluptuous, pensive animal" John Ledyard to Isaac Ledyard, April 9, 1786; original in NYHS.

## Honest Fame

"Blushes commonly beget blushes" See Ledyard to Isaac Ledyard, August 8. 1786; original in Dartmouth College Library. Another long rambling letter, written from Saint-Germain, covering various incidents from Ledyard's arrival in L'Orient in 1784, almost all the way to his abrupt departure from Paris, in mid-August of 1786. (In fact this letter was mailed from London, with another dated August 18.)

"two Great Dogs, an Indian pipe and a hatchet" Ledyard to Jefferson, August 16, 1786, from London, in JLP.

"I will name it La Fayette" Ledyard to Jefferson, August 16. 1786; original in Dartmouth College Archives.

"It is a daring, wild attempt" W.S. Smith to John Jay, September I, 1786.

"boxing some Puppy at the Theatre" Ledyard to Isaac, November 1786, in JLP. He describes "thrashing" "5 or 6 of these haughty turbulent insolent people" to Jefferson, November 25, 1786.

Banks in his youth had been quite a traveler See Patrick O'Brian's brief, readable biography, *Joseph Banks: A Life* (Chicago, 1997).

"The Enterprize is to cross the continent of north America" The subscription for Ledyard's journey across North America, signed by Banks, Hunter, et al., dated November 1786, is at NYHS, copy in Watrous, pp. 117–18.

"I dare not write you any more" Ledyard to Isaac from London, November-December 1786; original in Dartmouth College Archives.

PART FOUR · Kicked Round the World

Aurora Borealis

Many of the most important documents pertaining to Ledyard's Siberian journey, including the first-ever publication of his actual journals, are collected in Stephen Watrous's edition of John Ledyard's *Journey Through Russia and Siberia, 1787–1788* (Madison: University of Wisconsin Press, 1966). More recently, Nina Bashkina gathered documents regarding Ledyard's approach to, arrest in, and removal from Russia in *The United States and Russia: The Beginning of Relations*. General background on Catherine and Russia can be found in Henri Troyat, *Catherine the Great;* and Carolly Erickson, *Great Catherine.* There is no shortage of great trans-Siberian travel narratives, but Anton Chekhov's *A Journey to Sakhalin Island* is among the best. Also noteworthy is George F. Kennan, *Tent Life in Siberia* (despite its somewhat optimistic view of Tsarist rule), and Jules Verne's novel, *Michel Strogoff.* Ledyard's Cairo journey is best chronicled in the *Proceedings of the Association for the Discovery of the Interior Parts of Africa*, by Henry Beaufoy; and in the more detailed *Records of the African Association*, ed. Robin Hallett. Anthony Sattin's *The Gates of Africa* provides a superbly researched and readable overview of British exploration of Africa.

"I could go to heaven with Madam Parish" See Ledyard to Smith, December 20, 1786, in JLP, reprinted in Watrous, pp. 119–20. For background on John Parish, see Ernst Samhaber, *Merchants Make History.*

the mysterious Major William Langborn Details about the enigmatic Langborn from Curtis Carroll Davis, "The Curious Colonel Langborn," in *The Virginia Magazine of History and Biography*, vol. 64, no. 4, (1956), pp. 402–32.

"I will fly to him with my little all" John Ledyard to William Stephens Smith, December 20, 1786, in JLP.

"**However abridged, it would be too long**" Ledyard to Jefferson, March 19, 1787, in NYHS. Letter was received on May 25, 1787.

"**one would have supposed all the inhabitants to be dead**" Maupertuis, quoted in Acerbi, *Travels Through Sweden, Finland, and Lapland*, p. 543.

"**I immediately uncocked**" Acerbi, *Travels*, p. 255.

"**He set out for Tornea**" Sparks, *Life of Ledyard*, p. 243.

**they soon realized that Ledyard could never have covered** Peter Bohler and Peter Brewitt, personal communication. Their journey is chronicled online at http://www.dartmouth.edu/~doc/tripreports/ledyardtrek/

"**I believe that wolves rocks woods & snow understand it**" Ledyard to Jefferson, March 19, 1787; original in NYHS.

"**I am accustomed to hardships**" In Beaufoy, *Proceedings*, p. 45.

"**more shirts than shillings**" Jefferson to John Banister Jr., June 19, 1787, in PTJ, 11:476–77. Also see Ledyard to Jefferson, March 19, 1787.

"**well qualified for such a command**" See Burney, 1819, *A Chronological History of North-eastern Voyages of Discovery*, p. 271.

"**charming little blue-eyed German lass**" Ledyard to Pallas, October 18, 1787 (copy in Natural History Museum).

"**the manners & dispositions of the inhabitants**" Ledyard to Smith, May 15, 1787; original in NYHS.

## Walking to Yakutsk

**the Great Siberian Trakt** For early travelers' accounts of the Trakt, see George Kennan, *Siberia and the Exile System* (1891); and Anton Chekhov, *The Island: A Journey to Sakhalin.*

"**began . . . first to feel the want of houses**" Most details of Ledyard's journey are taken from his Siberian journal, in Ledyard and Watrous, 1966, *Journey Through Russia and Siberia, 1787–1788*, pp. 142ff.

"**They are the same people**" See Ledyard to Jefferson (from Barnaul), July 29, 1787; original in NYHS. For more background on racial theories of the time, including those of Jefferson, see Daniel Boorstin, *The Lost World of Thomas Jefferson;* also Malone, *Jefferson and the Rights of Man.*

**Chippewa, Ojibway, and Nootka languages** Ledyard's impressively large linguistic chart is also at NYHS.

"**Would a Tartar live on *Vive le Roi*?**" Watrous, p. 145.

"**They have been a long time Tartars**" Ledyard to Jefferson, July 29, 1787, in NYHS. The story of Russia's conquest of Siberia is well told by Anna Reid, in *The Shaman's Coat* (London: Weidenfield & Nicholson, 2002).

"**How I have come this far**" Ledyard to Jefferson, July 29, 1787, in NYHS.

"without a hat & very drunk" Watrous, p. 146.

"I was never so ill after a debauch" Watrous, p. 149.

"ruinous éclat of Petersburg" Watrous, p. 152.

"miserable receptacles" Ledyard passed through Barabinsk on his return journey from Irkutsk (Watrous, p. 204). For the state of contemporary Siberia, see Colin Thubron, *In Siberia*; and excellent analyses in the *Economist*, including "Siberia," November 6, 2003; and "Travels in Siberia," August 1, 2002.

Shelikhov was a born explorer See Lydia Black, *Russians in Alaska: 1732–1867*, pp. 104ff.

"Perhaps Shelikhov had been drinking" Ledyard's version of their meeting in Watrous, p. 159 (see also author's footnote). Shelikhov's notes are reprinted in Bashkina, pp. 232–235.

"He is a pretty good man" Iakobi letter, in Sparks MS 112; and reprinted in Watrous, p. 131.

"My rascal of a soldier stole our brandy" Watrous, p. 165.

no traveller ever passed by scenes Ledyard to Smith, in Watrous, pp. 137–140. Two more contemporary Americans have descended the Lena: C. W. Gusewelle (*Great Current Running*, 1993) and Jeffery Tayler (*River of No Reprieve*, 2006).

## The Icebox

"He did not burden himself with baggage" Pallas, in Bashkina, p. 228.

spinning their tops on the ice Ledyard to Smith, October 22, 1787, in NYHS.

"that meager devil POVERTY" Watrous, p. 167.

proto-Bolshevik conspiracy Augur, *Passage to Glory*, pp. 214–27.

"all Nature groans beneath its Rigour" Watrous, p. 194. Sparks edits this sentence to read, "All nature groans beneath the rigorous winter." Indeed, the sentence is part of an entirely cobbled-together passage. Sparks, p. 335.

"A pretty little puppy has come to me one day" Watrous, p. 181.

"the most consummate Scoundrels in the Universe" Watrous, p. 174.

"The Tartar is a Man of Nature" Watrous, p. 176.

"Steller ought to have been hung and Le Bruyn burned" Georg Steller (1709–1746) was a German naturalist who traveled on Bering's second expedition, which was shipwrecked on Bering Island (where Bering died). Captain Cook carried copies of his journals, translated by Pallas, which Ledyard might have read on board *Resolution*. Le Bruyn traveled from Archangelsk to Astrakhan.

a vast "Tartar" nation See Anna Reid, *The Shaman's Coat*.

"Will you come and live with me at Kamchatka?" Watrous, p. 171.

Small Pox Watrous, p. 204.

"a prison without walls" During World War II, a group of prisoners actually dared to escape from a gulag near the Lena River. They marched south through Siberia and into Mongolia, then across China; their story is told in the classic but controversial epic, *The Long Walk*, by Slavomir Rawicz (New York: Lyons Press, 1997).

**"There are but very few of the Yakutee"** Watrous, p. 175.

## Prisoner without a Crime

**"Unfortunately he has too much imagination"** Jefferson to Charles Thomson, September 20, 1787, in PTJ, vol. 12, p. 159.

**via a coded system of tattoos** Jefferson told this story to Nathaniel Cutting, who jotted it down in his diary on October 1, 1789, months after Ledyard had died. In Watrous, pp. 257–259; original MS in Massachusetts Historical Society.

**Iakobi informed Prince Alexander Bezborodko** Governor-General Iakobi's letter is in Bashkina, pp. 241–44.

**"At Yakutsk we found, to our great surprise, Mr. Ledyard"** Sauer, *Account of the Geographical and Astronomical Expedition to the Northern Russia*, p. 99.

**"I had a clear sky & smooth waters"** Ledyard to Sir James Hall, May 31, 1788; original in Scottish Record Office.

**"and Ledyard . . . would have been appointed to supply his place"** Burney, *Chronological History*, p. 279.

**Thomas Pennant . . . and Jonathan Carver** See Carol Urness, ed., *A Naturalist in Russia: Letters from Peter Simon Pallas to Thomas Pennant* (Minneapolis: University of Minnesota Press, 1967); and Norman Gelb, *Jonathan Carver's Travels Through America, 1766–1768* (New York: Wiley, 1993).

**"taking the Foreskins of the Enemy"** Watrous, p. 194.

**"having suffered inconceivable hardships from the severity of the cold"** Sauer, pp. 97–98.

**"with astonishing composure leapt into the kibitka"** Sauer, pp. 100–101.

**"the impropriety of his behaviour"** Sarychev, in *Account of a Voyage of Discovery*, in Watrous, p. 236; Sauer, p. 101.

**"like a vile Convict"** Watrous, p. 200.

**"what sort of treatment he should be given"** Iakobi, in Bashkina, p. 245.

**His primary error** Russia has a long history of arresting unauthorized travelers in Siberia. In 2005, for example, the British explorer Karl Bushby was apprehended after walking across the half-frozen Bering Strait. Like Ledyard, he lacked a proper vision.

**"I myself would contend to lop it off"** Watrous, p. 209.

**"he would certainly be hanged"** Beaufoy, p. 42.

**"that he might be avaricious of it"** Watrous, p. 197.

## The Saturday's Club

**The Saturday's Club** See Sattin, *The Gates of Africa*, pp. 13–27; also Hallett, *Records of the Africa Association*, pp. 13–18, on formation of the association.

**"an adventure almost as perilous"** Beaufoy, *Proceedings*, p. 18.

**"Had I been inclined for a wife"** Beaglehole, ed. *The Endeavour Journal of Sir Joseph Banks*, pp. 31–56.

**"Africa explored"** Watrous, p. 167.

**"'Tomorrow morning' was his answer"** Beaufoy, p. 19.

**the Green Man and Still** Ledyard's itemized receipts from his four-week stay in London, including his tavern bill, can be found among the Banks papers at the Sutro Library in San Francisco. The pub still existed a few years ago (on Whitecross Street), but has since closed.

**"I was so weak & ill with fatigue"** Watrous, p. 204.

**few Europeans had actually penetrated beyond the coast** For the early history of African travel, see Natalie Davis's biography of Leo Africanus, *Trickster Travels: A Sixteenth-Century Muslim between Worlds* (New York: Hill & Wang, 2006).

**Simon Lucas, a thirty-year-old who had been kidnapped** Sketch of Lucas in Hallett, *Records of the African Association*, p. 26.

**"no expence is to be spared"** Ledyard to Isaac Ledyard, dated June 1788; original in DCA.

**The association allocated seventy guineas . . . for Ledyard** Hallett, *Records of the African Association*, p. 51.

**"My heart is on your side of the Atlantic"** Ledyard to Isaac Ledyard, early June 1788; original in NYHS, transcript in JLP. In this long letter, Ledyard recounted his travels in Siberia and sent home six fur coats and boots.

**"leathern pantaloons"** Ledyard's itemized receipts in Banks papers, Sutro Library, San Francisco.

**"I want to talk a month with you without interruption"** Ledyard to Sir James Hall, May 31, 1788.

**"For death cancels all bonds"** Beaufoy, *Proceedings*, p. 45.

## Almost Universal Blindness

**"poverty, rapine, murder"** Ledyard to Jefferson, August 15, 1788, in NYHS.

**he somehow managed to avoid Jefferson** Ledyard to Jefferson (brief note) July 4, 1788: "Mr. Ledyard presents his compliments to Mr. Jefferson. . . . He is ill with a cold & fever or he would have waited on Mr. Jefferson."; in British Library.

**"he rather strove to prevent my embarking"** Ledyard to Jefferson, August 15,

1788; see also Cathalan to Jefferson, November 17, 1788, in PTJ; and Jefferson's reply of November 25, in PTJ.

**"Sweet are the songs of Egypt on paper"** Ledyard to Jefferson, September 10, 1788, in NYHS.

**"I told him, that it formed a part"** Ledyard's Cairo journal, in Hallett, *Records*, p. 57.

**"that they should make a King of me"** Hallett, *Records*, p. 59.

**"a London Jew in deep mourning"** For Lucas's travels, see Sattin, *The Gates of Africa*, pp. 52–62.

**"transported to anger"** Baldwin's and Rosetti's accounts of Ledyard's death are contained in Thomas Paine's letter to Jefferson of June 18, 1789, in *The Complete Writings of Thomas Paine*, pp. 1,292–93.

**instructed in basic medicine** Beaufoy to unidentified Lord (Rawdon?), July 16, 1788; original in DCA.

**the "incautious draught"** Beaufoy, *Proceedings*, pp. 40–41.

**"Born in obscure little Groton"** John Ledyard to Abigail Ledyard Moore, June 1, 1788; copied by Jared Sparks, in Sparks MS 112.

## PART FIVE · Passage to Glory

## Afterlife

**A "gentleman in New Hampshire"** Sparks's advertisement appeared in the *Intelligencer* and other papers; original in Sparks MS.

**"although very averse to this gentleman's intentions"** Daniel Ledyard to Richard Bartlett, November 21, 1821, in Sparks MS; also Bartlett to Sparks, December 5, 1821.

**"having never before heard of you"** Richard Price to Isaac Ledyard, June 19, 1790; original in NYHS.

**"an invincible desire"** Beaufoy, *Proceedings*, p. 14.

**"not a fit person for the expedition"** William Browne to Sir Joseph Banks, January 30, 1792, in the Dawson Turner Collection, of the Natural History Museum.

**by 1791, the African Association would have 109** See Hallett, *Records of the African Association*, pp. 22–24.

**Major Daniel Houghton set out in Ledyard's footsteps** For more on Houghton's fate, see Sattin, pp. 91-109.

**a restless young medical student named Mungo Park** The Mungo Park shelf is much longer than the John Ledyard shelf, starting with Park's own excellent *Travels in the Interior Districts of Africa*.

**"I have always remarked that women, in all countries, are civil"** The original passage may be found in Ledyard's Siberian journal, in Watrous, p. 183. Beaufoy excised Ledyard's reference to the foul-mouthed women of London's Billingsgate fish market.

**"Thro' many a land and clime a ranger"** This particular bit of doggerel appeared in the North American Calendar and Rhode Island Almanac in 1802. It, of course, bears little resemblance to Ledyard's actual words.

**"the life, character & adventures of our Dec'd relative"** Isaac Ledyard to Henry Seymour, January 9, 1790, in Sparks MS.

**he'd developed an adolescent fascination with the legend** Sparks's juvenile notebooks are carefully preserved by Harvard, in Sparks MS.

**"into Africa at Tetuan, or Mogadore"** See Herbert B. Adams, *The Life and Writings of Jared Sparks*, p. 94.

**lengthy negotiations with the Ledyard family** This apparently took Sparks more than a year, aided by a mutual friend. "But the most interesting part of his life—his tour to Siberia—I fear is a blank," Sparks wrote to another friend; in Adams, p. 180.

**"I hope it will be finished next year"** Adams, p. 202.

**to create a "Washington myth"** See Willard Randall, *George Washington: A Life*, pp. 14-15, 57; Sparks also reputedly sold some valuable Washington papers, such as a journal from the French and Indian War. He was called to account by Lord Mahon; see Adams, *The Life and Writings of Jared Sparks*; and Sparks's own *A Reply to the Strictures of Lord Mahon* (1852).

**"I was left to the longest interviews with my own imaginations"** William Cowper Prime, *Among the northern hills*.

**Jared Sparks himself had proposed erecting a monument** Adams, p. 387.

## EPILOGUE · The River

**his classmate Ebenezer Mattoon** This incident reported in the *Dartmouth* newspaper in 1874.

**"the patron saint of freshmen who run away"** Frost said this in his 1955 commencement address at Dartmouth. The other famous runaway freshman was Fred Rogers, better known as Mr. Rogers.

**his old shipmate Simeon Woodruff** Malloy, *"Boston Men,"* p. 27.

**"We observe only his transit"** Thoreau, *A Week on the Concord and Merrimack Rivers* in *The Writings of Henry David Thoreau*, vol. I, p. 122 (Houghton Mifflin, 1906).

# BIBLIOGRAPHY
# AND FURTHER READING

Acerbi, Giuseppe. *Travels Through Sweden, Finland, and Lapland, to the North Cape, in the Years 1798 and 1799.* London: Printed for J. Mawman, 1802.

Adams, Herbert Baxter. *The Life and Writings of Jared Sparks, Comprising Selections From His Journals and Correspondence.* Freeport, NY: Books for Libraries Press, 1970.

Adams, William Howard. *The Paris Years of Thomas Jefferson.* New Haven: Yale University Press, 1997.

Alexander, John T. *Catherine the Great: Life and Legend.* New York: Oxford University Press, 1989.

Alexander, Michael. *Omai, Noble Savage.* London: Harvill Press, 1977.

Ambrose, Stephen E. *Undaunted Courage: Meriwether Lewis, Thomas Jefferson, and the Opening of the American West.* New York: Simon & Schuster, 1996.

Anderson, Fred. *Crucible of War: The Seven Years' War and the Fate of Empire in British North America, 1754–1766.* 1st ed. New York: Alfred A. Knopf, 2000.

Augur, Helen. *Passage to Glory; John Ledyard's America.* 1st ed. Garden City, NY: Doubleday, 1946.

Banks, Joseph, and A. M. Lysaght. *The Journal of Joseph Banks in the Endeavour.* Guildford, Surrey, England: Genesis Publications in association with Rigby, 1980.

Bashkina, Nina N., and David F. Trask. *The United States and Russia: The Beginning of Relations, 1765–1815.* Washington, DC: U.S. Government Printing Office, 1980.

Beaglehole, J. C. *The Life of Captain James Cook.* Stanford, CA: Stanford University Press, 1974.

———. *The Death of Captain Cook.* Wellington: Alexander Turnbull Library, 1979.

Bederman, Sanford Harold. *The Ethnological Contributions of John Ledyard.* Atlanta: Georgia State College, 1964.

Bentwich, Norman De Mattos. *Josephus.* Philadelphia: The Jewish Publication Society of America, 1914.

Beston, Henry. *The Book of Gallant Vagabonds, By Henry Beston.* New York: George H. Doran Company, 1925.

Black, Lydia. *Russians in Alaska, 1732–1867.* Fairbanks: University of Alaska Fairbanks, 2004.

Blodgett, Harold William. *Samson Occom.* Hanover, NH: Dartmouth College Publications, 1935.

Boorstin, Daniel J. *The Lost World of Thomas Jefferson.* Chicago: University of Chicago Press, 1981.

Brooks, Richard. *The Royal Marines: 1664 to the Present.* Annapolis, MD: Naval Institute Press, 2002.

Burney, James. *A Chronological History of North-Eastern Voyages of Discovery; and of the Early Eastern Navigations of the Russians.* London: Payne and Foss [etc.], 1819.

Bushman, Richard L. *The Great Awakening; Documents on the Revival of Religion, 1740–1745.* 1st ed. Documentary problems in early American history, New York: Published for the Institute of Early American History and Culture at Williamsburg, Va. [by] Atheneum, 1970.

Carver, Jonathan, and John Coakley Lettsom. *Travels Through the Interior Parts of North America, in the Year 1766, 1767, and 1768.* London: Sold by J. Walter, 1778.

Caulkins, Frances Manwaring, and Emily Serena Gilman. *The Stone Records of Groton.* Norwich, CT: Free Academy Press, 1903.

Caulkins, Frances Manwaring, and Cecelia Griswold. *History of New London, Connecticut, From the First Survey of the Coast in 1612 to 1860.* New London, CT: H. D. Utley, 1895.

Chase, Frederick. *A History of Dartmouth College and the Town of Hanover, New Hampshire.*

Chekhov, Anton Pavlovich. *The Island: a Journey to Sakhalin.* New York: Washington Square Press, 1967.

Chernow, Ron. *Alexander Hamilton.* New York: Penguin Press, 2004.

Cook, James, J. C. Beaglehole, and R. A. Skelton. *The Journals of Captain James Cook on His Voyages of Discovery.* Cambridge: Published for the Hakluyt Society at the University Press, 1955.

Cook, James, and James King. *Captain Cook's Third and Last Voyage to the Pacific Ocean in the Years 1776, '77, '78, '79, and '80.* New York: Printed by Mott and Hurtin for Benjamin Gomez, 1795.

Davis, Natalie Zemon. *Trickster Travels: A Sixteenth-Century Muslim Between Worlds.* 1st. ed. New York: Hill and Wang, 2006.

Dawson, Warren R. *The Banks Letters; A Calendar of the Manuscript Correspondence of Sir Joseph Banks, Preserved in the British Museum, the British Museum (Natural History) and Other Collections in Great Britain.* London: Printed by order of the trustees of the British Museum, 1958.

Delbanco, Andrew. *Melville: His World and Work.* 1st ed. New York: Alfred A. Knopf, 2005.

Demos, John. *The Unredeemed Captive: A Family Story From Early America.* 1st ed. New York: Alfred A. Knopf, 1994.

Dicharov, Zakhar. *Neobychaæinye Pokhozhdeniëiìa V Rossii Dzhona Lediarda-Amerikanëtìsa.* Sankt-Peterburg: Nauka, 1996.

Edwards, Jonathan, and Perry Miller. *The Works of Jonathan Edwards.* New Haven: Yale University Press, 1957.

Eisler, Kim Isaac. *Revenge of the Pequots: How a Small Native American Tribe Created the World's Most Profitable Casino.* New York: Simon & Schuster, 2001.

Ellis, Joseph J. *Thomas Jefferson: Genius of Liberty.* New York: Viking Studio in association with the Library of Congress, Washington, DC, 2000.

Erickson, Carolly. *Great Catherine.* 1st ed. New York: Crown Publishers, 1994.

Feldman, Louis H., and Gōhei Hata. *Josephus, the Bible, and History.* Leiden: E. J. Brill, 1989.

Field, Cyril. *Britain's Sea-Soldiers; a History of the Royal Marines and Their Predecessors and of Their Services in Action, Ashore and Afloat, and Upon Sundry Other Occasions of Moment.* Liverpool: The Lyceum Press, 1924.

Forster, Georg, and Johann Reinhold Forester. *A Voyage Round the World, in His Britannie Majesty's Sloop, Resolution.* London: B. White [etc.], 1777.

Forsyth, James. *A History of the Peoples of Siberia: Russia's North Asian Colony, 1581–1990.* Cambridge and New York: Cambridge University Press, 1992.

Gelb, Norman. *Jonathan Carver's Travels Through America, 1766–1768: An Eighteenth-Century Explorer's Account of Uncharted America.* New York: Wiley, 1993.

Golder, Frank Alfred. *Russian Expansion on the Pacific, 1641–1850; an Account of the Earliest and Later Expeditions Made By the Russians Along the Pacific Coast of Asia and North America; Including Some Related Expeditions to the Arctic Regions.* Cleveland: The Arthur H. Clark Co., 1914.

Gunther, Erna. *Indian Life on the Northwest Coast of North America, as Seen By the Early Explorers and Fur Traders During the Last Decades of the Eighteenth Century.* Chicago: University of Chicago Press, 1972.

Gusewelle, C. W. *A Great Current Running: The U.S.-Russian Lena River Expedition; With Lena Reunion.* 1st ed. Kansas City: Lowell Press, 1994.

Haefeli, Evan, and Kevin Sweeney. *Captors and Captives: The 1704 French and Indian Raid on Deerfield.* Native Americans of the Northeast. Amherst: University of Massachusetts Press, 2003.

Hallett, Robin. *Records of the African Association, 1788–1831.* London and New York: T. Nelson, 1964.

Hallett, Robin. *The Penetration of Africa; European Enterprise and Exploration Principally in Northern and Western Africa Up to 1830.* London: Routledge & K. Paul, 1965.

Harris, William Wallace, and Charles Allyn. *The Battle of Groton Heights: A Collection of Narratives, Official Reports, Records, Etc. Of the Storming of Fort Griswold.* Mystic, CT: Seaport Autographs, 1999.

Hempstead, Joshua. *Diary of Joshua Hempstead: A Record of Life in Colonial New London, Connecticut, 1711–1758.* New authorized ed. New London, CT: New London County Historical Society, 1998.

Hetherington, Michelle. *Cook & Omai: The Cult of the South Seas.* Canberra: National Library of Australia, 2001.

Holmes, Maurice. *Captain James Cook; a Bibliographical Excursion.* New York: B. Franklin, 1968.

Horwitz, Tony. *Blue Latitudes: Boldly Going Where Captain Cook Has Gone Before.* 1st ed. New York: Henry Holt, 2002.

Hough, Richard. *Captain James Cook.* 1st ed. The adventure library. North Salem, NY: Adventure Library, 2003.

Howay, Frederic William, Robert Haswell, John Box Hoskins, and John Boit. *Voyages of the "Columbia" to the Northwest Coast, 1787–1790 and 1790–1793.* North Pacific studies series; no. 13. Portland, OR: Oregon Historical Society Press in cooperation with the Massachusetts Historical Society, 1990.

Isaacson, Walter. *Benjamin Franklin: An American Life.* New York: Simon & Schuster, 2003.

Jefferson, Thomas, and Julian P. Boyd. *The Papers of Thomas Jefferson.* Princeton: Princeton University Press, 1950.

Jones, John Paul, and James C. Bradford. *The Papers of John Paul Jones.* Cambridge, UK, and Alexandria, VA: Chadwyck-Healey, 1986.

Jones, John Paul, Robert Charles Sands, and Janette Taylor. *Life and Correspondence of John Paul Jones, Including His Narrative of the Campaign of the Liman.* New York: [D. Fanshaw, printer], 1830.

Kennan, George. *Tent Life in Siberia, and Adventures Among the Koraks and Other Tribes in Kamtchatka and Northern Asia.* New York and London: G. P. Putnam & Sons, 1870.

———. *Siberia and the Exile System.* New York: The Century Co., 1891.

Kochan, Miriam. *Life in Russia Under Catherine the Great.* London and New York: Batsford Putnam, 1969.

Lawlor, Laurie. *Magnificent Voyage: An American Adventurer on Captain James Cook's Final Expedition.* 1st ed. New York: Holiday House, 2002.

Ledyard, John. *John Ledyard's Journal of Captain Cook's Last Voyage.* Corvallis: Oregon State University Press, 1963.

Ledyard, John, and Stephen D. Watrous. *Journey Through Russia and Siberia, 1787–*

*1788: The Journal and Selected Letters.* Madison: University of Wisconsin Press, 1966.

Ledyard, John, and James Zug. *The Last Voyage of Captain Cook: The Collected Writings of John Ledyard.* National Geographic adventure classics. Washington, DC: National Geographic Society, 2005.

Lehmann-Haupt, Hellmut, Lawrence C. Wroth, and Ruth S. Granniss. *The Book in America: A History of the Making, the Selling, and the Collecting of Books in the United States.* New York: R.R. Bowker Co., 1939.

Love, William DeLoss. *Samson Occom and the Christian Indians of New England.* 1st ed. The Iroquois and their neighbors. Syracuse, NY: Syracuse University Press, 2000.

Lupton, Kenneth. *Mungo Park, the African Traveler.* Oxford and New York: Oxford University Press, 1979.

Lyte, Charles. *Sir Joseph Banks: 18th Century Explorer, Botanist, and Entrepreneur.* North Pomfret, VT: David & Charles, 1980.

M'Clure, David, and Elijah Parish. *Memoirs of the Rev. Eleazer Wheelock, D.D., Founder and President of Dartmouth College and Moor's Charity School; With a Summary History of the College and School.* Newburyport: E. Little & Co., 1811.

Malloy, Mary. *Boston Men on the Northwest Coast: The American Fur Trade, 1788–1844 (Alaska History).* University of Alaska Press, 1998.

Malone, Dumas. *Jefferson and His Time.* 1st ed. Boston: Little, Brown, 1948.

McCallum, James Dow. *Eleazar Wheelock: Founder of Dartmouth College.* Hanover, NH: Dartmouth College Publications, 1939.

McCallum, James Dow, and Eleazar Wheelock. *The Letters of Eleazar Wheelock's Indians.* Hanover, NH: Dartmouth College Publications, 1932.

McCullough, David G. *John Adams.* New York: Simon & Schuster, 2001.

Melville, Herman, Harrison Hayford, and Hershel Parker. *Moby-Dick: An Authoritative Text.* 1st ed. New York: W. W. Norton, 1967.

Moore, Charles B. *The New York Genealogical and Biographical Record* 7, no. 1 (1876).

Morgan, Edmund Sears. *Benjamin Franklin.* New Haven: Yale University Press, 2002.

Morison, Samuel Eliot. *John Paul Jones, a Sailor's Biography.* 1st ed. Boston: Little, Brown, 1959.

Morris, Robert. *Papers of Robert Morris.*

Morris, Robert, E. James Ferguson, and John Catanzariti. *The Papers of Robert Morris, 1781–1784.* Pittsburgh: University of Pittsburgh Press, 1973.

Moulton, J. L. *The Royal Marines.* London: Leo Cooper, 1972.

Munford, James Kenneth. *John Ledyard; an American Marco Polo.* Portland, OR: Binfords & Mort, 1939.

O'Brian, Patrick. *Joseph Banks: A Life.* Chicago: University of Chicago Press, 1997.

Occom, Samson, and Joanna Brooks. *Samson Occom: Collected Writings From a Founder of Native American Literature.* New York: Oxford University Press, 2006.

Paine, Thomas. *Papers of Thomas Paine.*

Pallas, Peter Simon, Carol Louise Urness, and Thomas Pennant. *A Naturalist in Russia; Letters From Peter Simon Pallas to Thomas Pennant.* Minneapolis: University of Minnesota Press, 1967.

Park, Mungo. *Travels in the Interior of Africa.* Trafalgar Square Publishing, 2005.

Parker, Hershel. *Herman Melville: A Biography.* Baltimore: Johns Hopkins University Press, 1996.

Prime, William Cowper. *Among the Northern Hills.* New York: Harper & Brothers, 1895.

Randall, Willard Sterne. *Benedict Arnold: Patriot and Traitor.* 1st ed. New York: Morrow, 1990.

Randall, Willard Sterne. *George Washington: A Life.* 1st ed. New York: Henry Holt & Co., 1997.

Rawicz, Slavomir. *The Long Walk.* New York: Lyons Press, 1997.

Reid, Anna. *The Shaman's Coat: A Native History of Siberia.* London: Weidenfeld & Nicolson, 2002.

Rickman, John. *Journal of Captain Cook's Last Voyage to the Pacific Ocean.* March of America facsimile series, no. 47. Ann Arbor, MI: University Microfilms, 1966.

Roberts, Richard Owen. *Salvation in Full Color: Twenty Sermons By Great Awakening Preachers.* Wheaton, IL: International Awakening Press, 1994.

Robson, John. *Captain Cook's World: Maps of the Life and Voyages of James Cook R.N.* Auckland: Random House New Zealand, 2000.

Robson, John. *The Captain Cook Encyclopædia.* Milsons Point: Random House Australia, 2004.

Rodger, N. A. M. *The Wooden World: An Anatomy of the Georgian Navy.* Annapolis, MD: Naval Institute Press, 1986.

Salmond, Anne. *The Trial of the Cannibal Dog: The Remarkable Story of Captain Cook's Encounters in the South Seas.* New Haven: Yale University Press, 2003.

Samhaber, Ernst. *Merchants Make History; How Trade Has Influenced the Course of History Throughout the World.* Translated By E. Osers. 1st American ed. New York: John Day Co., 1964.

Sattin, Anthony. *The Gates of Africa: Death, Discovery, and the Search for Timbuktu.* 1st U.S. ed. New York: St. Martin's Press, 2005.

Sauer, Martin. *Expedition to the Northern Parts of Russia.* Richmond, UK: Richmond Publishing Co., Ltd., 1972.

Schama, Simon. *Citizens: A Chronicle of the French Revolution.* 1st ed. New York: Alfred A. Knopf, 1989.

Schmucker, Samuel Mosheim. *The Life of Dr. Elisha Kent Kane, and of Other Distinguished American Explorers; Containing Narratives of Their Researches and Adventures in Remote and Interesting Portions of the Globe.* Philadelphia: J. W. Bradley, 1858.

Sealts, Merton M. *Melville's Reading.* Rev. ed. Columbia, SC: University of South Carolina Press, 1988.

Shaw, Cass Ledyard Ruxton. *The Ledyard Family in America.* West Kennebunk, ME: Phoenix Pub., 1993.

Sobel, Dava. *Longitude: The True Story of a Lone Genius Who Solved the Greatest Scientific Problem of His Time.* New York: Walker, 1995.

Sparks, Jared. *The Life of John Ledyard, the American Traveller; Comprising Selections From His Journals and Correspondence.* Cambridge, MA, and New York: Hilliard and Brown G. & C. Carvill, 1828.

———. *Life of John Ledyard, American Traveller.* Boston: C.C. Little and J. Brown, 1847.

———. *A Reply to the Strictures of Lord Mahon and Others, on the Mode of Editing the Writings of Washington.* London and Boston: Trübner and Co. and J. Munroe and Co., 1852.

Stannard, David E. *Before the Horror: The Population of Hawai'i on the Eve of Western Contact.* Honolulu, HI: Social Science Research Institute, University of Hawaii, 1989.

Stark, Charles Rathbone. *Groton, Conn. 1705–1905.* Stonington, CT: Printed for the author by the Palmer Press, 1922.

Stevens, John Austin. "The Ledyard Family." *The Magazine of American History,* 7 (1881).

Tayler, Jeffrey. *River of No Reprieve: Descending Siberia's Waterway of Exile, Death, and Destiny.* Boston and New York: Houghton Mifflin, 2006.

Thomas, Evan. *John Paul Jones: Sailor, Hero, Father of the American Navy.* New York: Simon & Schuster, 2003.

Thomas, Garth. *Records of the Royal Marines.* London: PRO Publications, Public Record Office, 1994.

Thomas, Nicholas. *Cook: The Extraordinary Voyages of Captain James Cook.* New York: Walker & Company, 2003.

Thompson, Julian. *The Royal Marines: From Sea Soldiers to a Special Force.* London: Sidgwick & Jackson, 2000.

Thompson, Julian. *The Royal Marines: From Sea Soldiers to a Special Force.* Pan, 2001.

Thubron, Colin. *In Siberia.* 1st ed. New York: HarperCollins, 1999.

Tracy, Joseph. *The Great Awakening. A History of the Revival of Religion in the Time of Edwards and Whitefield.* Boston and New York: Tappan & Dennet Dayton & Newman, 1842.

Troyat, Henri. *Catherine the Great.* 1st ed. New York: Dutton, 1980.

Ver, Steeg and Clarence Lester. *Robert Morris, Revolutionary Financier.* New York: Octagon Books, 1972.

Verne, Jules. *Michael Strogoff.* New York: G. Munro, 1877.

Wallace, Lee. *Sexual Encounters: Pacific Texts, Modern Sexualities.* Ithaca, NY: Cornell University Press, 2003.

Wheelock, Eleazar. *Papers.* In Dartmouth College Archives, Hanover, NH.

Whitaker, Epher. *History of Southold, L.I.: Its First Century.* Southold, NY: Printed for the author, 1881.

Whitman, Elnathan. *The Death of Good Men Compared to a Sweet, Refreshing Sleep.* Hartford, CT: Printed by Ebenezer Watson, 1771.

Wilderson, Paul W. *Governor John Wentworth & the American Revolution: The English Connection.* Hanover: University Press of New England, 1994.

Williams, Glyndwr. *Voyages of Delusion: The Quest for the Northwest Passage.* New Haven: Yale University Press, 2003.

Williams, John, Stephen Williams, and Thomas Prince. *The Redeemed Captive, Returning to Zion. A Faithful History of Remarkable Occurrences, in the Captivity and Deliverance, of Mr. John Williams; Minister of the Gospel in Deerfield, Who, in the Desolation Which Befel That Plantation, By an Incursion of the French and Indians, Was By Them Carried Away, With His Family, and His Neighbourhood, Unto Canada. Drawn Up By Himself. Whereto There is Annexeda Sermon Preached By Him, Upon His Return, At the Lecture in Boston, December 5, 1706.* 3rd ed. Boston: Printed and sold by S. Kneeland, 1758.

Zeichner, Oscar. *Connecticut's Years of Controversy, 1750–1776.* Hamden, CT: Archon Books, 1970.

Ziff, Larzer. *Return Passages: Great American Travel Writing, 1780–1910.* New Haven: Yale University Press, 2000.

Zimmermann, Heinrich, Elsa Michaelis, Cecil French, and Frederic William Howay. *Zimmermann's Captain Cook, an Account of the Third Voyage of Captain Cook Around the World, 1776–1780.* Toronto: The Ryerson Press, 1930.

Zug, James. *American Traveler: The Life and Adventures of John Ledyard, the Man Who Dreamed of Walking the World.* New York: Basic Books, 2005.

# INDEX